MODERN MUSLIM THEOLOGY

Engaging God and the World with Faith and Imagination

Martin Nguyen

ROWMAN & LITTLEFIELD
Lanham • Boulder • New York • London

Executive Editor: Rolf Janke
Editorial Assistant: Courtney Packard
Senior Marketing Manager: Kim Lyons

Credits and acknowledgments for material borrowed from other sources, and reproduced with permission, appear on the appropriate page within the text.

Published by Rowman & Littlefield
An imprint of The Rowman & Littlefield Publishing Group, Inc.
4501 Forbes Boulevard, Suite 200, Lanham, Maryland 20706
https://rowman.com

Unit A, Whitacre Mews, 26-34 Stannary Street, London SE11 4AB, United Kingdom

British Library Cataloguing in Publication Information Available

Library of Congress Cataloging-in-Publication Data
Names: Nguyen, Martin, author.
Title: Modern Muslim theology : engaging God and the world with faith and imagination / Martin Nguyen.
Description: Lanham : Rowman & Littlefield, [2018] | Includes bibliographical references and index.
Identifiers: LCCN 2018016752 (print) | LCCN 2018018380 (ebook) | ISBN 9781538115015 (electronic) | ISBN 9781538114995 (cloth : alk. paper) | ISBN 9781538115008 (pbk. : alk. paper)
Subjects: LCSH: Islam—Doctrines.
Classification: LCC BP166 (ebook) | LCC BP166 .N465 2018 (print) | DDC 297.2—dc23

∞ ™ The paper used in this publication meets the minimum requirements of American National Standard for Information Sciences Permanence of Paper for Printed Library Materials, ANSI/NISO Z39.48-1992.

Printed in the United States of America

In the name of God, the Merciful, the Compassionate

There is goodness for those who respond to their Lord.

Qur'an 13:18

Remember your Lord inwardly, in humility and awe, with a quietness of words, in the mornings and in the evenings—do not be among the heedless—those who are with your Lord are not too proud to worship Him: they glorify Him and prostrate before Him.

Qur'an 7:205–6

For Kiran Tahir

CONTENTS

ACKNOWLEDGMENTS

The book that rests in your hands was developed over the course of many years. For me to write Muslim theology as I have done here required two somewhat lengthy preliminary undertakings on my part. First, I had to discover that writing of this nature was even possible. Second, I had to determine the arc of ideas that would emerge from out of the words that I would write. The project overall took much longer than I expected, marked by a number of intervening interims in which the work in progress seemed to lie fallow. These periods of apparent silence, however, were welcome interruptions and critical interventions filled with shared experiences that served to refine, expand, and, at times, radically transform the ideas that I present herein. I take this opportunity, then, to acknowledge those with whom I have shared this endeavor.

I resolved to write *Modern Muslim Theology* in 2011 in the month of Ramadan after an earnest conversation with a friend. The very idea of a book such as this, however, had begun to crystallize weeks earlier after participating in the Wabash Center's Teaching and Learning Workshop for Pre-Tenure Asian and Asian-American Religion and Theology Faculty in Crawfordsville, Indiana. The conversations and experiences shared there directed me along a new trajectory. In fact, in the years to follow, my continued involvement with the Wabash Center as well as the Religious Studies Department at Fairfield University, the Scriptural Reasoning at the University group, and Georgetown University's Building Bridges Seminar provided important spaces for me to work through some of the questions I had in mind.

Once I began to write, I found support early on from Maria Dakake and Rumee Ahmed. By late March 2013, I presented what would eventually become the chapter on revelation at the Contemplating the Qur'an Conference at Howard Divinity School. Shortly afterward, R. David Coolidge, Michael Dann, and Wasim Shiliwala offered helpful comments on a draft chapter that I produced. In January 2014, I presented on the Muslim imaginative tradition at the Annual Meeting of the Society for the Study of Muslim Ethics in Seattle, Washington. At that time, Ingrid Mattson provided welcome direction and advice for further honing my understanding of the religious imagination. This conference paper eventually developed into my respective chapters on tradition and the religious imagination. In 2018, *Renovatio: The Journal of Zaytuna College* first published the article that is now the final section of the chapter on tradition. The resulting chapter on the religious imagination was further improved thanks to insightful comments from Cyrus Ali Zargar.

By October 2014, I had completed a first draft of the entire manuscript. The present book has been significantly revised since then because of the helpful feedback provided by several colleagues: Jawad Bayat read over the introduction and my chapter on theology; Yousef Casewit commented on theology, tradition, and revelation; and Sam Ross offered remarks on theology and what would eventually become the chapter on modern time. My departmental colleague John Thiel at Fairfield University very generously offered his remarks on the entirety of this initial iteration of the manuscript. As I undertook the lengthy revision process and sought a publisher, John Kelsay, Bruce Lawrence, and Ebrahim Moosa provided invaluable guidance. Additionally, the ability to write and then revise this work was made possible by Fairfield University through a Summer Research Stipend awarded in 2013, an Applied Research Grant awarded in 2016, and a sabbatical leave granted for the spring of 2018. I am thankful for the sustained institutional support.

At the 2015 Annual Meeting of the Society for the Study of Muslim Ethics, I presented an abbreviated version of the final chapter of the book. In early 2016, when I was invited to present at the College of the Holy Cross for the Future of Scholarship on the Qur'an Conference organized by Caner Dagli, I presented an adapted version of my work on the Qur'an as revelation. I benefited greatly from the insightful intersections with the work of my copanelists, Zareena Grewal and Juliane Hammer. An expanded version of this paper was first published as "Modern Scripturalism and Emergent Theological Trajectories: Moving Beyond the Qur'an as Text" in the *Journal of Islamic and Muslim Studies*. The final section of that article has been revised and is reprinted in chapter 5 with permission from Indiana University Press.

In the fall of 2016, I met with Sarah Stanton, then the senior acquisitions editor at Rowman & Littlefield, about having my manuscript published in the press's series Religion in the Modern World. I am immensely thankful for her diligent shepherding of this manuscript toward publication. From beginning to end, working with Rowman & Littlefield has been a rewarding experience thanks to Sarah, new senior acquisitions editor Rolf Janke, editorial assistant Courtney Packard, senior production editor Alden Perkins, the two series editors Kwok Pui-Lan and Joerg Rieger, and my five anonymous external reviewers. I am especially grateful to Pui-Lan for her sustained support of the project and her mentorship over the years.

I would also like to thank those friends and colleagues not yet mentioned who nonetheless welcomed (or were too polite to rebuff) my discussions of theology: Arshad Ali, Samy Ayoub, Omer Bajwa, Ayesha Chaudhry, Dale Correa, Aysha Hidayatullah, Mohammad Khalil, Melinda Krokus, Mahan Mirza, Younus Mirza, Jawad Qureshi, Hussein Rashid, Sa'diyya Shaikh, Mairaj Syed, Sarra Tlili, and Maheen Zaman. In particular, Najeeba Syeed and Nuri Friedlander have been truly invaluable conversation partners as we sought to imagine together the critically important theological work that still lies ahead. I am also indebted to three teachers from early on in my scholarly career: Abdulaziz Sachedina, Abdulkarim Soroush, and Farid Esack. Although the writing of this book did not begin until after my time with them, I recognize the indelible mark that each of them has left on me.

Finally, I completed the first draft of the manuscript seven months after our daughter was born. The expectation and then arrival of Maryam Ella unquestionably drove and shaped the writing of this book. Which brings me to the person who truly made this book possible, Kiran Tahir, my partner in life and love who has supported this endeavor of faithful engagement from its inception to its conclusion. She read with a careful and critical eye every draft of every chapter of this book as it was written and revised. She did so many times over. Her thoughts and comments on the work in progress were the most valuable of all. At every step of the way, Kiran and I have struggled together to bring this book to life. I dedicate this book to her, because were it not for Kiran, this book would not have come into being.

INTRODUCTION

> A man of little understanding may perhaps say: "There is already a sufficient abundance of books, there is no benefit in compiling new ones in this age." Such a man would be correct insofar as books are indeed abundant and should be sufficient; but not in saying that no benefit is to be gained from compiling further books now. People's hearts are naturally attracted to everything new, and God gives them at each time knowledge clothed in the form best suited to the age.
> —Imam ʿAbd Allāh Ibn ʿAlawī al-Ḥaddād, *The Book of Assistance*[1]

> I won't deny I don't know where I'm at. . . . But by the same token, how many of us put the finger down on one point and say, "I'm here."
> —Malcolm X[2]

WHY THEOLOGY?

This book is a foray into theology. Specifically, this book works to develop a *Muslim theology of engagement*. What do I mean, however, by a Muslim theology of "engagement"? More than that, what is "Muslim" theology? And perhaps most pointedly, why "theology" at all? This book, in its own way, works to answer these three questions. Although the full breadth of this text will be required to do so, something ought to be said now by way of introduction. To that end, it would be best to address these three questions in reverse.

Why "theology" at all? Admittedly, theology is not an easy subject to discuss. With the many and overwhelming concerns of everyday life and the world pressing upon us, why would anyone, even a person of faith, turn to "theology" for respite, relief, or resolution? What does theology—this seemingly outmoded and overly complicated way of thinking—have to offer to a world on quickly shifting ground? Many today dismiss theology altogether. It seems too antiquated and woefully ill equipped to respond adequately to the sophisticated challenges that assail us. Whether confronting concerns of science or sexuality, existential crises or systemic social injustices, or the perennial problems of sickness, suffering, and death, why indeed would anyone turn to theology? What use is "God talk" when confronting these utterly human questions? Although it may seem to fly in the face of all practical considerations, I argue the contrary. I believe that "theology" is of incredible—if not the utmost—importance for us in the here and now.

Admittedly, how I use the term *theology* differs from commonplace expectations. As many often think of it within the context of Islam, theology is a scholastic exercise. Its subject is faith, but its method demands a highly refined form of reasoned thinking. Moreover, the "God talk" that emerges is dry and overly rationalistic more often than not. It seems more focused on elaborating proofs, polemics, and apologetics than on fostering faith. That is one prevalent impression at least. Put another way, classical Islamic theology appears to be more cerebral than practical or pastoral. As a result, theology seems more suited for experts than everyday believers.

I contend that theology is more than merely an intellectual enterprise.[3] Let me be clear, then, at the outset that I am not using the word *theology* as a substitute or translation for an Arabic term like *ʿaqīda* ("creed"), *ʿilm al-kalām* ("scholastic theology"), or *uṣūl al-dīn* ("foundational principles of the religion"), though these important fields of religious inquiry invariably figure into the conversation. Nor do I agree with the fairly negative characterization just given. My aim, however, is not to rehabilitate the perception of these fields of religious knowledge. The concern is squarely on reconceptualizing "theology" broadly conceived, which I do in chapter 1. For the present, I will simply say that theology, if it is truly to be *theology*, must attend to the fostering of faith. The reality is that there are times—incredibly many times—when what one needs in this life is to have faith fostered—not proven, argued, or meticulously explained. As such, theology should not be the preserve of intellectual elites, but ought to be accessible in order to serve all.

In light of this expectation, I cast a wide net when speaking of theology in this book. I understand theology to encompass a great many things. It encompasses, as expected, matters of belief and doctrine, but it also encompasses ethics and spirituality. It encompasses devotional practices and religious sensibilities. It encompasses the practice of everyday life and life itself. In fact, I argue that theology is being done—negotiated and undertaken—all the time, whether we realize it or not. Theology simply *names* a life-encompassing and faith-affirming process with which every person is already engaged. It is an integral and intrinsic part of what it means to be human. By naming and better understanding the theological activity that is already underway in our lives, we may better shape and cultivate the life of faith that draws us closer to God and deepens our commitment to the righteousness to which God continually calls humankind. Although how all of this is so may not be immediately apparent, this book, from beginning to end, endeavors to make such a case.

MUSLIM THEOLOGY

But for whom is all of this important? This brings us to our second query about "Muslim" theology. At one level, this is a work abstractly intended for all those interested in the role of religion in contemporary life. The ideas, narratives, and symbols invoked throughout this book may find resonance with readers from different faith backgrounds, and it is my hope that these invocations spur discussion and dialogue broadly within and across communities of faith. Nevertheless, this book is a work of "Muslim" theology because I wrote it with a particular community of faith in mind. The same ideas, narratives, and symbols that I have just spoken of are Islamic in register, at least to my mind. Moreover, the decision to describe this theology as "Muslim" rather than "Islamic" is intentional. I am using "Muslim" in order to emphasize the human activity that animates it. As I will argue throughout this book, human agency and imagination are indispensible to theology. God, of course, is the central coordinate of theology, but I believe it important to speak of and to the innumerably many Muslims who are wrestling with and living out their theologies in the everyday.

Furthermore, this book is a "Muslim" theology in order to claim ownership of the work done herein. While the usage of "Islamic" might arguably be suitable for a historically descriptive treatment of theology, the book that rests in your hands is not this type of work. The author is not uninvolved with the subject at hand, standing at a scholarly distance. Rather, I speak herein as an adherent to the faith of Islam addressing the many Muslim communities with which I have intersected and continue to engage. At times, I speak directly and with concern. The choice is intentional. Theology, I believe, ought to be attentive to both homiletics (the art of writing and delivering sermons) and pedagogy (the method and practice of teaching), both of which have been long cultivated within Islam's tradition of preaching and spiritual instruction.[4] As to how these figure into the book, it is sometimes better to witness a thing in action rather than have to spell it out explicitly. I offer, therefore, the voice of this book from its beginning to its end as a testament to this aspiration.

I recognize as well that there is an inherent challenge when anyone speaks of an abstract "Muslim community." There is an ideal and a reality that must be continually negotiated. At an aspirational level, I am addressing an imagined Muslim community captured by a designation that has had enduring resonance within the Islamic tradition, namely the idea of *ahl al-qibla*, literally "the people of the direction of prayer." The *qibla* mentioned here refers to the direction of prayer to which all Muslims direct their ritual prayers, the Kaʿba or the house of God that resides at the heart of the city of Mecca. As God discloses in the Qur'an: *We shall turn you to a direction of prayer that is dear to you. Turn your face in the direction of the sacred place of prostration* (Q. 2:144). Although the Muslim community may differ over many things great and small with respect to faith, practice, and doctrine, it is bound together by its recognition that prayer *ought* to be oriented toward the house of God in Mecca. This is not to imply that all Muslims fastidiously pray or that all Muslims pray in the same way. God knows that the differences and difficulties of prayer are manifold. Whether one prays regularly, irregularly, or not at all, Muslims agree that prayer ought to be oriented toward that direction divinely established by God.

Additionally, the significance of the *qibla* extends beyond prayer. Muslims aspire to sojourn to it in pilgrimage, and when they pass from this life, they are laid to rest with their faces turned toward it. Ultimately, the designation *ahl al-qibla* names a community that is bound together by its common reverence for a site made sacred by God. It names a symbolic community rather than one defined by the right arrangement of beliefs. Thus, to avoid more particularistic and potentially divisive designations for the Muslim community, I choose to imagine the Muslim community as one united in a common inclination to God and for which prayer marks the means of knowing the way.

Nevertheless, particularisms cannot be entirely avoided. I recognize that during the course of this book I cite certain sources and not others and that I invoke some names and not others. These choices say much about to whom this work is directed and the memories and histories in which this Muslim theology is rooted. Furthermore, I recognize that works of theology very often bear the traces of the autobiographical. As the author of this book, I can attest that elements of the autobiographical mark this work. Just as the texts of the past reveal traces of the lives of their authors, this work most assuredly bears the markings of my own. Indeed, the theology that this book presents is born out of my own experiences: my experience as a person of color born and raised in a country so indelibly colored by race; my experience as a child of Vietnamese refugees who has only ever called this land of colonization home; my experience as a beneficiary of a largely secular Western education; my experience as an Asian American man, husband, and father raised in a southern blue-collar suburban family living in a time when identifiers such as these (and many others) are important to foreground; and my experience as a person of faith who came to faith out of reverence, love, and awe amid an English-speaking Muslim community in the United States. And perhaps most important of all, this book emerges from my experience as a person of faith for whom faith is an ongoing and lifelong undertaking. That is to say, the words and ideas expressed herein reflect where I have been and where I hope to go. So while I may broadly speak about the imagined Muslim community, I also acknowledge that this work of theology emerges from a particular horizon of life that some, but not all, may share or be able to appreciate. In the end, horizons of understanding are opened for whom God wills.

A MUSLIM THEOLOGY OF ENGAGEMENT

With those words said, what then is a Muslim theology of "engagement"? In order to answer this last query, something must be said about what I hope to accomplish during the course of this book. First, I contend that theology today needs to be viewed in a new light. As Imam al-Ḥaddād expresses above, every age has its own needs and challenges. The world we live in is continually changing. Our understanding of theology, then, ought to adapt accordingly. Toward that end, this work brings into relief concepts that I believe are key for developing a modern Muslim theology: theology, revelation, tradition, faith, and imagination. Stated differently, this book seeks to provide a suitable and relevant language through which Muslims today can foster their faith. This faith, however, must be lived. Understanding is not enough. Faith must seek engagement—engagement with the Divine, engagement with the world, engagement with different orders of society, engagement with one another, and engagement with our own humanity. We must embody and live our theologies, not just believe in them. As a result, this work also presents the beginnings of a theology that is as much experiential as it is conceptual.

The theological trajectory of this book, however, does not land us where some might expect. The arc of this work does not alight us upon some lofty height of self-realization or divine disclosure. My aims are not so ambitious or far-reaching. Other avenues are better suited for such ends, the foremost of which remain the Qur'an and the practice of the Prophet Muhammad. Rather, the arc of this book is inspired by the arc of the obligatory ritual prayer, *ṣalāh*, which has attained a special iconic place across Muslim consciousness as well as within popular perceptions of the faith. Moreover, no posture is more emblematic of ritual prayer in specific and Islam in general than the prostration of head to earth, *sajda*. As the Iranian philosopher Abdulkarim Soroush states, "We need to bring religious experiences back to life in order to allow the construction of a new theology."[5] The Muslim theology of engagement that I develop here is aimed at practice, prayer foremost of all.

Ultimately, the theology of engagement that I develop herein is a theology of prostration. As a result, where we are headed and where this book will end is not high above, but down below in that lowest position of prayer, prostration. While important questions will be asked about God, revelation, tradition, and ourselves, my final aim is to bring us to a deep and meaningful understanding of this simple act of submission. Sometimes it is better to address that which afflicts us on low so that we might better orient ourselves to God on High. At this point, it should be clear that this book has much work to do. The case to be made will require careful deliberation and the industry of our imaginations.

GENEALOGY OF THE BOOK

As may be obvious at this point, this is not a traditional, let alone conventional, approach to Muslim theology. At least, it may not seem so. My concern here is neither rational argumentation nor the finer points of doctrinal belief. I am not challenging the tenets of faith. I do not claim to speak from the position of a particular classical theological school or perspective. Nor is the book an argument for faith in modern times. My concern is to spell out what the work of theology entails. I am trying to trace out where theology ought to lie within our lives and to indicate the resources and avenues that we have at our disposal so that we may each pursue the life of faith in our own ways. In other words, I am concerned with the *practice* of theology. Rather than provide a lengthy theoretical exposition on theological principles or rational arguments, I present in the course of these many pages a series of demonstrations that I hope are lucid, vivid, and memorable for those who take the time to engage with them. Faith figures only insomuch as it is hoped that the faith-seeking and the faithful might find their faith nurtured through the act of practicing or, better yet, living one's theology in today's world.

Nevertheless, despite the initial impressions, what I present to you in the forthcoming pages is in fact not a new or singular phenomenon. This book is an expression of a current that has been long present in the storied Islamic tradition. This is all to say that similarly spirited voices precede mine. All thought has its genealogy, and I want to acknowledge the genealogy of the present work. Two texts in particular were especially influential to me in how I frame and develop the present book: *The Revival of the Religious Sciences* by the seminal medieval theologian Abū Ḥāmid al-Ghazālī (d. 505/1111) and *The Reconstruction of*

Religious Thought in Islam by the modern South Asian philosopher and poet Muhammad Iqbal (d. 1938). Both of these works seemed unconventional for their respective periods of time.

Al-Ghazālī's *Revival* was a work that defied scholarly genres. Frank Griffel, a scholar of al-Ghazālī, writes, "*Revival* was an unusual book for its time," while Kenneth Honerkamp, one of the modern translators of the *Revival*, notes "the non-scholastic nature of Imām al-Ghazālī's prose."[6] Not conforming to widely known standards, the *Revival* marked the genesis of a new genre of religious writing.[7] In his own words, al-Ghazālī describes his project as follows: "For although the scholars follow one course, there is no reason one should not proceed independently and bring to light something unknown, paying special attention to something his colleagues have forgotten."[8] The "unknown" and "forgotten" matter that al-Ghazālī addresses with his *Revival* is the relationship of ethical conduct to the attainment of a goodly Hereafter. His concern was primarily practical.[9] The resulting discourse, then, is not driven by legalism or scholasticism, but by spiritual revival. In book after book of the *Revival*, al-Ghazālī addresses the spiritual dimensions of everyday undertakings, from ablutions, prayer, and fasting to marriage, bodily appetites, and travel. As Muslim ethicist Ebrahim Moosa describes, "Ghazālī's primary desire was to see his heart come alive, and the result is a book with admirably sensitive readings of the Muslim tradition with a *carnavalesque*, even festive, eclecticism toward its revered subject: the sciences of religion."[10] The revival that al-Ghazālī envisioned, then, was not purely individual but aimed ultimately at the broader tradition of his time.[11] Al-Ghazālī was trying to uplift an entire community and how it engaged with faith.

Eight centuries later in the twentieth century, Muhammad Iqbal pursued a similar end of reviving the tradition with the series of lectures that constitute *The Reconstruction of Religious Thought in Islam*. Instead of focusing on ethical conduct, however, Iqbal turned to philosophy, writing, "In these Lectures . . . I have tried to meet, even though partially, this urgent demand by attempting to reconstruct Muslim religious philosophy with due regard to the philosophical traditions of Islam and the more recent developments in the various domains of human knowledge."[12] Hardly interested in merely rehashing the religious discourses of the past, Iqbal was, by his own account, engaged in a more "constructive" endeavor, arguing, "Nor can the concepts of theological systems, draped in the terminology of a practically dead metaphysics, be of any help to those who happen to possess a different intellectual background. The task before the modern Muslim is, therefore, immense. He has to rethink the whole system of Islam without completely breaking with the past."[13] While their approaches differed, both al-Ghazālī and Iqbal were united in their desire to see the living tradition nourished and sustained in their respective contemporary contexts.[14] Their solution was to undertake the construction of a new way of speaking and thinking about faith and tradition. Positioned humbly in the shadow of its predecessors, this work—a Muslim theology of engagement—is similarly concerned with constructing a new way of understanding matters of faith that is both revivifying and ethically grounded. And although I have confined myself to sharing only two historical examples, I gratefully acknowledge that Muslims throughout the tradition have undertaken the task of theology with similar creativity in their approaches and equal concern for their changing contexts.[15]

ARRANGEMENT OF THE BOOK

With all that said, I have divided the book into seven chapters, each of which seeks to reframe key concepts that I believe are critical for the work of modern Muslim theology. Chapter 1, "The Language of Theology," is concerned with laying out the fundamental premises for the present theological venture. Naturally, I begin by discussing what I mean by "theology" itself. Given the term's centrality to the project at hand, it is necessary to foreground my reconceptualization of theology at the outset. The remainder of the chapter addresses what I believe to be the contextual horizon of engagement before ending with a preliminary treatment of revelation, a concept that is treated at length in chapter 5.

With chapter 2, "The Measure of Modern Time," I delineate some of the challenges presented by the contemporary context. In particular I focus on how modern conceptions of death, time, and the end times differ radically from their religiously grounded predecessors. My aim with this chapter is to delineate the stakes of the theological endeavor. Nevertheless, the sense of crisis to which the present theological undertaking is responding is placed in its historical context by chapter's end.

With chapter 3, "Imagining Tradition," I address the concept of tradition and its relationship to theology and revelation. The chapter begins with an exploration of the many registers that tradition has come to possess before turning to a number of compelling theoretical conceptions. In response, I offer a theological intervention in which the Ka'ba, the house of God in Mecca, is presented as a figuration of tradition. Then, in chapter 4, "The Religious Imagination," I explore how the imagination has been understood and employed by the Muslim tradition before grounding it for the work of modern Muslim theology.

Chapter 5, "Revelation and Response," turns to God at last. Herein I seek to answer several questions: What does it mean for God to speak to us? And how ought that experience figure into the matrices of our lives? What does it mean for the eternal, unchanging speech of God to continually speak to humankind across place and time with prescience, wisdom, and relevance? Theology, I contend, must always be conceived as a response to revelation. This chapter marks my attempt to imagine how this relationship ought to be.

In chapter 6, "Faith in the Tradition," I present a historical theology of faith. I examine how the question of faith has changed over time, bookending the chapter with two testimonies of faith. I open with the autobiographical account of Abū Ḥāmid al-Ghazālī and then close with the life of faith of Malcolm X (d. 1965) in order to demonstrate the changing nature of faith across history and the changing nature of the tradition itself.

Finally, with chapter 7, "Theology in Prostration," I develop a practical theology of prayer oriented toward righteous engagement. This final chapter is a translation, so to speak, of prayer and prostration for our times. It is also a demonstration of what an imaginative theology can achieve. However one chooses to do the work of theology, theology itself is an ongoing project. This book offers a possible beginning—and not an ending—for how we might practice theology today.

CONVENTIONS OF THE BOOK

Throughout the course of this book, I have endeavored to keep Arabic terminology to a minimum; the reasoning for this is presented in the second section of chapter 1, entitled "The Horizon of Engagement."

When it was necessary, however, I have always provided an accompanying English equivalent, while also transliterating the term according to the conventions established by the *International Journal of Middle East Studies* (IJMES)—a standard in the field—in order to allow readers familiar with the language ease in determining the original. Citations of the Qur'an are provided parenthetically with the abbreviation "Q." followed by the numerical citation of the chapter and then verse. All translations of the Qur'an are my own unless otherwise noted in the endnotes. Nonetheless, I have regularly consulted and adapted from the excellent work of three sets of translators: M. A. S. Abdel Haleem, Tarif Khalidi, and Seyyed Hossein Nasr's team of translators.[16] Finally, at the first mention of historical Muslim figures, I follow their names with the year of death in parenthesis with the abbreviation "d." When doing so I provide two dates: first, the year of death according to the Islamic calendar (AH for *anno hegirae*, "in the year of the Hijra"), for which year 1 AH is 622 CE, followed by the year of death according to the Common Era calendar (CE for "Common Era").

NOTES

1. 'Abdallah Ibn 'Alawi al-Haddad, *The Book of Assistance*, trans. Mostafa al-Badawi (Louisville, KY: Fons Vitae, 2003), 5.
2. Malcolm X, *February 1965: The Final Speeches* (New York: Pathfinder, 1992), 173. The quotation originally appears in Theodore Jones, "Malcolm Knew He Was a 'Marked Man,'" *New York Times*, February 22, 1965.
3. I am not alone, of course, in conceiving theology more broadly. Many other scholars have recognized the pervasiveness of "theology" across the intellectual and cultural horizons of Islam. To offer one illustrative example, in *The Cambridge Companion to Classical Islamic Theology*, several of the volume's contributors, including its editor, define theology as more than the scholastic tradition. Tim Winter, in his introduction to the volume, states that the "book does not identify 'theology' as conterminous with this *kalām* tradition" and that "it acknowledges many issues which most readers will recognise as theological were treated by Muslim civilisation in a wide range of disciplines." Tim Winter, "Introduction," in *The Cambridge Companion to Classical Islamic Theology*, ed. Tim Winter (Cambridge: Cambridge University Press, 2008), 2. Similarly, Oliver Leaman recognizes that the work of theology was undertaken by Muslim scholars across a number of fields of learning writing: "There often exists

no clear distinction between Islamic theology, in the sense of *kalām*, and the other Islamic and not so Islamic sciences, such as grammar, jurisprudence (*fiqh*), philosophy (*falsafa/ḥikma*), Sufism, and the even more specific activities of learning how to operate with the Traditions of the Prophet, and how to assess and rank the chains of narrators which differentiate their levels of reliability. Islamic theologians did not usually strictly separate what they did from all these other activities, and so it is not easy to provide a neat account of precisely what is 'theological' and what is not." Oliver Leaman, "The Developed *Kalām* Tradition," in *Cambridge Companion to Classical Islamic Theology*, 77. Notably, these descriptions still focus on theology as a form of knowledge that is primarily treated through particular disciplines. What is not emphasized, though it is likely implied, is the application and practice that follows thereafter. William Chittick's articulation, which addresses the aim of Islamic theology, moves more explicitly in this direction with his language of relatability. Chittick describes theology as "God-talk in all its forms" and explains that it "is concerned with clarifying the reality of the Object of Worship, the Absolute *Ḥaqq*, so that people can relate to it in the right and appropriate manner." William C. Chittick, "Worship," in *Cambridge Companion to Classical Islamic Theology*, 221.

4. With respect to homiletics, the sermon (*khuṭba*) and the preacher (*wāʿiẓ*) have been the central concern for a number of classical works produced by religious scholars. The concern for pedagogy is evident throughout the tradition, but is especially apparent within the domain of Sufism, whose exponents were particularly attentive to the nature and form of spiritual instruction. On the historical significance of Muslim homiletics, see Jonathan P. Berkey, *Popular Preaching and Religious Authority in the Medieval Islamic Near East* (Seattle: University of Washington Press, 2001); Linda G. Jones, *The Power of Oratory in the Medieval Muslim World* (Cambridge: Cambridge University Press, 2012). For Sufi models of pedagogy, see Margaret Malamud, "Gender and Spiritual Self-Fashioning: The Master-Disciple Relationship in Classical Sufism," *Journal of the American Academy of Religion* 64 (1996): 89–117; Seyyed Hossein Nasr, *Sufi Essays*, 3rd ed. (Chicago: ABC International Group, 1999), 57–67; Laury Silvers-Alario, "The Teaching Relationship in Early Sufism: A Reassessment of Fritz Meier's Definition of the *shaykh al-tarbiya* and the *shaykh al-taʿlīm*," *Muslim World* 93 (2003): 69–97; Carl W. Ernst, *Sufism: An Introduction to the Mystical Tradition of Islam* (Boston: Shambhala, 2011), 120–46; Martin Nguyen, *Sufi Master and Qur'an Scholar: Abū'l-Qāsim al-Qushayrī and the Laṭāʾif al-ishārāt* (Oxford: Oxford University Press, 2012), 55–79, 242–50.

5. Abdulkarim Soroush, *The Expansion of Prophetic Experience: Essays on Historicity, Contingency and Plurality in Religion*, ed. Forough Jahanbakhsh, trans. Nilou Mobasser (Leiden: Brill, 2009), 239.

6. Frank Griffel, *Al-Ghazālī's Philosophical Theology* (Oxford: Oxford University Press, 2009), 48; al-Ghazālī, *Kitāb al- ʿilm, The Book of Knowledge: Book 1 of the Iḥyāʾ ʿulūm al-dīn—The Revival of the Religious Sciences*, translated by Kenneth Honerkamp (Louisville, KY: Fons Vitae, 2015), xxxiv.

7. Griffel states, "*Revival* creates a new genre of literature by combining three earlier ones: the genre of *fiqh* books on the individual rulings (*furūʿ*) of Shari'a, the genre of philosophical tractates on ethics and the development of character such as Miskawayh's (d. 421/1030) *Refinement of Character* (*Tahdhīb al-akhlāq*), and the genre of Sufi handbooks such as Abū Ṭālib al-Makkī's (d. 386/998) *Nourishment of the Hearts* (*Qūt al-qulūb*)." Griffel, *Al-Ghazālī's Philosophical Theology*, 48.

8. Al-Ghazālī, *Kitāb al- ʿilm*, xliv.

9. Kenneth Garden, another scholar of al-Ghazālī, uses the phrase "Science of Praxis" to describe the main concern of the *Revival*. Kenneth Garden, *The First Islamic Reviver: Abū Ḥāmid al-Ghazālī and His Revival of the Religious Sciences* (Oxford: Oxford University Press, 2014), 66.

10. Ebrahim Moosa, *Ghazālī & the Poetics of the Imagination* (Chapel Hill: University of North Carolina Press, 2005), 115.

11. With respect to the *Revival*, Garden writes, "Its aim was nothing less than the transformation of the religious landscape of his age." Garden, *First Islamic Reviver*, 68.

12. Muhammad Iqbal, *The Reconstruction of Religious Thought in Islam*, ed. M. Saeed Sheikh (Stanford, CA: Stanford University Press, 2012), xlv.

13. Iqbal, *Reconstruction*, 78. With respect to the "constructive" nature of his work, in 1928 Iqbal wrote in a letter to Muhammad Ali Jinnah, the future founder of Pakistan, "My task is merely constructive, and in this construction I shall take into consideration the best traditions of Islamic philosophy." This line is quoted in Annemarie Schimmel, *Gabriel's Wing: A Study into the Religious Ideas of Sir Muhammad Iqbal* (Lahore: Iqbal Academy Pakistan, 2000), 49.

14. In fact, there is likely a genealogical connection between the *Revival* and the *Reconstruction* as Annemarie Schimmel, a scholar of Iqbal, observes of Iqbal's chosen title. Schimmel writes, "The title is likely to bear an implied allusion to the *Vivification of the Science of Religion*, Imām Ghazzālī's great theological work." Schimmel, *Gabriel's Wing*, 49.

15. The works that I would classify as modern Muslim theology are too numerous to catalogue exhaustively here. Nevertheless, several developments are worth mentioning. In a separate article I have used Aysha Hidayatullah's

analysis of the modern feminist exegetes, which focuses on Riffat Hassan, Azizah al-Hibri, Amina Wadud, and Asma Barlas, to delineate what I believe is a significant emergent theological trajectory. Feminist theology, of course, extends beyond Qur'anic exegesis and includes contributions and critiques in other fields, like Kecia Ali's work in law and ethics. Intersecting with this discourse is the liberation theology developed by South African scholar and activist Farid Esack. See Martin Nguyen, "Modern Scripturalism and Emergent Theological Trajectories: Moving Beyond the Qur'an as Text," *Journal of Islamic and Muslim Studies* 1, no. 2 (November 2016): 61–79; Aysha Hidayatullah, *Feminist Edges of the Qur'an* (Oxford: Oxford University Press, 2014); Amina Wadud, *Qur'an and Woman: Rereading the Sacred Text from a Woman's Perspective* (Oxford: Oxford University Press, 1999); Amina Wadud, *Inside the Gender Jihad Women's Reform of Islam* (Oxford: Oneworld, 2006); Asma Barlas, *"Believing Women" in Islam: Unreading Patriarchal Interpretations of the Qur'an* (Austin: University of Texas Press, 2002); Kecia Ali, *Sexual Ethics and Islam: Feminist Reflections on Qur'an, Hadith, and Jurisprudence* (Oxford: Oneworld, 2006); Farid Esack, *Qur'ān, Liberation and Pluralism: An Islamic Perspective of Interreligious Solidarity against Oppression* (Oxford: Oneworld, 1997).

Some Muslim scholars have turned to comparative theology or the theology of religions to produced works aimed at unearthing, reexamining, and at times reframing the Islamic tradition to address the lived realities of modern Muslim communities living among the religious other. This includes the work of Mahmoud Ayoub, Mona Siddiqui, Jerusha Lamptey, Mohammad Khalil, Muhammad Legenhausen, Reza Shah-Kazemi, and Aref Nayed. See Mahmoud Ayoub, *A Muslim View of Christianity: Essays on Dialogue*, ed. Irfan A. Omar (Maryknoll, NY: Orbis, 2007); Mona Siddiqui, *Christians, Muslims, and Jesus* (New Haven, CT: Yale University Press, 2014); Mona Siddiqui, *Hospitality in Islam: Welcoming in God's Name* (New Haven, CT: Yale University Press, 2015); Jerusha Tanner Lamptey, *Never Wholly Other: A Muslima Theology of Religious Pluralism* (Oxford: Oxford University Press, 2014); Mohammad Hassan Khalil, *Islam and the Fate of Others: The Salvation Question* (Oxford: Oxford University Press, 2012); Reza Shah-Kazemi, *The Other in Light of the One: The Universality of the Qur'ān and Interfaith Dialogue* (Cambridge: Islamic Text Society, 2006); Aref Nayed, *Growing Ecologies of Peace, Compassion and Blessing: A Muslim Response to "A Muscat Manifesto"* (Dubai: Kalam Research & Media, 2009).

The project of the "Islamization of knowledge" was first articulated by Malaysian scholar Syed Muhammad Naquib al-Attas and then echoed by Palestinian American scholar Isma'il al-Faruqi (d. 1986). It marks an attempt to ground ethically aspects of modernity in Muslim traditions of knowledge. Other attempts at articulating a reconciliation of Islamic and "Western" traditions include the thought of philosopher Shabbir Akhtar and ʻAlija Izetbegovic (d. 1996), the first president of the Republic of Bosnia and Herzegovina. Similar to al-Attas, the eminent Iranian philosopher Seyyed Hossein Nasr has developed an abiding school of thought deeply rooted in Islamic metaphysics and spirituality aimed at responding to the crises of the modern world. William Chittick has also contributed substantially along this line of thought. See Syed Muhammad Naquib al-Attas, *Islam and Secularism* (Kuala Lumpur: International Institute of Islamic Thought and Civilization, 1978); Syed Muhammad Naquib al-Attas, *Prolegomena to the Metaphysics of Islām: An Exposition of the Fundamental Elements of the Worldview of Islām* (Kuala Lumpur: International Institute of Islamic Thought and Civilization, 1995); Isma'il R. Al-Faruqi, *Islāmization of Knowledge: General Principles and Work Plan* (Washington, DC: International Institute of Islāmic Thought, 1982); Shabbir Akhtar, *The Final Imperative: An Islamic Theology of Liberation* (London: Bellew, 1991); ʻAlija ʻAli Izetbegovic, *Islam Between East and West* (Indianapolis: American Trust Publications, 1993); Seyyed Hossein Nasr, *Man and Nature: The Spiritual Crisis of Modern Man* (Chicago: ABC International Group, 1997); William C. Chittick, *Science of the Cosmos, Science of the Soul: The Pertinence of Islamic Cosmology in the Modern World* (Oxford: Oneworld, 2007).

Finally, several critical Muslim thinkers have made important theological contributions to a number of fields. These include the Iranian intellectual Ali Shariati (d. 1977) with respect to the sociology of religion, Egyptian scholar Nasr Hamid Abu Zayd (d. 2010) with respect to Qur'anic hermeneutics, Algerian philosopher Mohammed Arkoun (d. 2010) with respect to "applied Islamology," Moroccan philosopher Taha Abderahmane with respect to logic and ethics, and Iranian thinker Abdulkarim Soroush with respect to a critical philosophy of religion. See Ali Shariati, *Religion vs. Religion*, trans. Laleh Bakhtiar (Chicago: ABC International Group, 2000); Ali Shariati, *School of Thought and Action*, trans. Cyrus Bakhtiar (Chicago: ABC International Group, 2000); Nasr Hamid Abu Zayd, *Reformation of Islamic Thought: A Critical Historical Analysis* (Amsterdam: Amsterdam University Press, 2006); Mohammed Arkoun, *Islam: To Reform or to Subvert?*, 2nd ed. (London: Saqi Books, 2006); Mohammed Arkoun, *The Unthought in Contemporary Islamic Thought* (London: Saqi Books, 2002); Ṭāhā ʻAbd al-Raḥmān, *Fī uṣūl al-ḥiwar wa-tajdīd ʻilm al-kalām* (Casablanca: al-Muʼassasa al-Ḥadītha, 1987); Ṭāhā ʻAbd al-Raḥmān, *Al-Ḥaqq al-Islāmī fī-l-ikhtilāf al-fikrī* (Casablanca: al-Markaz al-Thaqāfī al-ʻArabī, 2005); Abdolkarim Soroush, *Reason, Freedom, and Democracy in Islam: Essential Writings of ʻAbdolkarim Soroush*, ed. and trans. Mahmoud Sadri and Ahmad Sadri (Oxford: Oxford University Press, 2000); Soroush, *Expansion of Prophetic Experience*.

16. *The Qur'an*, trans. M. A. S. Abdel Haleem (Oxford: Oxford University Press, 2005); *The Qur'an: A New Translation*, trans. Tarif Khalidi (London: Penguin, 2008); *The Study Quran: A New Translation and Commentary*, trans. Seyyed Hossein Nasr, Caner K. Dagli, Maria Massi Dakake, Joseph E. B. Lumbard, and Mohammed Rustom (New York: HarperCollins, 2013).

I

THE LANGUAGE OF THEOLOGY

THEOLOGY

> With the reawakening of Islam . . . it is necessary to examine, in an independent spirit, what Europe has thought and how far the conclusions reached by her can help us in the revision and, if necessary, reconstruction, of theological thought in Islam.
> —Muhammad Iqbal, *The Reconstruction of Religious Thought in Islam*[1]

Theology is *how we respond to God.* I am not describing with these few words theology at its barest level; I am speaking to what theology means in its *fullest* sense—at its utmost. The entirety of this book rests upon this definition. This reading of theology is based on God's promise in the Qur'an: *There is goodness for those who respond to their Lord* (Q. 13:18). Theology encompasses the totality of one's being. It is reflected in our very way of living—our thoughts and feelings, our inclinations and dispositions, our intentions and actions, our habits and observances. How we live in the world is how we express our theology, because how we live in the world is precisely how we respond to God the Creator, our Lord and Sustainer.

Even so, theology is more than a reflection of how we live in the world. It is also a means for changing one's condition in the here and now, in the Hereafter, and—above all—before God. If how one lives in the world is indeed how one responds to God, then changes made in that life invariably alter one's relationship with the Almighty. Theology and life are intertwined. As such, theology—expressing simultaneously a state of being and the aspiration for faith—determines the nature of one's perpetually changing relationship with God.

The Qur'an emphasizes that a life oriented toward God lies at the core of what it means to be human. Throughout the scripture, the human being is called to be a servant of God. Servanthood, then, is an expression of our humanity. What does it mean, though, to be a "servant" of God? How does one serve the Divine? It is not inconsequential that the Arabic word for "worship" in the Qur'an, *'ibāda*, is etymologically related to the word for "servant," *'abd*.[2] Worship and servanthood are not two entirely different matters, but intimately connected. The Qur'an is quite intentionally signaling that serving God and worshiping God are coterminous. To worship God is to serve God. It is as if one's humanity finds fulfillment when these two dimensions of life, service and worship, are made to intersect and align as closely as possible. Put another way, God is disclosing to us that to worship is human.[3]

Worship, however, is more than rites and prayers alone. The worship that God speaks of in the Qur'an is far more extensive. Worship is existential. For humankind, and indeed all of creation, worship is woven into the bonds of existence. As the Qur'an states: *Whatever is in the heavens and the earth is glorifying God, the Almighty, the All-Wise* (Q. 57:1). Every creature, by its nature, is engaged in the praise and worship of God. Every act that is committed can carry the weight of worship. Every breath that is taken draws a person closer to God. Worshipfulness runs through life itself. After all, the presence of the Divine is always before us. *To God belong the East and the West. Wherever you turn there is the face of God. God is the All-Encompassing, the All-Knowing* (Q. 2:115). It does not matter wherever one is in this world or whenever one is in this life, God is with us. However our lives turn or are overturned, we are always turning *to* God, whether we realize it or not. It is in this perpetual "turning" or *tawliya*—a state that the human being continually experiences—that lies at the heart of theology. A faithful theology seeks to transform every turn of life into a worshipful response to the Creator. Its aim is to remind the human being that one is always responding to God, whether one is conscious of it or not.

Theology and life, however, are not one and the same. While a faithful theology will inform all ways of living, not all ways of living express a faithful theology. To live, in and of itself, is not enough. God may always be before humanity, but humanity does not always recognize God's presence or heed God's call. Indeed, there are ways of living that can distance one further from God. There are ways of living that diminish, disrupt, and damage one's relationship with the Creator. Human beings are a forgetful lot, prone to obliviousness. We not only transgress against God, we transgress against each other and we transgress against our own selves. We exact pain and suffering against one another. We have sown discord and violence in this world since nearly the beginning. In the Qur'an's account of humankind's creation, the angels decried to God the depravity that human beings would come to commit: *Will You place upon [the earth] one who will cause corruption and shed blood?* (Q. 2:30) Humankind is capable of horrible, reprehensible things. Such ways of living are not the ground of theology. They do not represent how humanity is meant to respond to God. The verse of the angels' complaint, however, is not merely a humbling admonishment of the human condition. It is also a challenge to humankind to rise above and transform for the better. The question is whether or not the challenge is accepted. Will we choose to find God at each moment and at every turn? Theology, then, entails choice. When we choose to pursue a life of faith, when we consciously attend to how we respond to God, we are undertaking the work of theology. We are choosing to do so. Successful or not, one ought to, at the very least, choose to try.

Furthermore, theology is manifold in form. There are as many theologies possible as there are ways of living that nurture a life of faith. Whether grounded in prayer or seclusion, in charity or fellowship, or in the loving care of child, parent, or partner, the possibilities are numerous. We are doing theology whenever we undertake any of these activities. Every person is enlivened to faith according to a different array of ways. It should not be supposed, however, that one theology stands categorically above the rest. The appropriateness of one theology over another is shaped by the circumstances and challenges of time, place, and person. And in the end, the efficacy of a theology is ultimately mediated by the providence of God and the nature and needs of each individual servant. Every person is drawn to God in his or her own manner, just as every person will return to God at his or her appointed time. And in turn, God shapes each life in accordance with that person's capacities. *God does not burden a soul with more than it can bear* (Q. 2:286). Again, theology is not some remote preserve accessible only to a few, nor is it a narrow and exacting path upon which the entirety of humankind must uniformly embark. Rather, theology is something that every person continually discovers, undertakes, and shapes in pursuit of faith. We are responding to God whether we are conscious of it or not. We are making choices that affect our faith, our relationship with God, whether we realize it or not. The ties of faith are bound and loosened by the character of our respective theologies. Given the heavy world in which we live, we cannot afford to be negligent or oblivious of our theological responsibilities.

Theology is for even the most troubled among us. It does not serve the pious and strong of heart alone. It has the potential to strengthen, deliver, and radically transform the least of us. Whether one's faith is taxed and wavering or uplifted and ascending, a heart turned toward a faithful and fulfilling theology can draw any of us closer to God. No move is too little. Even the most incremental of steps is significant. As God affirms in a soundly transmitted sacred report or *ḥadīth qudsī*: "And if he draws nearer to Me by a handsbreadth, I draw nearer to him by an armslength; and if he draws nearer to Me by an armslength, I draw nearer to him by a fathom; and if he comes to Me walking, I come to him running."[4] It does not matter where we begin or when we begin; what matters is that we begin at all. God responds to the slightest of our moves toward Him. If pursued with faithful deliberation, our theologies can be powerfully transformative.

THE HORIZON OF ENGAGEMENT

> In my slow, painstaking, ragged handwriting, I copied into my tablet everything printed on that first page, down to the punctuation marks. I believe it took me a day. Then, aloud, I read back, to myself, everything I'd written on the tablet. Over and over, aloud, to myself, I read my own handwriting. I woke up the next morning, thinking about those words—immensely proud to realize that not only had I written so much at one time, but I'd written words that I never knew were in the world.
>
> —Malcolm X, *The Autobiography of Malcolm X*[5]

> I say the word again, as he would want me to: Afro-American—Afro-American Malcolm, who was a master, was most meticulous in his

> use of words. Nobody knew better than he the power words have over the minds of men.
> —Ossie Davis, eulogy delivered for Malcolm X, Faith Temple Church, February 27, 1965[6]

Words matter. What words we use are important because it is by our words that we are distinguished. As related in the Qur'an, when the angels ask God why He would place humans upon the earth, especially given the harm that they would invariably inflict, God responds that He knows that which the angels do not. Then God proceeds to impart to Adam, the first human being, something of great import: *And He taught Adam all the names* (Q. 2:31). It is by *all the names* that humankind, the innumerable descendants of Adam, stand apart from the angels. These names make us who we are. They are not merely a distinguishing feature. These names—the words that we declare publicly—represent an important form of power because to name a thing is to assert knowledge over it. Indeed, as the Qur'anic account relates, God proceeds to then ask Adam to speak the names aloud so that the angels may come to know that despite our faults, there is wisdom and purpose to humanity's collective existence upon the earth. Our destiny rests in our words, so we must approach the words that we use with care. For this reason, then, it is through words that I now demarcate the horizon of engagement that this book assumes.

I approach the work of Muslim theology by embracing the task fully within the "logosphere" of English. The choice of English is intentional. This book is written for those of us who live and struggle upon that linguistic horizon. But a logosphere is more than merely language. We are not just bound by a common spoken tongue. We are also bound by a common experience and faith. As described by the Algerian thinker Mohammed Arkoun, "A logosphere is the linguistic mental space shared by those who use the same language with which to articulate their thoughts, their representations, their collective memory, and their knowledge according to the fundamental principles claimed by a unifying *weltanschaung*."[7] The common ground presumed here is a logosphere of English accented and accentuated by the language of the Qur'an, the speech of God. We benefit from certain privileges and are marginalized in particular ways that are historically and socioculturally specific to our context and condition. As a result, the theological framework that I am presenting depends upon appreciating the conceptual genealogies of words as they are used across English-speaking Muslim horizons. English is not just a language. It is *our* language texturing the world that we inhabit.

And why should this not be the case? Muslim communities have come of age in the Anglophone world. Perhaps no life better reflects this development than the life of Malcolm X. Near the end of his life (though he did not know it then, he could only suspect), Malcolm X described to Alex Haley part of the manner of his education in English.

> In my slow, painstaking, ragged handwriting, I copied into my tablet everything printed on that first page, down to the punctuation marks. I believe it took me a day. Then, aloud, I read back, to myself, everything I'd written on the tablet. Over and over, aloud, to myself, I read my own handwriting. I woke up the next morning, thinking about those words—immensely proud to realize that not only had I written so much at one time, but I'd written words that I never knew were in the world.[8]

From "aardvark" to the end, Malcolm X came to learn and live the English language word by word. The end result was a powerful mastery of the language, a distinction honored by Ossie Davis in his eulogy for Malcolm X—"a master . . . most meticulous in his use of words"—and a distinction to which Malcolm X's later life amply attests.[9] This mastery of the word carried Malcolm from prison to the Nation of Islam to the holy vicinities of the Kaʿba itself. In both spoken and written form, Malcolm X harnessed the English language in all its starkness and complexity that his words elevated us in powerful and unimagined ways. To be sure, his words, spoken with clarity and fierceness, elevate us still. Though uttered many decades ago, the words of Malcolm X—carefully cultivated from the copied pages of an English dictionary—have unquestionably made an indelible impression on the ongoing communities of today. Malcolm has played no small part in our linguistic coming of age.

Thus, when speaking of theology, it is not always necessary for us to seek out a classical equivalent, Arabic or otherwise. We English speakers pursue our lives of faith in an English logosphere. Is not our horizon of meaning covalent with Malcolm's? Should it not be? Moreover, not all concepts pertinent to our discourse are easily or even possibly translatable.[10] As I stated in the introduction, what I mean by theology is not

ʿaqīda, *ʿilm al-kalām*, *uṣūl al-dīn*, or some other classical formulation. It is greater than all these. The sense of theology that we are dealing with here and what I have described as "how we respond to God" has a genealogy and significance that is rooted to our English-speaking context. Furthermore, it has developed a range of meanings that is specific to the concerns and understandings of our Muslim communities. So taking into account these baseline considerations, when I say "theology" I mean *theology*, which literally means "discourse on God" and refers to the human attempt to apprehend, make sense of, and find fulfillment in a transcendent reality.

I understand theology as a relational act. It does not abide in isolation but always exists in relation to something else. More pointedly, theology unfolds in relation to God. As the etymological root of the word indicates (*theos* + *logos*, "an account of God"), theology is our attempt to put into words our understanding of the Divine. This discussion—this discourse—is not merely a philological or intellectual exercise. The "account" entailed by theology demands more than our words or our cognitive assent. It means more than simply saying, "I believe . . ." In undertaking the work of theology, we move beyond the mental act of conviction toward something more encompassing—living a life of faith. Theology entails the resolve to transform our lives in accordance with our convictions. This is because the one of whom we are making an account, God, is no ordinary, commonplace thing. He is God the Eternal and the Almighty, the Creator of the heavens and the earth and all that is between it. How can we speak of this extraordinary subject without also being drawn into its orbit and being changed by it? Any proper "accounting" of God, then, demands the entirety of one's being. In trying to understand the Divine, we are invariably changed ourselves. One cannot come to know God without being transformed oneself. More than talking *about* God, we are, at the end of it, also talking *with* God.

THE MEASURE OF REVELATION

> *In the name of God, the Merciful, the Compassionate. Alif Lām Mīm. This is the Scripture in which there is no doubt.*
> —Qur'an 2:1–2

We speak to God because God is speaking to us. Revelation is the means by which the eternal presence of God is made known to history-bound humanity. It is through revelation that we come to know God. While much will be said of revelation in the pages to come, something must be said of revelation now before we can properly proceed to other important theological subjects. After all, if theology is indeed a response to God, then we must take into account the nature of God's address to humankind.

Revelation may be understood as divine communication, with the Qur'an representing the most decisive and clear form of revelation that God has sent. Nevertheless, God's means of divine disclosure are manifold, a point the Qur'an repeatedly stresses. As Japanese scholar of Islam Toshihiko Izutsu has delineated, revelation appears in one of two modes.[11] According to the first mode of revelation, God makes Himself known through nonverbal, phenomenal "signs"—signs that are replete in nature. All of creation, including the human self, are signs of the Creator. The Qur'an repeatedly exhorts this point:

> *We shall show them Our signs upon the horizons and within themselves, until it becomes clear to them that it is the truth.* (Q. 41:53)

> *In the creation of the heavens and the earth; and the alternation of night and day; and the ships that plough the sea with what benefits humankind; and the water God sends down from the sky to revive the earth after it is dead; and His scattering of all manner of creatures over it; and the shifting of the winds and the clouds subdued between the sky and earth—in all these are signs for a people who understand.* (Q. 2:164)

All manner of natural phenomena are a revelatory testament to God. It is as if this mode of revelation, the natural sign, is woven into the fiber of all existent things. The very fact of our createdness discloses in some way the will and presence of God. The question is whether or not one is able to read these signs of God. *Have they not seen the birds above them spreading out their wings and closing them?* (Q. 67:19). *Have they not seen how many generations We destroyed before them?* (Q. 6:6; 36:31). As the admonishing tone of these Qur'anic verses implies, it is clear that many falter in this task. We fail to witness God's guidance inscribed in the phenomenal world around us. A rich natural theology might be constructed if we were to grant greater attentiveness to the nature of the cosmos and the guidance of God therein.

According to Izutsu's second mode of revelation, God also makes Himself known through verbally articulated "signs" made manifest through human language. This is the kind of revelation received by the prophets. Its form was typically a body of communicated text, sent down successively throughout history and preserved as scripture. The Qur'an names several of these scriptural revelations in addition to itself: the Scrolls (*Ṣuḥuf*) of Abraham, the Torah (*Tawrāh*) of Moses, the Psalms (*Zabūr*) of David, and the Gospel (*Injīl*) of Jesus. The Qur'an sent to the Prophet Muhammad marks the culmination and fulfillment of this mode of revelation. This mode of revelation speaks more directly to humanity than the signs of nature. According to Muslim theologians, this form of revelation issues from the "speech of God" or *kalām Allāh*, an eternal attribute of the Divine. In effect, God's timeless and transcendent word is made manifest in human history and through human language. The Qur'an, then, is a form of revelation made for human ears to hear, human tongues to recite, and human hearts to preserve. *God was truly gracious to the faithful when He sent to them a Messenger from among themselves, reciting to them His signs, purifying them, and teaching them scripture and wisdom when before they had been in manifest error* (Q. 3:164). God may speak to creation in myriad ways, but scriptural revelation, as we know it, is a form of revelation aimed at and attuned to our human ways of being.

As helpful as Izutsu's classification of revelation is, we would be mistaken to imagine the Qur'an, or any of the earlier scriptures, as purely or even primarily verbal revelations. Revelation, rather, possesses a dynamism that extends beyond the human word. For instance, the Qur'an is also phenomenally experienced within the mesh of creation. Its recitation creates a distinctive aural landscape for those who hear it, and its performance transforms the space that it fills. The Prophet himself describes the first words of revelation as if they were inscribed upon his heart.[12] To experience the Qur'an is to be indelibly marked by it. Even its physical presence, whether embodied in calligraphic artistry or carefully bound between two covers, has a palpable bearing to it. It is not insignificant that the religious scholars prescribe that one should approach the scripture with a reverential degree of respect and ritual purity.[13] The Qur'an exudes a presence to which the faithful are called and compelled to respond.[14]

While much could be said of the signs of creation and earlier scriptures, it is the Qur'an that serves as our most direct and decisive criterion for "reading" God's revelation. It is through the Qur'an that God most clearly addresses us and invites our response. The Qur'an, then, is theology's foremost interlocutor. If theology is indeed a relational act performed in conjunction with the Divine, then theology must also be understood as our considered response to the message conveyed by the Qur'an. Through it God speaks and to it we respond.

NOTES

1. Iqbal, *Reconstruction*, 6.

2. The two Arabic words *'abd* ("servant, slave, bondsman") and *'ibāda* ("worship") are derived from the same triliteral root in Arabic (*'ayn - bā' - dāl*) and thus share a root meaning. William Chittick has explored this relationship with greater subtlety in his study of worship. Chittick, "Worship," 218–19.

3. This idea finds limited accord with Mircea Eliade's idea of *homo religiosus* ("religious man"). He writes, "Whatever the historical context in which he is placed, homo religious always believes that there is an absolute reality, *the sacred*, which transcends this world but manifests itself in this world, thereby sanctifying it and making it real. He further believes that life has a sacred origin and that human existence realizes all of its potentialities in proportion as it is religious—that is, participates in reality. The gods created man and the world, the culture heroes completed the Creation, and the history of all these divine and semidivine works is preserved in the myths. By reactualizing sacred history, *by imitating the divine behavior*, man puts and keeps himself close to the gods—that is, in the real and the significant." Mircea Eliade, *The Sacred and the Profane: The Nature of Religion*, trans. Willard R. Trask (San Diego: Harcourt Brace & Company, 1959), 203 (emphasis added); see also 14–15, 116–18, 138. See also John A. Saliba, *"Homo Religiosus" in Mircea Eliade: An Anthropological Evaluation* (Leiden: E. J. Brill, 1976), 45–65.

4. William A. Graham, *Divine Word and Prophetic Word in Early Islam* (The Hague: Mouton, 1977), 127, saying 12; *110 Ahadith Qudsi: Sayings of the Prophet Having Allâhs Statements*, ed. Ibrahim M. Kunna, trans. Syed Masood-ul-Hasan, 3rd ed. (Riyadh: Darussalam, 2006), 11, hadith 1.

5. Malcolm X and Alex Haley, *The Autobiography of Malcolm X* (New York: Grove Press, 1965), 173.

6. Manning Marable and Garrett Felber, eds., *The Portable Malcolm X Reader* (New York: Penguin, 2013), 402.

7. Arkoun, *Unthought in Contemporary Islamic Thought*, 12.

8. Malcolm X, *Autobiography*, 173.

9. Marable and Felber, *Portable Malcolm X Reader*, 402.

10. I will return to this point when discussing "tradition" in chapter 3, "Imagining Tradition."

11. Toshihiko Izutsu, *God and Man in the Qur'an: Semantics of the Qur'anic Weltanschauung* (Kuala Lumpur: Islamic Book Trust, 2002), 142–213.

12. The Arabic reads: *ka-innamā kataba fī qalbī kitāban*. Abū Jaʿfar Muḥammad b. Jarīr al-Ṭabarī, *Tārīkh al-umam wa-l-mulūk: Tārīkh al-Ṭabarī*, ed. Abū Ṣuhayb al-Karamī (Amman: Bayt al-Afkār wa-l-Dawliyya, n.d.), 310; al-Ṭabarī, *The History of al-Ṭabarī, Volume VI: Muḥammad at Mecca*, trans. W. Montgomery and M. V. McDonald (Albany: State University of New York Press, 1988), 71.

13. For a prominent example of Qur'anic etiquette literature or *adab al-Qurʾān*, see Yaḥyā b. Sharaf al-Nawawī, *Al-Tibyān fī adāb ḥamalat al-Qurʾān*, ed. ʿAbd al-ʿAzīz ʿIzz al-Dīn al-Sayrawān (Beirut: Dār al-Nafāʾis, 1984); al-Nawawī, *Etiquette with the Quran: Al-Tibyān fī Ādāb Ḥamalat al-Qurʾān*, trans. Musa Furber (Chicago: Starlatch Press, 2003).

14. See al-Shāfiʿī, *The Epistle on Legal Theory*, ed. and trans. Joseph E. Lowry (New York: New York University Press, 2013), 14–45; Daniel W. Brown, *Rethinking Tradition in Modern Islamic Thought* (Cambridge: Cambridge University Press, 1996), 51–52; Abdullah Saeed, *Interpreting the Qurʾān: Towards a Contemporary Approach* (London: Routledge, 2006), 18; Aisha Y. Musa, *Ḥadīth as Scripture: Discussions on the Authority of Prophetic Traditions in Islam* (New York: Palgrave Macmillan, 2008), 5; Rumee Ahmed, *Narratives of Islamic Legal Theory* (Oxford: Oxford University Press, 2012), 79–80; Jonathan Brown, *The Canonization of al-Bukhārī and Muslim: The Formation and Function of the Sunnī Ḥadīth Canon* (Leiden: Brill, 2007); Jonathan A. C. Brown, *Hadith: Muhammad's Legacy in the Medieval and Modern World* (Oxford: Oneworld, 2009). Complicating matters further, hadith or reports that relate the sayings, deeds, and indications of the Prophet Muhammad are also considered a form of revelation. Specifically, scholars designate the Qur'an as "recited revelation" (*waḥy al-maṭlū*) and the life of the Prophet Muhammad as "unrecited revelation" (*waḥy ghayr maṭlū*). The formalization of this distinction within Islamic legal discourse is likely rooted in al-Shāfiʿī's inclusion of prophetic practice or Sunna as an expression of divine legislation, or *bayān* (and hence revelation), in his seminal legal treatise *Al-Risāla*. The immense body of prophetic reports, then, also represents a real

and meaningful means of accessing God's revelation. The very life of the Prophet, divinely guided in many avenues—though not all—can also serve as a form of revelatory guidance if the hadith are properly evaluated, interpreted, and arrayed. The scholarly disciplines that arose to meet this monumental task are unquestionably sophisticated and diverse. I use the cautionary "though not all" because not every action of the Prophet was "prophetic" in directive. Consider, for example, this episode from the life of the Prophet, which took place during the preparations for the Battle of Badr: "al-Ḥubāb b. al-Mundhir b. al-Jamūḥ said to the apostle: 'Is this a place which God has ordered you to occupy, so that we can neither advance nor withdraw from it, or is it a matter of opinion and military tactics?' When he replied that it was the latter he pointed out that it was not the place to stop but that they should go on to the water nearest to the enemy and halt there, stop up the wells beyond it, and construct a cistern so that they would have plenty of water; then they could fight their enemy who would have nothing to drink. The apostle agreed that this was an excellent plan and it was immediately carried out." Other incidents from the life of the Prophet also indicate that not every dimension of his life was prophetically driven. See Ibn Isḥāq, *The Life of Muhammad: A Translation of Isḥāq's Sīrat Rasūl Allāh*, trans. A. Guillaume (Oxford: Oxford University Press, 1955), 296–97; Abū Muḥammad ʿAbd al-Malik b. Hishām al-Muʿāfirī, *Al-Sīra al-nabawiyya li-Ibn Hishām*, ed. Walīd b. Muḥammad b. Salāma and Khālid b. Muḥammad b. ʿUthmān, 4 vols. (Cairo: Maktabat al-Ṣafā, 2001), 2:175.

2

THE MEASURE OF MODERN TIME

A POUND OF FLESH

> It was all so very businesslike that one watched it fascinated. It was pork-making by machinery, pork-making by applied mathematics. . . . It was like some horrible crime committed in a dungeon, all unseen and unheeded, buried out of sight and of memory.
> —Upton Sinclair, *The Jungle*[1]

> The Islamic slaughtering process is like a form of worship. . . . This animal just gave its life so that a human could eat. It is not a process to be taken lightly. You have to do the slaughter with presence. It is a physical, spiritual, and technical act.
> —Ibrahim Abdul-Matin, *Green Deen*[2]

The measure of modernity can be found in a pound of flesh. Walk into your typical grocery store and steer down to the meat aisle. Then gaze upon the refrigerated shelves and behold pound after pound of flesh, tightly packed, stacked, and arrayed in neat order. Each package has been weighed, valued, and marked with its calculated worth. Whether cubed, cut, or ground, each pound on display is presented to us as an abstract mass of semigelatinous muscle, sinew, and fat. This is the meat that we eat. Do we know from whence it came? How conscious are we of the cost of life incurred? These denuded and disembodied hunks of flesh arrive to us anonymously, disconnected from the animal life from which they were efficiently cleft. Our relationship to animals has been radically reconfigured, and each pound of faceless flesh is a testament to this change.

I am drawing attention to this pound of flesh as one way of making sense of the dizzying series of transformations at play when we speak of modernity. This particular social shift is one that historian Richard Bulliet has incisively identified as a move from "domesticity" to "postdomesticity," by which he means the following:

> "Domesticity" refers to the social, economic, and intellectual characteristics of communities in which most members consider daily contact with domestic animals (other than pets) a normal condition of life: in short, the farming existence of a bygone generation for most Americans, but contemporary reality for most of the developing world. "Postdomesticity" is defined by two characteristics. First, postdomestic people live far away, both physically and psychologically, from the animals that produce the food, fiber, and hides they depend on, and they never witness the births, sexual congress, and slaughter of these animals. Yet they maintain very close relationships with companion animals—pets—often relating to them as if they were human. Second, a postdomestic society emerging from domestic antecedents continues to consume animal products in abundance, but psychologically, its members experience feelings of guilt, shame, and disgust when they think (as seldom as possible) about the industrial processes by which domestic animals are rendered into products and about how those products come to market.[3]

The societies in which we live are increasingly postdomestic. Our contact with the rhythm of farm life has been diminished—if not severed—and we have lost, as a result, our once intimate exposure to the cycles of life and death that unfold therein. The occluded processes by which the meat that we eat is procured only insulate us further from the reality of death. The meat we eat comes precut and prepackaged and in some cases is already precooked. It arrives faceless and in embarrassing abundance. The lives that are taken for our consumption are so far removed and abstracted that we more often than not fail to recognize that a life was taken at all.

A similar distancing informs how many Muslims in postdomestic societies celebrate the religious holiday that memorializes the Prophet Abraham's test of faith, the sacrifice of his son for the sake of God, known as Eid al-Adha or the Feast of the Sacrifice. As described in the

Qur'an, Abraham is instructed at the last moment to sacrifice a substitute in his son's place, having proven his obedience and commitment to God (Q. 37:104–8). In commemoration of this act, a domestic animal, typically a cow, goat, or sheep, is sacrificed on Eid so that its meat may be shared with those in need. For those of us living in postdomesticity, we oftentimes insist on taking our children, at least once in their lifetime, out to witness the slaughtering of the animal intended for sacrifice. So infinitesimally scant is our contact with death in this manner (or any death for that matter) that the visit becomes an event. It is hoped that this one-time occasion, the ritual slaughter, will somehow reinstill an appreciation for the loss of life that our meat consumption incurs. Yet our consumption of meat and the death it necessarily entails is far from a singular event. It is a regularity—a mechanized and industrialized reality—that our postdomestic societies willfully obscure. We no longer see the blood that is shed in both birth and death as it was once witnessed in domestic farm life. And hand in hand with our diminished witnessing of life and death is the diminishment of our ethics and expectations surrounding them.[4]

LIFE WITHOUT END

> Know that the heart of the man who is engrossed in this world and is given over to its vanities and harbours love for its appetites must certainly be neglectful of the remembrance of death.
> —Abū Ḥāmid al-Ghazālī, *Iḥyā' 'ulūm al-dīn*[5]

> We fear death because we resist passing time. If other animals do not fear death as we do, it is not because we know something they do not. It is because they are not burdened by time.
> —John Gray, *Straw Dogs*[6]

Our increasingly postdomestic existences, our advances in health and medicine, and our outlook of continual progress further hide the reality of death from our view. Death is still present, but it has been compartmentalized into various forms of entertainment: dramatized violence, death-defying undertakings, graphic horror, and dystopian or postapocalyptic imaginings. Death is a plot device for Hollywood fantasies. It is only memorialized for celebrities. In effect, death has been sufficiently distanced from our lived reality. In the other direction, every effort is made to extend life and to build therein leisure and convenience. We imagine the passage of life to be far more pristine and never ending than it really is. As the German sociologist Norbert Elias succinctly states, "Life grows longer, death is further postponed. The sight of the dying and dead people is no longer commonplace. It is easier in the normal course of life to forget death."[7] This is part of our modern predicament. It is harder and harder for us to imagine our own impending end, but the truth is we are as much the dying as we are the living.

The elderly among us once served as a constant reminder of our own mortality. In the past, as our loved ones aged, we lived alongside them with care and reciprocity. Now even this facet of existence is disappearing. The aesthetics of youth are glorified, while the signs of aging are deemed unbecoming. We find it hard now to live with reminders of our own mortality, the aged foremost of these. And so the dying are sequestered to die alone. In Elias's analysis of death in developed societies, he observes, "The tendency to isolate and conceal it [death] by turning it into a special area has hardly decreased since the last century, and has possibly increased."[8] The elderly are withdrawn to hospices and hospitals to spend their final moments in bland white rooms under flickering fluorescent lights. We are more likely than not to find ourselves alone or served by strangers in the twilight of our lives. We are willing to subject ourselves to unfamiliar settings and inhospitable conditions because our scientific knowledge works tirelessly to extend life, though it can never stave off death completely. We would rather live meekly in sterile settings than die in familiar ones.

Our confidence in our personal selves, achieved through the modern rise of individualization, also translates into isolation. As Elias contends, as death experientially approaches with aging, we begin to wrestle with and are tormented by the meaningfulness and meaninglessness that we judge our lives to have been.[9] When others pass or are passing, we no longer know what words to offer to them or those who will survive them. We are verbally and emotionally impotent with the approach of death, its arrival, and its completion. We no longer know how to express or find ourselves when confronted with it. We flounder in its wake. Rather than confront our insecurities, we hide the dying in both body and mind. The "natural" death has become incredibly remote from the everyday existence of many of us.

The consequences of the modern occultation of death are theologically profound. When death itself is no longer witnessed and experienced in all its possible tenderness and terribleness, we begin to lose sight of our own mortality and limitations. In death's absence, we begin to imagine that our lives will go on in perpetuity. As foolhardy and dangerous as such a view is, a greater transgression looms larger. When we lose sight of our mortal createdness, we fall deaf to the Creator Himself. As the Qur'an emphasizes, God both *gives life and death* (Q. 57:2).[10] Our masking of death in effect masks the fullness of God from our view. Death, that ultimate reminder that our time in this world is limited and that judgment in the Hereafter awaits, recedes before the intense press of modern times, and with it slips our mindfulness of the Divine. Hubris festers in its place.

I opened this chapter with a meditation on flesh, death, and postdomesticity to bring into relief at least one frame of reference through which our lives today can be understood as modern. While I believe this particular perspective to be significant, it is certainly not exhaustive of "modernity" or what it means to be modern. How we experience and conceive of our modernness can be framed through a multitude of possibilities. The analytical threads that one could follow with respect to modernity, modernism, and postmodernity are far too numerous to fully explore here. All of the intricacies bound up in this shadowy and shape-shifting cluster of concepts need not be unraveled at once, however, in order to appreciate the overarching power and effect that modernity possesses. For the purpose of this work, I will focus on time—that perceived axis of human experience—and the different ways that we live and die by it.

I admit that time may seem to be a minor concern when assessing the dilemmas and crises of the present era. Devastating wars and military occupations, worldwide population displacement, precipitous climate change, widening wealth and health disparities, and global white supremacy are much more visceral realities assailing communities today. An element of time, however, underlies all these troubles of the world. Moreover, from the perspective of theology, none of these matters falls outside the reach of God. Alongside human struggle, suffering, and affliction, God is ever present. Indeed, God's revelation addresses each of these dilemmas in its own way, although His word may not always be heard.[11] It is imperative, then, to take the time to hear once more the Divine. How one understands time determines to a great degree how one hears and responds to God's revelation.

THE TIME THAT REMAINS

> The moment is what you are in [now]. If you are in this world, then your moment is this world. If you are in the Hereafter, then your moment is the Hereafter. If you are in joy, then your moment is joy. If you are in sorrow, then your moment is sorrow.
> —Abū ʿAlī al-Daqqāq, in *Al-Qushayrī's Epistle*[12]

Time. We seek it. We cherish it. We nurture and cultivate it each in our own way, though we might not realize how much of ourselves we pour into it. Time is a human universal. How we measure it and how much we value it might differ, but it nevertheless is an inescapable part of the fabric of our existence. We plot our thoughts, actions, memories, and expectations against our projections of past, present, and future. We conceptualize life itself as the passage of time even though all that we ever experience is the present moment in the here and now. Our sense of self is suspended between the person we once were and the person we hope to become. We experience life through the lens of time.

Until recently, our sense of time was intimately connected to the world in which we lived. As British sociologist Anthony Giddens describes, our sense of when, time, has been traditionally linked to either the observable cycles of nature or to a specific where, place.[13] We pursued our daily labor by the available light of night and day. We lived in expectation of the incoming seasons. We measured our activities against the celestial theater of the sun, moon, and stars above. We witnessed the world in an immediate and deeply rooted way and kept time by it.

With respect to time and the rhythm of nature, the Qur'an repeatedly raises the intimate relationship between human life, time, and the created world in order to emphasize the workings of God underlying it. *It is He who made the Sun a radiance and the moon a light and determined its phases so that you may know the number of years and the reckoning [of time]* (Q. 10:5). As a result, the days are marked from one sunset to the next and the year measured by the monthly waxing and waning of the moon. Moreover, the timing of devotional acts is pinned to observable natural phenomena. Both prayer and fasting are connected with the position of the sun and diminishment of its light. *Perform the prayer at the declining of the sun until the darkening of the night* (Q. 17:78). *And eat and drink until the white thread of dawn becomes distinct from the black thread* (Q. 2:187). The Prophet Muhammad and the early followers who survived him elaborated upon these Qur'anic descriptions, referring in like fashion to the phenomena of the created world. For example, when asked about the timings of prayer, they frequently referenced the lengthening of shadows, the changing brightness of the sun, and the degree of perceptible sunlight at twilight and dawn.[14] A prayer could even be delayed, according to the Prophet, on account of the intensity of the noonday heat.[15]

Place was also important for Islamic conceptions of time. In pre-Islamic Arabia, sacred sites had periods of inviolable time attached to them in which pilgrims were expected to wear specific attire, observe specific patterns of behavior, and refrain from bearing arms.[16] With the coming of Islam, four months of the calendar continued to be recognized as sacred months. *Indeed the number of months in the eyes of God is twelve months, [ordained] in the book of God on the day God created the heavens and the earth; of them four are sacred* (Q. 9:36). Three of those sacred months, Dhū al-Qaʿda, Dhū al-Ḥijja, and Muḥarram, were established as sacred with a clear sense of place in mind because it is in the midst of this three-month span that the Hajj pilgrimage to the Kaʿba, also known as *al-masjid al-ḥarām* or "the sacred mosque," takes place. The tabulation of years within Islam is also tied to a sense of place. According to tradition, in 17 AH/638 CE the second Caliph, ʿUmar b. al-Khaṭṭāb, retro-dated the years of the Islamic calendar to begin with the year of the *hijra*, 1 AH/622 CE, when the Prophet Muhammad and his nascent community fled from Mecca to Medina to escape intensifying persecution.[17]

Whether tied to the observable rhythm of the created cosmos or to places of special significance, these anchored measures of time have been dislodged with the advent of modernity. As historian Vanessa Ogle has demonstrated, the late-nineteenth- and early-twentieth-century European–American imposition of standard mean time was met with varying degrees of resistance from Beirut to Bombay.[18] Communities were reticent to surrender their local time for the coldly calculated Greenwich Mean Time of the North Atlantic empires. Increasingly, time has been made to stand alone, unanchored and unmoored. As Giddens describes it, we now live with "empty time." He explains:

> The invention of the mechanical clock and its diffusion to virtually all members of the population (a phenomenon which dates at its earliest from the late eighteenth century) were of key significance in the separation of time from space. The clock expressed a uniform dimension of "empty" time, quantified in such a way as to permit the precise designations of "zones" of the day (e.g. the "working day").[19]

Time is no longer connected to what we witness or where we live. We have instead devised means to keep time that are free of experience and relationship. Time may now be unified, but it no longer has a meaningful connection to anything. Time has been taken out of the world and placed into the void. And so we live by the emptiness of the mechanical clock. There is perhaps no better expression of this within the Muslim community than the mathematical calculation of the Islamic calendar. For an increasing number of the faithful, the visual witnessing of the new moon seems no longer necessary to signal the start of Ramadan. Instead, deference is granted to the ingenuity of computations and equations.[20] Time has become literally clockwork.

Empty time has progressively made its way into all forms of social life across all corners of the world. Its allure and force are irresistible. While time has arguably gained in its human utility, it comes at the cost of its relational meaningfulness. We have traded "quality time" for "quantity time," replacing the metaphysical with the mechanical. Creation and Creator no longer figure in this new time's measure. The belief is that our modern sense of time is more vibrant, advanced, and forward looking. We imagine that it will make us better than we once were. We have made time into something altogether new and unprecedented and speak of it in a radically different way than in times past. "Time is of the essence." "Time is money." "Time well spent." "Putting in the hours." "Overtime." "Downtime." "Killing time." "A race against the clock." "Like clockwork." These idioms and axioms reflect modern time's effect upon our everyday existences. Our lives are dictated by demanding schedules, clocked hours, and incessant deadlines. We mark our calendars excessively. We watch the clock incessantly. We schedule our days to fit in as much as we can. We want to maximize our productivity. We want every moment to count.

Our societies move ever toward a *mastery of time*. Time has become a resource to be collected and stockpiled. Instruments have been devised to track and measure time with the utmost subatomic precision. Every moment must count. How else can we maximize our productivity and refine our calculations? Time, in the modern sense, is something that we can handle and manipulate, each to our own ends. We believe that we have incredible agency over our chronology. We want to make the most of *our* time. As beneficial as some of these endeavors may be, there is nonetheless a cost. Empty time focuses our attention so concertedly on time itself—the time that remains—that we lose sight of the world to which time was once so intimately connected. The Qur'an is incisive in its rejoinder to the contemporary cooptation of time. However commodified, time does not run on endlessly. Each life has its apportioned duration before its mortal expiration. Even the world itself—all of the created cosmos—has a stunning conclusion in store. Creation, time included, shall come to an end—by the will of God.

END OF THE END TIMES

> *Among humankind are those who say, "We believe in God and in the Last Day," yet they do not believe.*
> —Qur'an 2:8

Modern time has been marshaled to refine and expand innumerable fields of knowledge, though its efficacy falters with respect to knowledge of the end or eschatology. In contrast, the Qur'an foregrounds the end times as a central concern. That the end is coming is one of the scripture's more persistent and incisive refrains. Although this world may seem ever enduring, God repeatedly assures that it too will inevitably be unmade. *That day We shall roll up the skies like the rolling of scrolls for writings. As We began the first creation, so shall We repeat it—a promise upon Us; truly shall We do it* (Q. 21:104). Indeed, the reversal of creation will be so complete that nothing will remain but God alone. *All who are upon it shall perish, while the face of our Lord perdures, glorious and noble* (Q. 55:26–27). This dramatic ending, however, is not the product of God's wrath. Rather, there is divine purpose to it. The end times figure into Islam's economy of salvation. Our time in this world is intimately tied to an eternal life to come. Following our individual deaths and the end of all things is a promised resurrection and a divine judgment where we receive from God our eternal recompense. Rather than marking a true terminus, the end times open the way to the eternal Hereafter, *al-Ākhira*.[21]

The advent of modern time, however, signals the sublimation or displacement of this divinely determined drama of the life to come. Modernity refocuses attention on life in this world. Progress, rather than salvation, is the prevailing aspiration. Instead of an impending end times, modern time sets an open-ended future abounding with dizzying possibilities before our gaze, and we, for our part, proceed toward it undaunted. Surely, we imagine, our historical agency and human ingenuity can domesticate this horizon of uncertainties. Just as we have commodified time for our worldly pursuits, so too do we subject time to innumerable calculations aimed at eliminating and controlling the unknown variables of the future. We have turned away from eschatology for a framework of constant "prognostication."

The German historian Reinhart Koselleck first drew attention to "prognostication" or the modern desire to predict endlessly the future in an incisive study of modern European political history.[22] As both Christian church and empire lost their ability to instill eschatological expectations upon their followers, time became increasingly calculable in quality. The future was no longer held captive to religious visions of the end times. Instead, those vying for power began to forecast rationally the time ahead. As Koselleck describes:

> The future became a domain of finite possibilities, arranged according to their greater or lesser probability. . . . Weighing the probability of forthcoming or non-occuring events in the first instance eliminated the conception of the future taken for granted by religious factions: the certainty that the Last Judgment would enforce a simple alternative between Good and Evil through the establishment of a single principle of behavior.[23]

The cosmological end time was dispensed with for a more tangible and rational future. This dramatic development from within Christian Europe has since been disseminated farther afield through the sprawl of its colonial holdings and policy of cultural imperialism.

The impulse toward prognostication has become pervasive. From political outcomes to data analytics, modern societies are increasingly obsessed with rational prediction. We consult weather forecasts religiously to prepare for what the future will bring. We map our routes constantly to ensure the fastest path to our destinations. We insure and secure our present moment against the innumerable unknowns that may befall us. We develop statistical models to predict the volatility of markets, the outcome of elections, life expectancies, and all manner of other temporal matters. We harness empirical data to concretize and commodify the unpredictability of the future as much as humanly possible. We turn time, that once ever-present unknown variable in our lives, into a resource that we can harness and control and know through and through. The unknown shall be known. Time has become a variable for us to control and master.

In centuries past, much of humanity lived with a sense of *fortuna*, a sense of fate or destiny. The accidents of life were once understood as a matter of fortune or divine decision. We believed the unexpected occurred because of forces beyond our control. We once imagined that the course of our lives unfolded according to a transcendent power beyond our full knowledge and certainly beyond our meager influence and agency. Cause and reason were deferred or consigned to a greater cosmological system. When disease, disaster, or death struck, it was in accordance with a power greater than our own. Nor were our futures our own, but woven into a larger narrative of metaphysical magnitude. In the Qur'anic worldview, *fortuna* lay with nothing less than the power and providence of God. Across the centuries, the faithful have humbly recognized that the designs of the Creator exceeded human comprehension and kept faith in the fact that *God is the best of planners* (Q. 8:30). In the face of this experienced reality, trust in the Divine or *tawakkul* was cultivated. With modernity, trust is increasingly placed elsewhere.

Modern societies, according to Giddens, have largely traded the language of *fortuna* for that of risk.[24] Whereas *fortuna* is connected to a higher power, risk, in contrast, is rooted in ourselves. For what is risk? It is the idea that we can minimize the dangers ahead by either pursuing more cautious plans or taking a chance—temporarily place ourselves in potentially dangerous and trying situations—in hopes of securing a better future outcome. Is not risk-taking so very often equated with success? If we subject ourselves to certain degrees of risk, we might be able to seize a brighter future, a more lucrative one, or a more worthwhile one. In the end it does not matter, though, what kind of life we are hoping for. In this age, where risk has overshadowed *fortuna*, the defining factor is that our lives are seemingly *in our own hands* rather than that of a higher power. Rather than acknowledging greater, unknown forces at work, we instead believe that we can control or mitigate the unexpected. Our actions and our choices are now seen to be a determining force. We have agency. History is ours alone to change and make; God has been brushed to the margins.

Think upon how we live our lives. We imagine that our life will be long, not because it has already been apportioned by God, but because of the things that we can do to lengthen and preserve it. We eat more consciously and subscribe to intense and regimented programs of exercise. We subject ourselves to increasingly impressive medical procedures and incredibly questionable medications. We purchase vehicles equipped with greater safety features. We adopt an array of impressively engineered technologies of convenience. We erect buildings that are taller, sounder, stronger, and able to withstand the forces of nature. We are mapping the human genome in hopes that we can anticipate, forestall, or even circumvent the debilitating afflictions, disorders, and illnesses that lie within our genes. On hundreds of fronts we work and endeavor to live longer and better through a confidence in our human ability to do so.

Even our lives are carefully planned for years in advance. Marriage and children are weighed and delayed against careers and opportunities for life-changing experiences. Insurance policies, educational funds, and retirement plans are now integral parts of our future calculations. We carefully plot out how our lives are going to unfold. We make certain sacrifices now, expecting to capitalize on them in the future, confident that there is a future waiting for us. The specter of the end and its suddenness and finality rarely factor into the meticulous planning that we weave into our lives. We imagine we have all the time in the world. While all these many undertakings may be noble in objective, what is so very often lacking is the reality of the Divine itself. Where is God amid these predictions, calculations, and mitigations?

We are modern through and through. Our sense of time is radically different, and it cannot be undone. Empty time permeates us thoroughly. It cannot be filled over, so to speak. The world we live in will continue to be a world ordered and run according to risk and prognostication. For those who seek a life of faith, our age seems to be an age of crisis because it has become so very hard to hear, much less witness, the Divine. Our confidence in ourselves grows inordinately greater. What is to be done in a world that has drowned out the voice of God with the din of statistical oracles and human hubris? How can the radical and transformative power of death and the end times be maintained in social worlds that continually occlude or domesticate them? How can faith be sustained in a world where faith has no utility?

CRISIS CONTINUOUS

> Now the current state of the people of this ancient path is deplorable. Generally speaking, we are powerless, bereft, morally bankrupt—objects of history rather than subjects of history, as were our pious predecessors who engaged the world with the power of truth and dispelled darkness with their spiritual light. Our condition is far from that of our noble forebearers.
> —Hamza Yusuf and Zaid Shakir, *Agenda to Change Our Condition*[25]

> The condition of the world and of nations, their customs and sects, does not persist in the same form or in a constant manner. There are differences according to days and periods, and changes from one condition to another. Such is the case with individuals, times, and cities, and it likewise happens in connection with regions and districts, periods and dynasties.
> —Ibn Khaldūn, *Al-Muqaddima*[26]

The above-cited quote from Hamza Yusuf and Zaid Shakir, leading Muslim American scholars, comes from an incisive assessment of "our current state" published in 2013.[27] Speaking with the Muslim community in mind, especially the Anglophone Muslim one, they express poignantly the deep trouble and malaise experienced across the present age. The sentiment is neither isolated nor unique. Countless other voices from our era could have been quoted in their place. The feeling of crisis, however we choose to imagine it, is far reaching and pervasive for those of us who aspire to a life of faith. What is to be done? What can be done when the problems at hand seem so immense and unavoidable?

The modern era in which we live is not an easy age, but no era, I argue, has ever been free of crisis. For all the "emptiness" that our modern sense of time imposes, it also allows us to see the past in a more clear-sighted way. Our keen and penetrating sense of the past—our historical consciousness—continually informs our sense of now. As Dutch historian Johan Huizinga aptly states, "Historical thinking has entered our very blood."[28] History now informs every dimension of our human experience, and we are, in our own ways, aware of this new fact of life. I offer this point in order to place the present sense of "crisis" into historical perspective while still appreciating the specific challenges of our particular context.

As acute as our modern sense of crisis feels, history reveals to us that our lot is not unique. Others in the past have struggled similarly to overcome or endure the crises of their respective times. While the form and substance of our perceived crises have unquestionably changed over time, the deep and abiding sense of crisis itself is persistent, if not constant, across human history. Modernity may seem terrible and insurmountable, but we have born a strikingly similar sense of peril in countless generations in the past. The present moment has always presented itself as daunting, desolate, and bleak. The rhythmic recurrence of messianic and apocalyptic expectations across the centuries is but one symptom of the human disposition toward crisis. The feeling of crisis pervades, if not defines, human experience. It was felt by the first of us—Adam and Eve, who were brought low so long ago. Indeed, what prophet from the past did not encounter and confront their share of crisis?

Our remembered past is pockmarked with divisive ordeals and terrible tribulations. A palpable sense of alarm and doom accompanied every moment of our history's steady unfolding. Mere decades after the death of the Prophet Muhammad, a series of civil wars irrupted among those who survived him, his revered companions.[29] The Prophet's own grandson, al-Ḥusayn b. ʿAlī b. Abī Ṭālib (d. 61/680), was slain in the most tragic of circumstances by those who claimed the mantle of authority over the Muslim community. Even at this early hour in postprophetic history, the sense of crisis was already intense.

In the centuries that followed, numerous voices from within the Islamic tradition would continue to give cry to that feeling of crisis. For many, the crisis concerned our hold over the faith itself. Less than a century after the Prophet's death, the Umayyad Caliph ʿUmar b. ʿAbd al-ʿAzīz (d. 101/720) confessed, "I fear the ruin of the *ʿilm* [religious knowledge] and the disappearance of the scholars."[30] A generation later, the great scholar of Medina Mālik b. Anas (d. 179/795) spoke likewise: "It [religious knowledge] has not stopped diminishing after the prophets and the (revealed) Books."[31] The eleventh-century sage and theologian Abū al-Qāsim al-Qushayrī (d. 465/1072) lamented the religious decline of his era, despite living in the scholastic metropolis of Nishapur, writing,

> This path has been overcome by weakness, nay the path has in fact completely disappeared. Gone are the elders, in whom one could find guidance; few are the young men, whose deeds and customs deserve to be emulated. Scrupulosity has disappeared from this world and rolled up its prayer rug, whereas greed has gained strength and tightened its stranglehold. Respect for the Divine Law has departed from the hearts of men and they have chosen the neglect of the religion as their support and rejected the difference between the permissible and the forbidden. They have made disrespect and shamelessness their religion. They have set no store in the devotional acts and become remiss in fasting and praying; they have galloped around in the field of neglectfulness and leaned toward those who blindly follow their lists. They have thought little about committing sinful deeds.[32]

This dire sentiment had hardly subsided by the next century. Abū Ḥāmid of al-Ghazālī (d. 505/1111) opened his religious magnum opus *The Revival of the Religious Sciences* with a similarly spirited admonition:

> The guides to the way are the learned who are the heirs of the prophets, but our age is void of them, and only the superficial remain, and Satan has mastery over most of them. All of them were so engrossed in their worldly fortunes that they came to see good as evil and evil as good, so that the science of religion disappeared and the light of guidance was extinguished all over the world.[33]

Down to the present, lamentations of this nature would reoccur periodically in the tomes of the scholars, as attested by the above-cited words of Hamza Yusuf and Zaid Shakir.

The failure to maintain and adhere to the faith, however, is only one manifestation of our sense of continual crisis. At other times and in other places, the seemingly relentless march of death has prompted our trepidations and concern. The great Sufi master Ibn al-ʿArabī linked his vision of the apocalyptic end with the city of Acre, which was occupied by crusaders during his lifetime in the twelfth to thirteenth centuries.[34] For the Muslims of Spain, the crisis at hand was the *Reconquista*, as city after city fell from Muslim rule over the slow grind of the years leading to 1492.[35] At roughly the same time at the other end of the Muslim world, another crisis was spiraling out of control. The historian ʿIzz al-Dīn Ibn al-Athīr (d. 630/1233) wrote of the early Mongol onslaught as their conquest of Muslim lands was still underway:

> For some years I continued averse from mentioning this event, deeming it so horrible that I shrank from recording it, and ever withdrawing one foot as I advanced the other. To whom, indeed, can it be easy to write the announcement of the death-blow of Islam and the Muslims, or who is he on whom the remembrance thereof can weigh lightly? O would that my mother had not born me, or that I had died and become a forgotten thing ere this befell! Yet withal a number of my friends urged me to set it down in writing, and I hesitated long; but at last came to the conclusion that to omit this matter [from my history] could serve no useful purpose. I say, therefore, that this thing involves the description of the greatest catastrophe and the most dire calamity (of the like of which days and nights are innocent) which befell all men generally, and the Muslims in particular; so that, should one say that the world, since God Almighty created Adam until now, hath not been afflicted with the like thereof, he would but speak the truth. For indeed history doth not contain aught which approaches or comes nigh unto it. . . . For these were a people who emerged from the confines of China, and attacked.[36]

Such was the terror instilled by this inauspicious invasion. The sense of crisis would only escalate in the decades to follow as the Mongols drove farther westward toward Baghdad and beyond.

Crisis was not always linked with conquest and falling blades. Its arrival was sometimes more subtle and insidious like the Black Death of the fourteenth century. The historian Ibn Khaldūn (d. 808/1406), living in the aftermath of this devastating plague, reports the deleterious effects that it had upon those who suffered through it:

> In the middle of the eighth [fourteenth] century, civilization both in the East and the West was visited by a destructive plague which devastated nations and caused populations to vanish. It swallowed up many of the good things of civilization and wiped them out. . . . Civilization decreased with the decrease of mankind. Cities and buildings were laid waste, roads and way signs were obliterated, settlements and mansions became empty, dynasties and tribes grew weak. The entire inhabited world changed. . . . It was as if the voice of existence in the world had called out for oblivion and restriction, and the world had responded to its call. God inherits the earth and all who dwell upon it.[37]

In every generation and in every age, the present moment has seemed imperiled and unprecedented. Many who have come before us have trembled with anxiety and concerns similar to our own. Wherever we are and whenever we are, that terrible sense of crisis persists.

The crisis that we face now, then, is merely an iteration of history. As the preceding testimonies bring to light, terribleness has visited humankind in generations past. It visits with great regularity and ease. It is as if we have never been without it. Did the tribulations of the prophets, the civil strife that wracked the early Muslim community, the martyrdom of al-Ḥusayn, the foreboding feeling of religious decline, the periodic tide of violence, death, and disease feel any less imposing, devastating, or irreparable than the perils of the modern world do for us now? Those who faced crises in the past felt just as viscerally as we do in the present that the world would never be the same again. My point here is theological. All of history is in continuous crisis, and it will continue to be so until the true final crisis arrives, the ending of all things followed by the resurrection and last judgment to come.

Know, then, that the deep and troubling feeling that overtakes humanity time and again serves a higher purpose. This life in this world is not the final abode. God did not place us here for our respite. Rather, our lot in this life is to be challenged, confronted, and tested. This is the nature of this life and this world. It is not that we are not headed or declining to lowness. We are already there. The Qur'anic term *dunyā*, used to refer to this life and this world, literally means "lowness." To live in this world is to abide in the depths. Our sense of continual crisis seeks to remind us that our lives are meant to be lived in the below.

Nonetheless, we must also recognize that there are significant differences in the crises that we experience across time and place. While the sense of crisis is perennial, the *form* of crisis changes. The challenge that this world presents—the face of lowness that we are made to confront—differs depending upon our circumstances and historical context. For the work of theology, then, taking into account the form of crisis also matters greatly. As Iqbal writes, "As knowledge advances and fresh avenues of thought are opened, other views . . . are possible. Our duty is carefully to watch the progress of human thought, and to maintain an independent critical attitude towards it."[38] We must realize that whenever and however we respond to God, we do so always in the midst of this world. The nature of our response cannot be separated out from the world in which we live.

Moreover, when we address the Creator, we address creation simultaneously, though admittedly in different ways and according to different registers. It is for these reasons that I have spent this time delineating what I believe are some of the most striking features of our modern predicament: the consequences of postdomesticity, the obfuscation of death, the prevailing culture of prognostication, and the general reorientation toward risk. These developments have dramatically altered our experience of this life. Despite the overwhelming nature of these developments, there is divine purpose to be discovered in them as well. Nothing transpires beyond the omniscience and providential omnipotence of God. All of history, its crises and its triumphs, has already been written. *No disaster befalls the earth nor yourselves except that it is in a Book before We bring it to pass—truly that is easy for God* (Q. 57:22). God is the ultimate determiner of our affairs, and it is God who has established for us the difficulties that we face. *Truly have We created all things in due measure* (Q. 54:49). Thus, however we imagine our modern crisis to be, know that it is by the will of God. Yet it is also by this same will that *God does not burden a soul with more than it can bear* (Q. 2:286). In the same vein, the Qur'an relates, *Say: "Nothing befalls us except that which God has decreed for us; He is our Master." Let the faithful trust in God* (Q. 9:51).[39] The world was not created for our failure but for our benefit. The crises that we confront ultimately exist so that we might learn to live and struggle through them and in doing so attain to God and the Hereafter. As antithetical or oppositional as aspects of modernity may seem to the life of faith, all of it is encompassed within the wisdom of God.

While this overarching reality may provide some consolation, a pressing set of questions remain: How are we to live for God and the Hereafter when modernity pushes so insistently against a life and time to come? How are we to weather the storm of this modern world when the very idea of God seems so remote, embattled, and marginal? How are we to respond at all? Our words, thoughts, and actions—our very means of responding to God—may seem fractured and broken in the midst of the modern, but we need only do what many generations before us have done to find our means of response again. We must seek God in all that we do. We must seek a life of faith that is attentive to the particularities of our context.

A theology for our time must involve an element of rediscovery. We must come to recognize the predispositions and prejudices that pervade our modern worldview and reincorporate within it those elements of our faith tradition that we have lost, overlooked, or misplaced. We must find the means of weaving the Divine back into the fabric of our daily existence. The hope that faith offers cannot be attained by argumentation alone. It will require imagination. It will require vulnerability. In this day and age, we must dare to hear God again amid and above the din of the world. We must render ourselves vulnerable by opening ourselves to a power greater and more deserving than anything that this world or our human selves could ever offer.

> *And surely We will test you with something of fear and hunger and of loss of wealth, lives, and fruits, but give glad tidings to the patient, those who, when disaster befalls them, say, "Truly we belong to God, and to Him we shall return."* Q. 2:155–56

NOTES

1. Upton Sinclair, *The Jungle* (New York: Grosset & Dunlap, 1906), 40–41.

2. Ibrahim Abdul-Matin, *Green Deen: What Islam Teaches about Protecting the Planet* (San Francisco: Berrett-Koehler, 2010), 176.

3. Richard W. Bulliet, *Hunters, Herders, and Hamburgers* (New York: Columbia University Press, 2005), 3.

4. Bulliet, *Hunters, Herders, and Hamburgers*, 1–35. Bulliet has linked many of the perceived excesses in modern forms of entertainment to our new postdomestic reality.

5. Al-Ghazālī, *The Remembrance of Death and the Afterlife—Kitāb dhikr al-mawt wa-mā ba ʿdahu: Book XL of the Revival of the Religious Sciences—Iḥyāʾ ʿulūm al-dīn*, trans. by T. J. Winter (Cambridge: Islamic Texts Society, 1989), 8; Abū Ḥāmid Muḥammad b. Muḥammad al-Ghazālī, *Iḥyāʾ ʿulūm al-dīn*, ed. Muḥammad Wahbī Sulaymān and Usāma ʿAmūra, 5 vols. (Damascus: Dār al-Fikr, 2006), 4:3310, *kitāb dhikr al-mawt.*

6. John Gray, *Straw Dogs: Thoughts on Humans and Other Animals* (London: Granta Books, 2002), 130.

7. Norbert Elias, *The Loneliness of the Dying*, trans. Edmund Jephcott (New York: Continuum, 1985), 8.

8. Elias, *Loneliness of the Dying*, 43.

9. Elias, *Loneliness of the Dying*, 58–66.

10. Elsewhere in the Qur'an, God proclaims, *It is We who give life and death; it is We who inherit [everything]* (Q. 15:23).

11. While the present book is concerned with establishing the parameters and starting principles for undertaking theology today, my next theological work will address some of the more concrete challenges that I have just named, specifically the intersection of race and displacement. I intend to explore the theological resources of Islam available for the ongoing struggle for racial justice and the growing refugee crisis.

12. Abū al-Qāsim al-Qushayrī, *Al-Qushayri's Epistle on Sufism*, trans. Alexander D. Knysh (Reading: Garnet, 2007), 75; Abū al-Qāsim al-Qushayrī, *Al-Risāla al-Qushayriyya*, ed. ʿAbd al-Ḥalīm Maḥmūd and Maḥmūd b. al-Sharīf, 2 vols. (Cairo: Dār al-Kutub al-Ḥadītha 1966), 1:188.

13. Anthony Giddens, *The Consequences of Modernity* (Stanford, CA: Stanford University Press, 1990), 17.

14. While numerous reports abound, consider the following prophetic reports and traditions ascribed to prominent companions of the Prophet Muhammad. The hadith scholar al-Tirmidhī reports: "Ibn Abbās said that the Prophet, may God's prayers and blessings be upon him, said, '[The angel] Gabriel led me [in prayer] twice before the House [of God]. The first time he performed the noon prayer when the shadow was like the strap of a sandal. Then he performed the afternoon prayer when everything was like its shadow [in length]. Then he performed the sunset prayer when the sun set and the

fasting person breaks their fast. Then he performed the night prayer when twilight faded. Then he performed the predawn prayer when eating becomes prohibited for the fasting person. The second time he performed the noon prayer with me was when the shadow of everything was like it [in length] at the time of the afternoon prayer of the previous day. Then he performed the afternoon prayer when the shadow of everything was twice its like [in length]. Then he performed the sunset prayer at its time from the first occasion. Then he performed the last night prayer when a third of the night had passed. Then he performed the morning prayer when the earth began to glow with light. Then Gabriel turned to me and said, "O Muhammad! These are the times of the prophets from before you. The times are what is between these two timings."'" A variation of the preceding hadith is also attested in the *Sunan* of Abū Dāwūd. Abū ʿĪsā Muḥammad b. ʿĪsā al-Tirmidhī, *Al-Jāmiʿ al-kabīr*, ed. Bashshār ʿAwwād Maʿrūf, 6 vols. (Beirut: Dār al-Gharb al-Islāmī, 1996), 1:195–96, *bāb mā jāʾa fī mawāqīt al-ṣalāh ʿan al-nabī ṣallā Allāh ʿalayhi wa-salām*, no. 149; Abū Dāwūd Sulaymān b. al-Ashʿath al-Azdī al-Sijistānī, *Sunan Abī Dāwūd*, ed. Shuʿayb al-Arnaʾūṭ and Muḥammad Kāmil Qarabalalī, 7 vols. (Beirut: Dār al-Risāla al-ʿĀlamiyya, 2009), 1:293, *bāb al-mawāqīt*, no. 393. In the *Muwaṭṭāʾ* of Mālik b. Anas, the following tradition is ascribed to ʿUmar b. al-Khaṭṭāb: "It was transmitted to me on the authority of Mālik, from his uncle Abū Suhayl from his father, that ʿUmar b. al-Khaṭṭāb wrote to Abū Mūsā. [He said] that he should pray *dhuhr* when the sun has begun to decline, *ʿaṣr* when the sun is still pure white before any yellowness enters it, *maghrib* when the sun has set, and to delay *ʿishāʾ* as long as he did not sleep, and to pray *subḥ* [*fajr*] when the stars are still visible, but intermingled. Read in it two long *sūras* from *al-Mufaṣṣal*." The section of the Qur'an designated *al-Mufaṣṣal* extends from Q. 49 *al-ḥujarāt* to Q. 80 *ʿabasa*. In the same collection is another tradition ascribed to Abū Hurayra: "It was transmitted to me on the authority of Mālik from Yāzīd b. Ziyād from ʿAbd Allāh b. Rāfiʿ, the *mawla* of Umm Salama, the wife of the Prophet, may God bless him and grant him peace, that he asked Abū Hurayra about the time of the prayer. Abū Hurayra said, 'Let me tell you. Pray *dhuhr* when the length of your shadow matches your height, *ʿaṣr* when your shadow is twice your height, *maghrib* when the sun has set, *ʿishāʾ* in the first third of the night, and *subḥ* [*fajr*] at the first light of dawn.'" Mālik b. Anas, *Al-Muwatta of Imam Malik ibn Anas: The First Formulation of Islamic Law*, trans. Aisha Abdurrahman Bewley (Inverness: Madinah Press, 2004), 4; Mālik b. Anas, *Al-Muwaṭṭāʾ*, ed. Muḥammad ʿAbd al-Raḥmān al-Marʿashlī (Beirut: Dār Iḥyāʾ al-Turāth al-ʿArabī and Muʾassasat al-Tārīkh al-Gharbī, 2003), 35–36, *kitāb wuqūt al-ṣalāh*.

15. The hadith scholar al-Bukhārī relates the following sound prophetic report: "Abū Dharr said that the muezzin of the Prophet, may God's prayers

and peace be upon him, gave the call to prayer for the noon prayer, but [the Prophet] said, 'Cooler, cooler' or 'Wait, wait.' He said, 'The severity of the heat is from the fury of hell. When the heat is severe, pray when it cools and the shadow of the hills appear.'" Abū ʿAbd Allāh Muḥammad b. Ismāʿīl al-Bukhārī, *Ṣaḥīh al-imām al-Bukhārī al-musammā al-jāmiʿ al-musnad al-ṣaḥīḥ al-mukhtaṣar min umūr rasūl Allāh wa-sunanihi wa-ayyāmihi*, ed. Muḥammad Zuhayr b. Nāṣir al-Nāṣir, 9 vols. (Beirut: Dār Ṭawq al-Najāh, 2002), 1:113, *bāb mawāqīt al-ṣalāh wa-fādlihā*, no. 535. This edition, which is cited throughout the book, is a reprint of the Būlāq edition first printed in 1311/1893–1894.

16. Robert G. Hoyland, *Arabia and the Arabs: From the Bronze Age to the Coming of Islam* (London: Routledge, 2001), 161.

17. F. C. De Blois, "Taʾrīkh, I. Dates and Eras in the Islamic World," in *Encyclopaedia of Islam*, 2nd ed., ed. P. J. Bearman, Th. Bianquis, C. E. Bosworth, E. van Donzel, W. P. Heinrichs, 12 vols. (Leiden: Brill, 1960–2005), 10:259.

18. Vanessa Ogle, "Whose Time Is It? The Pluralization of Time and the Global Condition, 1870s–1940s," *American Historical Review* 118, no. 5 (December 2013): 1376–1402. See also Vanessa Ogle, *The Global Transformation of Time: 1870–1950* (Cambridge, MA: Harvard University Press, 2015), 99–119.

19. Giddens, *Consequences of Modernity*, 17.

20. The debates on lunar calculation are heated and ongoing. My comment is not meant as an indictment. My point is that our increasing deference to calculation, and hence empty time, further marks our part in modernity. For arguments for and against visual moon sighting, see respectively Hamza Yusuf, *Caesarian Moon Births: Calculations, Moon Sighting, and the Prophetic Way* (Louisville, KY: Fons Vitae, 2008), and Zulfiqar Ali Shah, *The Astronomical Calculations and Ramadan: A Fiqhi Discourse* (Washington, DC: International Institute of Islamic Thought, 2009).

21. The Qurʾanic term *al-Ākhira*, which literally means "the last," is invoked to mean the Afterlife. Notable descriptions of *al-Ākhira* involve aspects of both time, the Afterlife, and space, an Afterworld felicitously with God and an Afterworld devastatingly devoid of God. The Hereafter, I believe, captures both these temporal and spatial dimensions to *al-Ākhira*. For more on the afterlife and the afterworld, see Nerina Rustomji, *The Garden and the Fire: Heaven and Hell in Islamic Culture* (New York: Columbia University Press, 2008), especially 5–28.

22. Reinhart Koselleck, *Futures Past: On the Semantics of Historical Time*, trans. Keith Tribe (New York: Columbia University Press, 2004), 9–25.

23. Koselleck, *Futures Past*, 18.

24. Giddens, *Consequences of Modernity*, 30–36; cf. Niklas Luhmann, *Risk: A Sociological Theory*, trans. Rhodes Barrett (New York: A. de Gruyter, 1993). Giddens is building upon and modifying the argument of German sociologist Niklas Luhmann.

25. Hamza Yusuf and Zaid Shakir, *Agenda to Change Our Condition* (n.p.: Sandala, 2013), 2.

26. Ibn Khaldūn, *The Muqaddimah: An Introduction to History*, trans. Franz Rosenthal, ed. N. J. Dawood (Princeton, NJ: Princeton University Press, 1967), 25.

27. An early version of this work was published by Hamza Yusuf alone in 2001 in which the same passage reads as follows: "Yet now, the present state of the people of this ancient path is as you see. We are powerless, bereft, morally bankrupt, and objects of history rather unlike our pious predecessors who were the subjects of history, engaging the world with the sword of truth and dispelling darkness with the power of their spiritual light. We are sad, anxious, impotent, indolent, debt-ridden, cowardly, miserly, and overpowered by the worst elements of humanity." Hamza Yusuf, *Agenda to Change Our Condition* (Hayward, CA: Zaytuna Institute, 2001), vi.

28. Quoted in John Lukacs, *Historical Consciousness or the Remembered Past* (New York: Harper & Row, 1968), 5.

29. For example, see Mahmoud M. Ayoub, *The Crisis of Muslim History: Religion and Politics of Early Islam* (Oxford: Oneworld, 2003); Marshall G. S. Hodgson, *The Venture of Islam: Conscience and History in a World Civilization*, vol. 1, *The Classical Age of Islam* (Chicago: University of Chicago Press, 1974), 197–230; Hugh Kennedy, *The Prophet and the Age of the Caliphates: The Islamic Near East from the Sixth to the Eleventh Century* (London: Longman, 1986), 50–90.

30. Houari Touati, *Islam and Travel in the Middle Ages*, trans. Lydia G. Cochrane (Chicago: University of Chicago Press, 2010), 27.

31. Touati, *Islam and Travel*, 27–28.

32. Al-Qushayrī, *Epistle on Sufism*, 2–3.

33. Al-Ghazālī, *Book of Knowledge*, xl–xli; al-Ghazālī, *Iḥyāʾ ʿulūm al-dīn*, 1:35–36.

34. Jean-Pierre Filiu, *Apocalypse in Islam*, trans. M. B. DeBevoise (Berkeley: University of California Press, 2011), 33.

35. For example, see the verses of the Andalusian poet Abū al-Baqāʾ al-Rūndī (d. ca. 684/1285) penned in the latter period of the *Reconquista*. A. R. Nykl, *Hispano-Arabic Poetry and Its Relations with the Old Provencal Troubadours* (Baltimore, MD: J. H. Furst, 1946), 337–39.

36. Edward G. Browne, *A Literary History of Persia*, vol. 2, *From Firdawsí to Saʿdí* (Cambridge: Cambridge University Press, 1956), 427–28.

37. Ibn Khaldūn, *The Muqaddimah*, 30.

38. Iqbal, *Reconstruction*, xlvi.

39. The Qur'an also states, *No disaster strikes except by the permission of God. And whoever believes in God—He will guide his heart. And God is Knowing of all things* (Q. 64:11).

3

IMAGINING TRADITION

THE QUESTION OF TRADITION

> Only through tradition are we an *umma semper reformanda.*
> —Abdal Hakim Murad, *Commentary on the Eleventh Contentions*[1]

Theology is negotiated between two important axes. As I mentioned at the outset, it is first and foremost a response to God and God's revelation. At the same time, theology also emerges out of tradition. We should not imagine our relationship with God to be a purely private matter. None of us lives in this world alone. We are part of a larger whole that bows in deference to the Divine. Our lives are enmeshed in a wider created cosmos. We are also part of communities of faith spread across space and time. Our response to God, then, is shaped inescapably and perpetually by our engagement with an ongoing, living tradition. But what is this tradition of which I speak? How ought it be understood? Whereas revelation is known through an array of disclosures made by God—the Qur'an, past scriptures, prophetic lives, and the signs of creation—tradition, in contrast, is more elusive. This is despite the fact that we call constantly upon "tradition," speaking at different times of prophetic traditions, an Islamic tradition, a written tradition, an oral tradition, a scholarly tradition, and so on. The dilemma, as we can see, is that we speak of tradition in a multitude of ways, not all of them congruent, making it difficult to define tradition with precision.

The problem is compounded in the English-speaking Muslim world, since no single classical Arabic term captures the many registers by which the English word *tradition* is invoked today. By tradition does one mean the Sunna or the "tradition of the Prophet," which represents his religiously normative legacy?[2] Or does one mean the tens of thousands of oral reports passed down by successive generations that recount and preserve the Prophet's words, deeds, and habits, better known as hadiths or "prophetic traditions"?[3] Or is tradition intended to be an equivalent of *naql*, which literally means "transmission" but more properly refers to the divinely transmitted body of knowledge disclosed by the Qur'an and Sunna together?[4] Or is tradition about a community living across history? The people of Medina, the descendants of those who had lived alongside the Prophet Muhammad, are understood to represent a "living tradition" whose customs and practices are worth honoring and preserving.[5] Or is tradition about an Islamic heritage imagined to encompass diverse bodies of knowledge and embodied by men of learning, wisdom, and piety?[6] The question of tradition is not new for the concerns underlying it are perennial.

From a theological perspective, tradition is ultimately about history and community or, more pointedly, whose history and which community. Tradition emerges in the space between the past and the present. It tells the story of from whence we came and, to some degree, shapes where we are going. The "we" here is significant as well, because the "we" differs depending on who tells the story. Tradition, then, is also about who belongs to this transhistorical community of faith and who does not. About whom and for whom are these stories told? In defining tradition, one is also defining who belongs and who does not. As a consequence, the question of tradition has been and continues to be a highly contested one. In both popular and scholarly circles, tradition is invoked frequently as a key concept for understanding the past, present, and future of communities of faith. For some, it represents a potentially productive good, if only tradition were properly observed, preserved, reformed, or revived. Tradition is not just worthwhile but vital and indispensible. For others, tradition is archaic, outmoded, and possibly deleterious to society—or worse "progress"—and must accordingly be restrained, resisted, or abolished altogether. Tradition has been wielded as a blunt instrument—an instrument of exclusion. However tradition is perceived, the concept has become a central preoccupation for many communities of faith as they come to terms with the myriad challenges and changes affecting the worlds in which they live.

Within Muslim contexts, tradition acquired seemingly existential significance. It has been the center of vigorous discussion and debate. Claims of ownership over the tradition abound. The chains of transmission (*asānid*, sing. *isnād*) painstakingly preserved in the study of hadiths, the licenses of instruction (*ijāzāt*, sing. *ijāza*) that accompany the copying and teaching of scholarly texts, and the genealogies of spiritual leadership (*salāsil*, sing. *silsila*) kept by Sufi orders demarcate in their own ways how claims to the past have been made across the fields of religious knowledge. Indeed, the Arabic designation from which the Sunni community derives its name, *ahl al-sunna wa'l-jamā'a* ("the people of the prophetic tradition and community"), is an explicit attempt to self-identify with tradition itself. This Sunni community, above all others—or so the designation presumes to claim—is the community that best honors, embodies, and exemplifies the tradition of the Prophet Muhammad.[7]

Far from perfect and harmonious, the tradition has always been a field of constant contestation. As time went on, latter-day Muslims increasingly valorized the earliest generations of the faithful, honorifically calling them the *salaf* or the pious forebearers of the Muslim community. This is despite the numerous Muslim historical chronicles that relate the civil strife (*fitna*), violence, and war that wracked the community in those early decades after the death of the Prophet Muhammad and then continued on incessantly for centuries afterward. Throughout Islamic history, numerous groups have argued for the rightness of their own particular lineage, ideology, or school of thought while decrying the legitimacy of others. Works of polemic and apologetics were composed and disseminated through the labor of the handwritten word all in the defense of the faith. That so many works of anathematization (*takfīr*), repudiation (*radd*), and heresiography were penned attests to the divisiveness that surrounds tradition and the questions of history and community it raises. Even the weekly congregational prayers could become an occasion for curses to be rained down from the pulpit against false claimants to the tradition. In fact, these passions periodically translated into violence, persecution, imprisonment, and execution, as the annals of the past diligently recount. The ardor with which Muslims have scrambled to stand sincerely with the tradition seems equally matched by the zealous fervor to determine the boundaries of it. The tradition, we cry, must be upheld, but what are we to make of the differences, divergences, and transgressions that we have committed in the name of tradition?

The problem persists today. In fact, with the rise of European colonialism and encroachment, a newfound urgency over tradition has emerged across different Muslim communities. Modern Muslim discourses continue to be replete with exhortations to the Islamic tradition, prophetic traditions, traditional learning, (neo)traditionalism, and the salvific "Tradition" in general. As South African scholar and ethicist Ebrahim Moosa elaborates, "Tradition is often confused and conflated with essentialist notions of 'authenticity' stemming from the politics of representation and identity."[8] The stakes of tradition are no longer framed primarily within a context of Muslim political primacy, but against a wider horizon of political subjugation, secular expectations, and social disenfranchisement. How ought we define tradition with these questions and problems in mind?

THE CONSTRUCTION OF TRADITION

> Although the tradition of talking about tradition has grown, it has not yet adequately appreciated a dimension of tradition that it has implicitly recognized: tradition as process—as a modality of change, as *a* way, but not *the* way, in which any society can cope with universal problems of human existence, such as legitimacy, authority, and change itself.
>
> —Marilyn Robinson Waldman, "Tradition as a Modality of Change"[9]

> What I am . . . is in key part what I inherit, a specific past that is present to some degree in my present. I find myself part of a history and that is generally to say, whether I like it or not, whether I recognize it or not, one of the bearers of a tradition.
>
> —Alasdair MacIntyre, *After Virtue*[10]

It is unsurprising that tradition has been the subject of critical inquiry, analysis, and theorization for many sociologists, anthropologists, historians, cultural theorists, philosophers, and scholars of religion seeking to better understand the social changes and processes underway, whether in Muslim societies or otherwise. The fruits of the resulting discourse have been manifold. Tradition has come to be understood as a dynamic means of societal adaptability, what historian Marilyn Robinson Waldman describes above as a "modality of change."[11] Tradition is a process that unfolds over time. Rather than being formed in the crucible of a specific past moment or period, tradition is diachronic. It is continually developing with each new era of human history and adapting to the new circumstances that invariably arise.

Furthermore, tradition is both of the past and of the present. According to the German philosopher of hermeneutics Hans-Georg Gadamer, tradition is precisely that which allows us to bridge the two.[12] Although the gulf between the past and our present moment is ever widening, we continually peer back into history for meaning, orientation, and guidance. Moreover, tradition possesses a critical element of malleability for Gadamer. He states, "Tradition is not simply a permanent condition; rather, we produce it ourselves inasmuch as we understand, participate in the evolution of tradition, and hence further determine it ourselves."[13] The British Marxist historian Eric Hobsbawm has analyzed how traditions of more recent "invented" construction are construed to possess a longer and more august "continuity with a suitable historic past."[14] What the broad-ranging modern analytical discourse over tradition has revealed is the degree to which human agency is at work in the formation, adaption, and perpetuation of a tradition. More than a repository of the past to be preserved or reformed, tradition is, at least in part, an ongoing human construct.

The words of Scottish philosopher Alasdair MacIntyre quoted above offer an important intervention with respect to our ongoing role in the construction of tradition. MacIntyre is asserting that a tradition—true to its Latin etymology *traditum*, meaning "what is handed down"—is inherited by new "bearers" with each successive generation.[15] Those who live in the present are as much involved in a tradition as those imagined to embody the past. It is not, however, only a matter of reception or blind imitation. Tradition is also about what *ought* to be handed down, for it is also etymologically related to *tradendum*, "what is supposed to be handed down."[16] Each of us, then, as the living bearers of tradition, has a role in discerning and perpetuating it. As Muslim American scholar Sherman Jackson elucidates,

> The past—as a simple matter of history—does not pass unprocessed and unmediated into the present. Instead, someone has to make decisions about which aspects of the past are non-essential and thus allowed to drop out, and which elements of the present are consistent with the past and thus eligible for admission into the sanctum of tradition.[17]

In order for a tradition to continue, its human adherents must construe it—construct and reconstruct it—as meaningfully continuous with the past with every successive generation.[18]

That process of deliberation and construction, of course, is neither straightforward nor unanimous in vision, but fraught with differences of opinion. Yet this is to be expected, MacIntyre explains, because "a living tradition . . . is an historically extended, socially embodied argument . . . an argument precisely in part about the goods which constitute tradition."[19] Tradition is formed and reformed within an ethos of questioning. Questions of whose past, of what ought to be handed down, of how we ought to live, and of what must be done drive the process. It is unsurprising, then, that tradition has been and continues to be the source and cause of much debate and division. "Traditions, when vital, embody continuities of conflict," as MacIntyre elaborates.[20] The energies that animate the debates over tradition, then, are not a problem but are integral to tradition itself. As divisive as they may be, these differences of opinion are an inescapable part of tradition itself and its unfolding within human history. They attest to its abiding relevance and vitality.

The human element is also the underlying principle of Talal Asad's notion of "discursive tradition," arguably one of the most influential anthropological theories of tradition within the Euro-American academy presently. Given its wide scholarly currency and because of its initial formulation for an anthropology of Islam, Asad's explanation is worth recounting at length:

> A tradition consists essentially of discourses that seek to instruct practitioners regarding the correct form and purpose of a given practice that, precisely because it is established, has a history. These discourses relate conceptually to *a past* (when the practice was instituted, and from which the knowledge of its point and proper performance has been transmitted) and *a future* (how the point of that

> practice can be best secured in the short or long term, or why it should be modified or abandoned), through *a present* (how it is linked to other practices, institutions, and social conditions) . . . it will be the practitioners' conceptions of what is *apt performance*, and of how the past is related to present practices, that will be crucial for tradition, not the apparent repetition of an old form.[21]

Asad's definition of tradition shifts the starting point for tradition away from ideas and onto practice—from orthodoxy to apt performance. Orthodoxy, of course, still matters, but it is not understood as a fixed or abiding "body of opinion." Rather, Asad argues, orthodoxy is as "a relationship of power," specifically "wherever Muslims have the power to regulate, uphold, require, or adjust *correct* practices, and to condemn, exclude, undermine, or replace *incorrect* ones."[22] Traditions are the means through which orthodoxy is developed in that they entail a constant process of negotiation, reasoning, and resistance. Or, as Moosa puts it, tradition can be said to "prefigure orthodoxy."[23]

My objective here is not to document exhaustively the theories of tradition that have emerged in the last two centuries, as potent and productive as they may be for understanding Islam and Muslim communities. I mention these particularly influential formulations because they share a common limitation, at least from the perspective of theology. Each of the preceding understandings is framed anthropocentrically; tradition is cast fundamentally as a human affair. Anthropological readings of tradition in particular tell only part of the story. While the light they shed on the human dimension of tradition is indispensible, this emphasis has become ascendant to the point that other dimensions of equal or arguably greater import are eclipsed. For the work of theology in particular, an intervention is in order. What is missing from the prevailing theoretical discussions of tradition is an accounting of the Divine. There is something deeply unsatisfactory, at least for a theologian, in focusing on primarily anthropocentric considerations. After all, theology is the business of talking of God—at the very least—and God ought to figure more prominently in theological conceptions of tradition.

Tradition partakes of both the human and the divine. While it is connected unquestionably to history and community, it also emerges from our abiding desire to remain bound in some meaningful way to revelation. A theological conception of tradition, then, ought to account for both revelation (its message, instantiation, and historical unfolding) and what we have made and continue to make of revelation. Tradition, then, is not merely about past and present, but about a past and present in which the workings of God are manifest. The initial irruption of the Qur'an onto the horizon of humanity nearly a millennium and a half ago will always be of incredible importance for the life of faith. So too is the legacy of the prophets sent by God in ages past. Yet access to that expansive, sacred past is always mediated through an ever-increasing historical interim, the growing record of our sincere and ongoing human effort to preserve and foster our connection to the Divine against the march of time. Rooted in revelation, our tradition represents over fourteen centuries of Muslim history in which we have continually negotiated the divide between a past and present marked by God. I am not arguing, however, for tradition to be granted sacrosanct status. It is decidedly not the same as revelation, though it must always account for it. As the preceding theoretical formulations attest and to which I largely agree, tradition is a construct of human making.

THE KAʿBA AS TRADITION

> I stand for my prayer and set the Kaʿba before my brow, the final crossing beneath my feet, Paradise to my right, the Hellfire to my left, and the angel of death behind me. I imagine it to be my last prayer.
> —Ḥātim al-Aṣamm, in al-Ghazālī's *Revival of the Religious Sciences*[24]

> The eye of imagination sees God as immanent. It recognizes God's signs and marks in all things. It perceives the universe as the theatre of divine significance, infused with intelligent and intelligible light. It finds God's names and attributes manifest everywhere in the world and the soul, and it describes God in the positive terms supplied by revelation and the natural realm. This is to say that the eye of imagination feeds on myth and symbol, and it sees things not simply as signs and pointers to God, but as the actual presence of the Real.
> —William Chittick, *Science of the Cosmos, Science of the Soul*[25]

My aim here is to offer a theological reading of the tradition that preserves the crucial role of the Divine in the unfolding of tradition while also critically accounting for our human role in the ongoing construction of it. To that end, let us step away from theoretical formulations and debates for the time being. To answer the question of tradition, I am taking recourse to the conventions of the religious imagination. Tradition, I believe, can be understood as a story, and what follows is a narrative theology of tradition that seeks to bring this out. What I am offering is a faith-oriented reading of history, specifically the life of the Kaʿba, the sacred structure that lies at the heart of the city of Mecca and to which Muslim prayer is perpetually oriented. I believe important dimensions of tradition can be elucidated through a narrative life of the Kaʿba. Alternatively, my treatment of tradition can be understood as a kind of figurative theology in that I am using the Kaʿba as a figuration or allegorical representation for tradition itself. Matters of the religious imagination, of course, are better demonstrated through the actual telling of the story rather than the analytic exposition of it.

Consider for the moment the house of God. Let us imagine the Kaʿba as our tradition. More than that, let us imagine the Kaʿba *is* our tradition. The Kaʿba is a powerful object and symbol in Islam that brims with significance. It is a thing that belongs to both the human and the Divine. Its origin is from the Eternal, but its life is lived alongside the lives of human beings. It is at once the house of God, a site declared sacred in the Qur'an—*God made the Kaʿba, the Sacred House, a sanctuary for humankind* (Q. 5:97)—while also an edifice of stone built by human hands. The stones that support it today have been changed many times over during the course of countless generations. In history, it has ever been the construct of man. In fact, it has been a thing of perpetual reconstruction. This is the Kaʿba—the house of God, *bayt Allāh*—protected from on high, but also maintained from down low. So too is the nature of tradition, born from revelation on high, but sustained and fostered by we who live ever so low.

Both the Kaʿba and tradition issue from a sacred source. Just as the Kaʿba's establishment is indebted to a divine decree, tradition likewise owes its genesis to God. Tradition would not exist were it not for God's sending down of revelation. On this register, tradition can continue to lay claim to a sustaining heavenly connection. Furthermore, the Kaʿba has played and continues to play a pivotal role in God's working within the world. It is a site where God has foreordained events of immense significance. To it God has sent a procession of His prophets, and to it still does God call the attention of the faithful. From Adam to Abraham and Ishmael to the Prophet Muhammad, the Kaʿba has figured into the many tales told of God's prophets and messengers. It has remained a testament and sign of God's presence in our world as history continues to unfold according to God's divine determination.

Moreover, the Kaʿba pervades the consciousness of believers in that it is the ritual axis around which both prayer and pilgrimage revolve. In a resounding moment of divine intervention, God reveals to the nascent Muslim community that the sacred sanctuary is in fact the new *qibla*, the direction of prayer. *We have seen you turning your face to heaven, so We shall turn you to a direction of prayer that is dear to you. Turn your face in the direction of the sacred place of prostration* (Q. 2:144). God, beholding the countenance of the Prophet lifted heavenward, compassionately responds. That response echoes through history. From that moment forward until the end of time, all prayers will be directed toward the Kaʿba. God recenters and returns the ritual attention of the community of faith upon His house. The Kaʿba's place in Islam is central. Is not tradition, the Islamic tradition, somehow the same? Is its sacred source not also God? And is its role not central to life in this world and the attainment of a goodly Hereafter?

Pressing further back into the past, the Kaʿba's beginnings lie in a time before time, *in illo tempore*. As related copiously in Qur'an commentaries, historical chronicles, and tales of the prophets, it is in the valley of Mecca where Adam and Eve reunite after having been brought low from Eden.[26] It is at that site that God commands them to honor the first sanctuary, the first iteration of the sacred house, as a site of remembrance and worship of God. Through their labor the valley of Mecca is made into "an earthly substitute for the garden of Eden."[27] The Kaʿba and its vicinities reflect the celestial realm, a now lost paradisiacal domain, while simultaneously being an accessible, physical reality in this world. Our continual orientation to the Kaʿba in this life is merely an echo of our true orientation to God in the realms of the Hereafter. At one and the same time, the hallowed grounds of the sacred house are a place of both heaven and earth. Here is Islam's *axis mundi*, the spiritual center around which the world is arrayed.[28] Tradition, in like fashion, exerts a centripetal force upon the believers as they abide in this passing world. It too is an axis that orients and directs the faithful to God.

Yet as much as the Kaʿba is the house of God, we must not forget that revelation also proclaims it to be a house of human making, as the Qur'an reminds: *As Abraham and Ishmael raised up the foundations of the house* (Q. 2:127). The Kaʿba's relationship to humanity is intimate. Anchored upon the earth, the house of God is a thing of history subject to the attention and negligence of its human custodians. Though built anew by Abraham and Ishmael, its stones are still subject to the vicissitudes of time. Each generation must tend to the Kaʿba's care lest it fall into ruin or disrepair. This too is true of tradition. Its life depends upon the work of generations, each laboring to protect and shepherd it through the ravages of history.

The fortitude of the Kaʿba's custodians, however, ebbs and flows over time. As centuries pass, those who cling to Abraham's legacy and continue to honor the Kaʿba's original purpose find themselves gradually driven to the periphery. Polytheism, with all its ease and lure, displaces monotheism until the Ka'ba is made into a sanctum for idols. Even the house of God can be made into a house of idolatry. Those who cleave still to the worship of the one God, known as the *ḥunafāʾ*, retreat to the vicinity's surrounding mountains, the margins of Mecca itself. The Kaʿba may abide, but it abides misremembered. Indeed, the pinnacle of negligence is reached only five years before the first Qur'anic revelation descends upon the Prophet Muhammad. At that time, when the mantle of prophethood was still some years off, the house of God had faded to a mere shadow of what it had once been. Early Muslim chronicles record that the Kaʿba stood as nothing more than loose stones rising to just above a man's height, plundered and left roofless by preceding generations.[29] It is only then, at such an abysmal low, that the tribe of Quraysh, the supposed custodians of Mecca and the Prophet Muhammad's kin, finally resolves to remake it. It is during this time that the Prophet Muhammad, years before receiving the Qur'anic revelation, worked with his kinsmen to physically restore the Kaʿba. Indeed, it was his hands that set back into place the sacred Black Stone, a celestial remnant originally sent to guide Adam and Eve. The Prophet would return decades later at the height of his prophetic mission to restore the Kaʿba yet again. This time, however, he did so by removing the idols and reinstating the monotheistic worship of God to its precincts.

As important as the prophets are, we should not dismiss the uncertain periods that emerged in between them. These times testify to how easily the human community of faith can stray and forget even when living in the presence of God's house. Consider how direly the fortunes of the Kaʿba fell from the time of Adam to the time of Abraham and then from the time of Ishmael to the time of Muhammad. In this way too, tradition resonates with God's sacred house. Is not tradition likewise a trust passed down by our successive generations to be preserved and protected? But has not this trust been relegated and neglected at times by those who are supposedly its guardians? Are we not also struggling to maintain the integrity of the tradition as we see it?

Nor does the saga of the Kaʿba conclude with the end of prophecy. The Day of Judgment looms ahead and time marches on while the wavering mass of humanity proceeds toward it. The history that stretches from the Prophet's passing to today is replete with accounts of the Kaʿba's travails and tribulations. God in His omniscience and omnipotence, His compassion and mercy, continues to watch over it while humanity in its forgetfulness and fragility continues to struggle before it. The Kaʿba lives on, and its physical remains are still subject to our very palpable care and neglect. As in times past, the state of the Kaʿba rises and falls with human fortune.

Half a century after the Prophet Muhammad, the early Muslim community finds itself divided and racked by seemingly unceasing civil war. How quickly is the light of prophecy eclipsed by darker times and murkier natures. Mecca and its recently restored sanctuary are soon besieged. ʿAbd Allāh b. al-Zubayr (d. 73/692), a companion of the Prophet born in the early years of Muhammad's time in Medina, decries the legitimacy of the Umayyad Caliph Yazīd b. Muʿāwiya (r. 60–64/680–683). He and his followers fortify themselves in Mecca. When forces loyal to the Umayyads march against Ibn al-Zubayr, he takes up arms and resists. Justifiable or not, it is under Ibn al-Zubayr's banner that the Kaʿba suffers its first real wound in the post-prophetic era. The chronicles report, "They [the supporters of Ibn al-Zubayr] were causing fires to be lit around the Kaʿbah. There was a spark which the wind blew; it set fire to the veil of the Kaʿbah and burned the wood of the Sacred House on Saturday, 3 Rabīʿ al-Awwal (October 31)" in the year 64/683.[30] One witness attests,

> I came to Mecca with my mother on the day the Kaʿbah was burned. The fire had reached it, and I saw that it was without its silk veil. I saw that the Yemenī corner of the Kaʿbah was black and had been cracked in three places. I asked, "What has happened to the Kaʿbah?" They pointed to one of Ibn al-Zubayr's followers and said, "It has been burned because of this man. He put a firebrand on the tip of his spear; the wind made it fly off. It struck the veils of the Kaʿbah between the Yemenī corner and the Black Stone."[31]

The house of God, although proclaimed by revelation to be a sanctuary for humankind, is made by men into the opposite. War fires and arms fill the Kaʿba's vicinities, and the followers of Ibn al-Zubayr lapse in their watchfulness and set God's house aflame. In the wake of the Prophet Muhammad, his divided community allows the sacred house to smolder and burn.

Nonetheless, the Kaʿba is restored, but the restoration is short-lived. Less than a decade later, ʿAbd al-Mālik, the fifth Umayyad Caliph (r. 65–86/685–705), sends al-Ḥajjāj b. Yūsuf (d. 95/714) to put an end to Ibn al-Zubayr's resistance in Mecca. Tensions reescalate, and blood is shed on the plains of ʿArafa, the supposed place of Adam and Eve's earthly reunion and the very site from which the Prophet Muhammad delivered his final sermon and received the last revelation: *Today I have perfected your religion for you, completed My blessing upon you, and chosen Islam as your religion* (Q. 5:3). Blood is shed on the very site where the Qur'anic revelation reaches its completion.

The trials of the sacred precinct do not end here. For six months and seventeen nights, al-Ḥajjāj besieges the city of the house of God. For six months and seventeen nights, engines made by men hurl stones at the sacred mosque and its quarters. For six months and seventeen nights, the walls of the Kaʿba are bombarded and shaken. One witness attests, "I saw the trebuchet (*manjanīq*) with which [stones] were being hurled. The sky was thundering and lightning, and the sound of the thunder and lightning rose above that of the stones, so that it masked it. The Syrians considered this ominous and withheld their hands. But al-Ḥajjāj . . . picked up the trebuchet stone and loaded it. 'Shoot,' he said; and he himself shot with them."[32] Here is a testament to human hubris—to transgress rather than uphold the sanctuary proclaimed sacrosanct by God. How often has the tradition been likewise subject to similar hubris? As for the Kaʿba, battered as it may be, its fallen and cracked stones will eventually be set aright.

This legacy of human devastation and ruination with respect to the Kaʿba continues. In the early fourth/tenth century, the zealous Qarmaṭīs of al-Baḥrayn bring trauma to Mecca once more. Under the leadership of Abū Ṭāhir al-Jannābī (d. 332/943–944), the Qarmaṭīs assault and capture cities throughout Iraq. Before long their sights turn to the holy city of Mecca, and on their push southward they attack caravans and pilgrims along the way. They arrive, no less, at the city on the 7th of Dhū l-Ḥijja, 317, one day before the Ḥajj pilgrimage is set to commence. The days that follow are filled with violence. Like a relentless wave, the Qarmaṭīs of Abū Ṭāhir crash upon Mecca. For eight horrific days, they plunder the city and massacre pilgrims. The blood of the pious carpets the grounds of the sacred house. In a final imperious act of defiance, the Qarmaṭīs tear the Black Stone from the Kaʿba and carry it away.[33] They carry away the stone sent down by God, the same blessed stone carried and cared for by the prophets of the past. The seemingly inviolable is violated. All is not lost, however. In 339/951, after twenty-two years of captivity, the Black Stone returns and the house of God is restored.

Even in recent times the Kaʿba continues to weather the storm of human history. On 20 November 1979, at the dawn of the fifteenth century of the Islamic calendar, Juhaymān al-ʿUtaybī and his fervent followers captured the sanctuary of the Kaʿba and held it and thousands of the pious hostage.[34] Just as in times past, war and bloodshed were brought into the holy sanctuary, and by force and violence are these things ushered out. The Kaʿba stood witness and endured the chaos and carnage surrounding it as the messianic expectations of Juhaymān al-ʿUtaybī were brought to naught. Even this trauma, which still lies within the grasp of living memory, was not beyond reversal. Time and again, we find the community of the faithful working and toiling to make and keep the house of God whole. However much we as a community have allowed blood, bitterness, and ruin to overtake the vicinity of the house of God, we have also diligently seen to the Kaʿba's eventual recovery and enduring survival. Such has been the life of the Kaʿba. Such *is* its life. Although great harm may be done to the sacred house, the wisdom and workings of God are greater. The Kaʿba's preservation and continuation through the ages has been rendered at the hands of a dedicated and faithful community acting in accordance with the will of God. Although many hands have clawed at its walls, many more have acted for its sake.

We can imagine the Kaʿba and tradition to be cut from the same cloth. God establishes both the sacred house and the tradition, and God continues to watch over them. The divine decree rests upon them both. At the same time, the Kaʿba and tradition are things of history, and their temporal lives yield to the volatility of human care and neglect. By the hands of the faithful, the Kaʿba and tradition have been preserved and perpetuated through so many long years, despite the turbulent nature of human piety and errancy. Moreover, it is through the Kaʿba and tradition that we find a connection with divinity. Although of human construct, both the Kaʿba and tradition stand as referents to God. How precious are the Kaʿba and tradition to Muslim sensibilities and how precarious do their lives seem when entrusted to human stewardship, yet how vital they also are in sustaining prayers and faith and how constant they have been as the community of faith struggles through this world.

This lengthy meditation on the Kaʿba is not a conventional definition of tradition, though it does the work of defining nonetheless. Nor, of course, do I mean to imply that the Kaʿba and tradition are true equivalents. In fact, the primary aim of the foregoing treatment was not to outline a life of the Kaʿba at all. Rather, I was using the Kaʿba and the religious expectations surrounding it as a means of conveying the very similar ways by which Muslims understand and relate to tradition.[35] The Kaʿba and tradition have a shared gravitas in the narratives of Islam, and so I invoked that shared gravitas to serve as a conceptual bridge and as a means of delineating significant shared features. Whether a Muslim has visited the vicinities of the Kaʿba or not (and I have not), the *idea* of the Kaʿba is a concrete reality in the religious imagination that allows us to access—with perhaps some unexpected insight—a more abstract, but no less serious, reality like tradition. The invocation of the Kaʿba allows us to discern with greater clarity how the tradition is a thing both of God and of humanity. It also allows us to imagine tradition as a thing undergoing constant change in one sense while simultaneously remaining fixed in another.

Finally, and perhaps most poignantly, the invocation of the Kaʿba's trials and tribulations exposes the emotional and religious investments that are folded into understandings of tradition. Much blood and ink have been spilled over tradition because of its overabundance of meaning. It embodies the diversity and vagaries of historic human communities while also symbolizing the singular unity of God's promise and providence. The significance of tradition is ultimately perspectival in nature. From the vantage of the Divine, it is protected and enduring. Its life is lived as God wills it. From the vantage of humankind, tradition requires both our concern and our labor for its continual restoration and perpetuation because our lives in this world and the Hereafter are intimately intertwined with it.

My aim throughout this final section, however, was not solely fixed upon tradition itself. I have also been making a case, by way of demonstration, for theology and the work of the religious imagination. As I hope this theological vignette on tradition demonstrates, there is great potential for the religious imagination for broadening and enriching the horizons of our present-day theologies. There are many avenues of approach that Muslim communities might follow for the pressing theological questions that they face in our day and age. Unsurprisingly, the doors of possibility opened by the imagination are manifold. Past generations found theological recourse in scholastic theology and in the rhetoric of eschatology. They found it in deep readings of the word of God. They found it in art, poetry, and sacred spaces. They found it in transformative experiences and pious pursuits of many varieties. The religious imagination can be used to access different perspectives and to foreground what is at stake. It should not be dismissed as useless fancy or reduced merely to creativity, although creativity is essential. Rather, I argue, the religious imagination is an important human faculty that can be marshaled like our senses and our reason in order to think theologically. The question now is the same as in times before: by what routes of the imagination can theologies be crafted that respond most faithfully and effectively to the religious expectations, lived realities, and salvific aspirations of communities of faith today? Or, to reframe the above exploration, where will our traditions take us and where will we take our traditions? Ultimately, what do we dare to imagine for the life of faith before us?

NOTES

1. As Murad explains, *umma semper reformanda* or "the community constantly reformed" is based on the Latin phrase *Ecclesia semper reformanda est* or "the church is constantly being reformed," which was first used by the Dutch Reformed Church and then the Catholic Church after the Second Vatican Council. Abdal Hakim Murad, *Commentary on the Eleventh Contentions* (Cambridge: Quilliam Press, 2012), 157, contention 89.

2. On a basic level, *sunna* means a "custom," "habit," or "course of conduct" and is literally "a clear path or a beaten track." The emergence of Islam, however, has transformed the general term *sunna* into the more definitive Sunna of the Prophet Muhammad. For this usage, see Brown, *Hadith*, 3; Mohammad Hashim Kamali, *Principles of Islamic Jurisprudence*, 3rd ed. (Cambridge: Islamic Text Society, 2003), 58; Bernard G. Weiss, *The Spirit of Islamic Law* (Athens: University of Georgia Press, 1998); Joseph E. Lowry, *Early Islamic Legal Theory: The Risāla of Muḥammad ibn Idrīs al-Shāfiʿī* (Leiden: Brill, 2007), 9 fn. 17.

3. Brown, *Hadith*, 7. Moreover, the hadith were of such paramount importance to the faithful that scholars dedicated their lives to the study of this transmitted literature. These scholars of hadith were called the *muḥaddithīn* or the traditionists, further reinforcing this particular association of hadith with tradition.

4. Jackson describes *naql* as the transmitted knowledge that is "located in the faithful transmission of scripture and its 'natural' extensions." Sherman Jackson, *Islam and the Problem of Black Suffering* (Oxford: Oxford University Press, 2009), 9.

5. Yasin Dutton, *The Origins of Islamic Law: The Qur'an, the Muwaṭṭaʾ and Madinan ʿAmal* (Surrey, UK: RoutledgeCurzon, 1999), 32–52; Lowry, *Early Islamic Legal Theory*, 6; Umar F. Abd-Allah Wymann-Landgraf, *Mālik and Medina: Islamic Legal Reasoning in the Formative Period* (Leiden: Brill, 2013), 183. This sentiment underlies the concept of *ʿamal* as articulated by the preeminent Medinan legal thinker Mālik b. Anas (d. 179/795).

6. A number of modernist Arab thinkers conceived of tradition as *al-turāth al-islāmī*, literally "the Islamic heritage." Ibrahim M. Abu-Rabiʿ, *Intellectual Origins of Islamic Resurgence in the Modern Arab World* (Albany: State University of New York Press, 1996), 3.

7. This was not the only designation of this sort forwarded by Muslim communities and schools of thought. For example, members of the Muʿtazilite school of theology called themselves *ahl al-tawḥīd wa'l- ʿadl*, literally "the people of God's oneness and justice," while religious scholars who specialized in

hadith and privileged it called themselves *ahl al-ḥadīth* or *aṣḥāb al-ḥadīth*, literally "the people of prophetic traditions" or more plainly "traditionists."

8. Moosa identifies the colonial encounter with Europe as the initial reason why many Muslim thinkers foreground the issue of tradition as a critical issue. Moosa, *Ghazālī and the Poetics of the Imagination*, 58–61, quotation on 60.

9. Marilyn Robinson Waldman, "Tradition as a Modality of Change: Islamic Examples," *History of Religions* 25, no. 4 (May 1986): 326.

10. Alasdair MacIntyre, *After Virtue*, 3rd ed. (Notre Dame, IN: University of Notre Dame Press, 2007), 221.

11. Waldman, "Tradition as a Modality of Change," 326.

12. Hans-Georg Gadamer, *Truth and Method*, 2nd rev. ed., trans. Joel Weinsheimer and Donald G. Marshall (New York: Continuum, 2002), 277–300.

13. Gadamer, *Truth and Method*, 293.

14. According to Hobsbawm, "'Invented tradition' is taken to mean a set of practices, normally governed by overtly or tacitly accepted rules and of a ritual or symbolic nature, which seek to inculcate certain values and norms of behaviour by repetition, which automatically implies continuity with the past. In fact, where possible, they normally attempt to establish continuity with a suitable historic past." Eric Hobsbawm, "Introduction: Inventing Traditions," in *The Invention of Traditions*, ed. Eric Hobsbawm and Terence Ranger (Cambridge: Cambridge University Press, 1983), 1.

15. MacIntyre, *After Virtue*, 221.

16. Josef Pieper, *Tradition: Concept and Claim* (South Bend, IN: St. Augustine's Press, 2008), 9–10. German Catholic philosopher Josef Pieper points out that both the sense of *traditum* and *tradendum* are contained within tradition.

17. Sherman Jackson, *On the Boundaries of Theological Tolerance in Islam: Abū Ḥāmid al-Ghazālī's Fayṣal al-Tafriqa Bayna al-Islām wa al-Zandaqa* (Karachi: Oxford University Press, 2002), 24.

18. To borrow a concept from classical Islamic theology, one might describe tradition as a kind of humanly determined "occasionalism." Like the continual instantiation of existence by the omnipotent Creator (the doctrine of occasionalism), tradition must be socially reconstituted in every moment. Tradition's human recipients, who are its participants at the same time, must be willing and able to maintain tradition's relevance in each generation. The bond between past and present is constantly being reaffirmed and reconfigured.

19. MacIntyre, *After Virtue*, 222.

20. MacIntyre, *After Virtue*, 222.

21. Talal Asad, *The Idea of an Athropology of Islam* (Washington, DC: Center for Contemporary Arab Studies, Georgetown University, 1986), 14–15, italics in original.

22. Asad, *Idea of an Athropology of Islam*, 15, italics in original.

23. Moosa, *Ghazālī and the Poetics of the Imagination*, 53. Moosa makes this precise point in his analysis of Asad.

24. Al-Ghazālī, *Iḥyā' 'ulūm al-dīn*, 1:351, *kitāb al-asrār al-ṣalāh, faḍīlat al-khushū'*. The Arabic word that I translate as "final crossing" is *ṣirāṭ*, which is traditionally understood to represent a bridge over hell over which every person must cross in the drama of last judgment. See Jane Idleman Smith and Yvonne Yazbeck Haddad, *The Islamic Understanding of Death and Resurrection* (Oxford: Oxford University Press, 2002), 78–80.

25. Chittick, *Science of the Cosmos*, 72.

26. Al-Ṭabarī, *Tārīkh*, 45; al-Ṭabarī, *The History of al-Ṭabarī*, vol. 1, *General Introduction and From the Creation to the Flood*, trans. Franz Rosenthal (Albany: State University of New York Press, 1989), 291–92; Abū 'Abd Allāh Muḥammad b. Sa'd al-Zuhrī, *Kitāb al-Ṭabaqāt al-kabīr*, ed. 'Alī Muḥammad 'Umar, 11 vols. (Cairo: Maktabat al-Khānjī, 2001), 1:23; Abū Isḥāq Aḥmad b. Muḥammad al-Tha'labī, *Qiṣaṣ al-anbiyā' al-musammā 'arā'is al-majālis*, ed. 'Abd al-Laṭīf Ḥasan 'Abd al-Raḥmān (Beirut: Dār al-Kutub al-'Ilmiyya, 2009), 34–35; al-Tha'labī, *'Arā'is al-majālis fī qiṣaṣ al-anbiyā' or "Lives of the Prophets,"* trans. William M. Brinner (Leiden: Brill, 2002), 60.

27. Brannon Wheeler, *Mecca and Eden: Ritual, Relics, and Territory in Islam* (Chicago: University of Chicago Press, 2006), 64.

28. In his immense chronicle, the Muslim historian al-Ṭabarī captures such a mythic assertion: "It has been said that God created the Ancient House (the Ka'bah) upon the water on four pillars. He did this two thousand years before He created this world, and the earth was then spread out underneath it." Al-Ṭabarī, *Tārīkh*, 23; al-Ṭabarī, *The History of al-Ṭabarī*, 1:216–17.

29. Ibn Isḥāq, *Life of Muhammad*, 84; al-Ṭabarī, *Tārīkh*, 305; al-Ṭabarī, *The History of al-Ṭabarī*, 6:51.

30. Al-Ṭabarī, *Tārīkh*, 1030; al-Ṭabarī, *The History of al-Ṭabarī*, vol. 19, *The Caliphate of Yazīd b. Mu'āwiyah*, trans. I. K. A. Howard (Albany: State University of New York Press, 1990), 224.

31. Al-Ṭabarī, *Tārīkh*, 1030; al-Ṭabarī, *The History of al-Ṭabarī*, 19:225.

32. Al-Ṭabarī, *Tārīkh*, 1142; al-Ṭabarī, *The History of al-Ṭabarī*, vol. 21, *The Victory of the Marwānids*, trans. Michael Fishbein (Albany: State University of New York Press, 1990), 225.

33. M. J. De Goeje, *Mémoire sur les Carmathes du Bahraïn et les Fatimides* (Leiden: E. J. Brill, 1886), 104–111; Shams al-Dīn Muḥammad b. Aḥmad b.

ʿUthmān al-Dhahabī, *Tārīkh al-islām*, ed. ʿUmar ʿAbd al-Salām Tadmūrī, 53 vols. (Beirut: Dār al-Kitāb al-ʿArabī, 1990-2000), 23:380–83.

34. Yasir Qadhi, "Mecca Under Siege: The Juhayman Crisis of 1979" (presentation at the Fifth International Conference on Islamic Legal Studies—Lawful and Unlawful Violence in Islamic Law and History, Harvard Law School, Cambridge, MA, September 10, 2006); Filiu, *Apocalypse in Islam*, 74–78; Yaroslav Trofimov, *The Siege of Mecca: The 1979 Uprising at Islam's Holiest Shrine* (New York: Doubleday, 2007).

35. I would note that Hamza Yusuf and Zaid Shakir of Zaytuna College have made similar use of the symbolic imagery of the Kaʿba elsewhere. An event in Anaheim, California, on May 18, 2013, was hosted entitled "Think Outside the Cube." The theme of the material distributed in the lead-up to the event discussed the incongruence of an enduring but incorrect conceptualization of the Kaʿba versus the documented history of it. The example cited by both Yusuf and Shakir is that we solely conceive of the Kaʿba as being draped in a black covering or *kiswa*, with the implication being that we could not conceive of the Kaʿba as otherwise. Yet, as they point out, the Kaʿba has borne many other variations in its history, including a red *kiswa* and a striped *kiswa* during the Abbasid period. The example is meant to illustrate the need to reevaluate current modes of thinking. As Shakir states, "We have to think outside of the cube, brothers and sisters, because we are encountering problems that are unique in human history. We are dealing with issues that are unique in human history . . . and to approach—or to find solutions rather—we have to think outside of the box." Zaid Shakir, "EVENT INVITE: May 18, 2013 Zaid Shakir, Think Outside the Cube," YouTube video, https://www.youtube.com/watch?v=Sy8_0uXMOJQ.

4

THE RELIGIOUS IMAGINATION

IMAGINE

> Worship God as though you see Him, for though you do not see Him, He sees you.
> —Hadith of the Prophet Muhammad[1]

At the heart of this prophetic report beats the pulse of the religious imagination. Carefully folded within the human self is a faculty from which springs our creativity, daring, insight, and wonder. This faculty, the imagination, works in conjunction with rationality and our sense perceptions to illumine the unseen, the unperceived, and the unfathomed. When faithfully marshaled, the imagination allows us to discover all that would incline us to the Divine, whether it emerges from out of the expanse of creation or rises from out of the depths of revelation. It is an imagination formed by faith that underlies those words of the Prophet Muhammad: "Worship God as though you see Him." The Prophet is directing us to draw upon this bursting bundle of cognitive and expressive potential within ourselves. The Prophet is inviting us to imagine, and in so doing to find God.

These words of the Prophet Muhammad are part of a larger narrative. According to one of his close companions, ʿUmar b. al-Khaṭṭāb (d. 23/644), the Prophet Muhammad was seated with some of his community when an unknown figure arrived in their midst.[2] The man's appearance was striking. The dusty signs of the road, which are expected of a traveler, were nowhere to be seen upon him. Nor did the visitor assume the reverential distance of a stranger. He instead drew close to the Prophet with startling familiarity. He sat in front of him knee-to-knee leaning in to place his hands upon the Prophet's thighs. Then, without greeting or introduction, the visitor began to question the Prophet (or so it seemed) on the meaning of weighty matters one after another: "O Muhammad, tell me about *islām*. . . . Tell me about *īmān*. . . . Tell me about *iḥsān*. . . . Tell me about the Final Hour."[3]

To the first two queries, the Prophet's answers were clear and categorical. "*Islām* is that you witness that there is no god but God and Muhammad is the Messenger of God, you establish the prayer, you give the prescribed charity, you fast during Ramadan, and you make pilgrimage to the House [the Kaʿba] if you are able to undertake the way there."[4] *Īmān* or "faith" is "that you have faith in God, His angels, His scriptures, His messengers, and the Last Day and that you have faith in foreordainment [*qadr*], its good and its evil."[5] Notably, the Prophet's reply to the third query of *iḥsān* or "spiritual excellence" differed dramatically.[6] With regard to *iḥsān*, he said, "that you worship God as though you see Him, for though you do not see Him, He sees you." This is no straightforward command because it concerns neither concrete actions nor specific tenets of belief. Instead, it is the delineation of an aspiration and the invocation of the imagination.[7] Although the word *imagination* never appears here or elsewhere in the hadith, the imaginative faculty is precisely what the community of faith is being asked to utilize in their pursuit of God. Moreover, no particular act of worship is singled out by the term *worship* here. Rather, the Prophet's exhortation was for something more comprehensive—a *life* of worship.[8]

When the exchange came to an end, the visitor left as abruptly and unceremoniously as when he arrived. Only after some time did the Prophet then turn to the gathered onlookers and ask, "O ʿUmar, do you know who the inquisitor was?" to which ʿUmar admitted his ignorance by saying, "God and His Messenger know best." In reply the Prophet said, "He was Gabriel who came to you to teach to you your religion."[9] But the Prophet's address here was not only aimed at those immediately present. The exchange between Gabriel, the angel of revelation, and the Prophet Muhammad addresses the faithful still. It remains vital and relevant for all those who would hear it across time and space.

Nonetheless, a question for us remains. What exactly is meant when the Prophet Muhammad says, "Worship God as though you see Him, for though you do not see Him, He sees you"? The Prophet is calling us to approach the life of worship as if God were present before us. This is not some unfathomable and abstract divine presence, however, but a request to behold the Almighty, the very vision of God, "as though you see Him." In sum, we are being asked to *imagine* that God could be visibly manifest before us.[10] It is a radical request, especially when recalling what the Qur'an discloses about the Prophet Moses's desire to behold his Lord:

> *And when Moses came at Our appointed meeting and his Lord spoke to him, he said, "My Lord, show Yourself to me so that I may behold You!" He said, "You shall not see Me, but behold the mountain! If it remains firm in its place, then you will behold Me." When his Lord disclosed Himself to the mountain, He made it crumble to dust, and Moses fell down senseless. When he recovered, he said, "Glory be to You! I turn to You in repentance! And I am the first of the faithful!"* (Q. 7:143)

Even Moses, a prophet and messenger of God, is unable to bear the sight of God in this life. In contrast, the Prophet Muhammad is instructing us to pursue the life of worship with what seems to be devotional abandon—behold the awesome Almighty! Yet devotional abandon is not the Prophet's intent. As the remainder of the prophetic saying makes clear, we are not expected to behold God through our sense perceptions—to "see" the Divine. Rather, the Prophet's words are directed at our imaginations. It is the "as though" embedded in the prophetic report that spares us the fate of Moses and the mountain. Those two words implicitly underscore the function of the imagination. We are to perform our worship "as though" we can visibly behold the Divine, knowing full well that we do not. Instead, the reality is the reverse, because "He sees you." We are the ones beheld by God, ever and always. It is our prayers and our lives of worship that are witnessed by the Divine. The least that we can do to better our prayers, our supplications, and our devotions is to imagine that God in all His might and glory is before us. Through the radicalness of the imagination, we can attain to a more excellent life of faith.

The hadith of Gabriel is far from the only scriptural reference to the religious imagination. The Qur'an and prophetic tradition are replete with the imagination's acknowledgment and invocation. The historical chronicles and prophetic biographies relate how the Prophet Muhammad appealed repeatedly to the imagination during the course of his prophetic mission. When commanded by God to begin his public preaching early in his career—*So proclaim that with which you are commanded and turn away from the idolaters* (Q. 15:94)—the Prophet first looked to his own kin, the tribe of Quraysh—*Warn your nearest kinsfolk* (Q. 26:214)—and addressed them from atop the hillock of al-Ṣafā in the city of Mecca. From this height, the Prophet called out, "'Beware this morning!' [The] Quraysh gathered around him and said, 'What is the matter?' Then he said, 'If I were to tell you that the enemy would come upon you this morning or this evening, would you believe me?' 'Certainly,' they replied. He said, 'I am a warner to you in the face of a terrible doom.'"[11] The Prophet Muhammad employs the imagination as a rhetorical device. He is asking the Quraysh that if they can imagine and believe in an imminent, physical threat, can they not imagine and believe in a greater "terrible doom" awaiting them in the Hereafter?

The rhetorical deployment of the imagination also infuses the preaching of the Prophet. For example, he admonishes, "Two ravenous wolves let loose among sheep are not as ruinous as greed for wealth and prestige are to a man's religion."[12] The Prophet summons to mind this arresting image in order to impress upon his community the danger inhering in worldly gain and ambition. Elsewhere, the Prophet paints a different picture that is just as evocative: "If the son of Adam were given a valley full of gold, he would love to have a second one; and if he were given the second one, he would love to have to have a third, for nothing fills the belly of the son of Adam except dust. And God forgives he who repents to Him."[13] Other sayings of the Prophet were aimed at bolstering the community of the faithful. According to one report, "The Prophet said, 'A believer to another believer is like a building whose parts enforce each other.' The Prophet then clasped his hands with the fingers interlaced."[14] Through this simple image, brought to life through his words and gestures, the importance of maintaining righteous relations with one another is memorably and directly conveyed. In a lengthier hadith, he states,

> The permissible is clear and the prohibited is clear and between them are uncertain matters of which many know not. Whoever is

> wary of uncertainties keeps their religion and honor sound and whoever falls into uncertainties falls into the prohibited. It is like the shepherd who herds his flock too close to the sanctuary; they will eventually graze in it. Every king has a sanctuary and the sanctuary of God is that which He prohibits. Within the body is a lump of flesh. If it is sound, the body is sound. If it is corrupt, the body is corrupt. Truly it is the heart.[15]

From straying flocks and protected preserves to the lump of flesh that beats within, the wisdom of the Prophet transports the listener from one striking image to the next.

The religious imagination is also powerfully used in discussions of eschatology and soteriology, knowledge of the end times and salvation, respectively. The Qur'an's terse evocations of the end times are stunning and dramatic.

> *Al-Qāri'a!*
> *What is al-Qāri'ā?*
> *What shall make you comprehend what al-Qāri'ā is?*
> *A day when humankind shall be like thickly scattered moths,*
> *And the mountains shall be like tufts of wool.*
> *As for the one whose scales are heavy,*
> *He shall be in a contented life,*
> *As for the one whose scales are light,*
> *His refuge shall be Hāwiya.*
> *And what will make you comprehend what that is?*
> *A raging fire!* (Q. 101:1–11)
>
> *Nay! He shall surely be thrown into al-Ḥuṭama.*
> *And what shall make you comprehend what al-Ḥuṭama is?*
> *The fire of God, fueled,*
> *Which engulfs hearts!* (Q. 104:4–7)

In these passages, enigmatic matters of the end times and the Hereafter—*al-Qāri'ā*, *Hāwiya*, and *al-Ḥuṭama*—are presented in such a way as to emphasize the difficulty of apprehending precisely what they are. They lie beyond the immediate ken of human perception and reason. Vivid images, visceral experiences, and confounding descriptions are summoned to mind instead in order to offer a glimpse of what these matters might mean. It is through the dynamism of imagination that God guides our understanding. This is not to say that the rational faculty is not also important to matters of faith. Both the Qur'an and the Prophet Muhammad regularly appeal to human reason as well. The relevant question here, then, concerns the relationship of reason to the imagination.

REASON AND RATIONALITIES

> Believers were brave indeed to invite such a corpulent guest as reason into their homes. The entry of reason into the realm of religions was a colossal, historical and ancient event, and the aftershocks produced more or less similar effects and consequences throughout the realm.
>
> —Abdulkarim Soroush, *The Expansion of Prophetic Experience*[16]

> When we look at what specific philosophers mean by reason and rationality, it quickly becomes obvious that they mean many different things. Most of the time philosophers claim to follow reason and rational methods, but it often seems that "rational" is no more than a philosopher's assertion that his methods and conclusions are obviously correct.
>
> —John Walbridge, *God and Logic in Islam*[17]

The scholarly tradition has generally afforded greater attention to the rational faculty—reason or the intellect—than to the imagination.[18] Created by God in the human being, reason was understood as a powerful means with which to engage God's revelation. What emerged over the course of early Islamic history, however, was a diverse array of positions as to reason's proper place within the Islamic schema.[19] For instance, the Muʿtazila, a theological school that flourished from the second/eighth century to at least the seventh/thirteenth century, seemed to grant reason primacy of place.[20] In their view, the human being, in principle, could come to know God and that which is good and evil through reason alone; Qur'anic revelation was not necessary.[21] Muslim philosophers like Ibn Sīna (d. 428/1037; known as Avicenna in Christian Europe) spoke of a preeminent "rational soul"—alongside a vegetative and animal soul—within the human being.[22] This perspective was based on the Aristotelian view that the defining and universal differentia attributable to the human being was a rational principle.[23]

Many Muslim scholars recognized, however, that rationality, while of great significance, was not universally constituted. The Māturīdīs, a mainstream school of Sunnī theology, maintain that although reason is essential to faith, reason also requires development. Human beings may all possess reason in potentiality, but they do not all exercise it with equal aptitude and facility. The rational faculty requires progressive refinement.[24] Ibn Sīna and other Muslim philosophers, for their part, understood their philosophical pursuits as an ongoing spiritual practice aimed at cultivating the immortal soul.[25] As God poses in the Qur'an, *Did We not grant you a long life enough for anyone capable of reflection to reflect therein?* (Q. 35:37). However formulated, the intellect was recognized as a matter of great importance, but in need of continual development over the course of one's life.

Nevertheless, as these preceding accounts indicate, there were clear differences of opinion as to what rationality was among the religious scholars. As John Walbridge astutely describes, "The problem with reason and rationality is that reason is, to a great extent, in the eye of the beholder, particularly with respect to starting points."[26] For example, the Muʿtazila and Muslim philosophers previously mentioned can be seen as "heir[s] to a concrete and very specific tradition of formal reasoning," an Aristotelian-Neoplatonic one, although their respective construals differ in significant ways.[27] As with tradition, then, human rationality may be described as socially and historically formed. What every generation invariably encounters, inherits, and develops are "constructions of reason," to borrow a phrase from Sherman Jackson.[28] He describes reason, or more precisely *al-ʿaql*, as

> a highly contested terrain of competing "regimes of sense" . . . the essential function of *al-ʿaql* is to adjudicate interpretive disputes and validate interpretive arguments in the public realm in a manner that is recognized as fair and impartial. While *al-ʿaql* is in one sense stable, it is also open to change and evolution, as its actual substance is not dictated by revelation but is negotiated in real space and time. Such change, however, occurs slowly, organically, within the recognized rules of the game, and—as with the rules of any sport—for the purpose of improving rather than destroying the game itself.[29]

While human beings may all possess reason in potentiality, there is no fixed, universal form of reason. Rather, there are *rationalities* that are conditioned by and developed within traditions.[30] How reason is formed and applied has changed and adapted to the shifting historical and social circumstances that we face. Our convictions, presuppositions, and prejudices—both personal and social—influence the form of our rationality and give shape to the logic by which we live our lives. Rationalities are derived from different genealogies, function in different ways, and are directed along different trajectories. These constructions of reason may come into conflict, but they are publicly negotiated with the aim of attaining to that which is perceived as good.

Indeed, rationality has its limits. The human self, if it is to attain to God in good faith, requires more than reason alone, as the renowned theologian al-Ghazālī famously attests in his autobiography. During the course of his life, he faced a number of existential questions of faith. While powerfully instrumental for matters of the mind, he found reason to be impotent in the face of doubt, skepticism, and religious crisis.[31] Al-Ghazālī only found succor in the "fruitional experience" offered through spiritual practice and the providence of God described as "a light which God Most High cast into my breast."[32] Rationality had been of limited use during his periods of questioning.

Although the idea that human beings are "rational animals" persists, rationality is not the defining differentia it is imagined to be.[33] Life in the everyday is hardly lived in accordance with it. The human complex of emotions, the amorphous nature of faith, and the range exhibited in artistic and aesthetic abilities all challenge the reduction of the human person to rationality. There are many other ways by which the human being might be known. The German philosopher Ernst Cassirer described the human being as a "symbolic animal."[34] The Scottish philosopher Alasdair MacIntyre and others speak of "a story-telling animal" in recognition of the integral role that narrative plays in human existence.[35] The Romanian historian of religion Mircea Eliade offers *homo religiosus*, "the religious man," in place of the self-styled *homo sapiens*, "the wise man."[36] In a similar spirit, the Canadian scholar of comparative religion Wilfred Cantwell Smith entertains faith as possibly "the most important of all human qualities."[37] Bringing together narrative, religiosity, embodiment, and ritual, the Canadian Reformed theologian James K. A. Smith describes human beings as "liturgical animals," for "to say that we are liturgical animals is simultaneously to emphasize that we are metaphorical animals, imaginative animals, poetic animals, 'storied' animals."[38] There is incredibly much that human beings do that might be described as integral to their existence.[39] We human beings tend to our dead when they pass from this world. We laugh and we weep. We make art and cherish it. We imagine. We pray and believe.

God repeatedly addresses us on a multiplicity of fronts, one of the foremost being as servants of God—*'ibād Allāh*: *His servants who have faith and do righteous deeds* (Q. 42:23)—an identification I first mentioned in chapter 1. To imagine that we are defined by rationality is to submit to an impoverished sense of who we are and how we ought to live. Instead, revelation reveals that we are defined by our relationship to God. We are meant to serve and worship, and we have been created with a nuanced matrix of faculties to fulfill that end. Reason, while important, is neither the sole nor ultimate recourse to the Divine. Instead, it is meant to operate in concert and balance with our sense perceptions, our consciousness, our emotions, our intuition, and our imagination. How we respond to God—how we relate to, serve, and worship Him—must be with all of who we are.

THE MUSLIM IMAGINATIVE TRADITION

> *And strike for them a parable of the life of this world . . .*
> —Qur'an 18:45

Many Muslim scholars have acknowledged, either implicitly or explicitly, the imaginative faculty as a significant aspect of the human person. It frequently figures in the constellation of faculties that constitute the human self as proposed by scholars, even if it was called by a number of different names.[40] For some the imagination was a faculty distinct from reason. In fact, the Sufi sage Ibn ʿAṭāʾ Allāh (d. 709/1309) considered the imagination one means of mitigating the dangers of reason. As Jackson describes, Ibn ʿAṭāʾ Allāh identified "a combination of confessional self-reflection, inspirational and humbling human experience, and unspoiled religious imagination . . . alongside a humble commitment to the religious law and following the example of the Prophet" as key to the life of faith.[41]

For others the imagination was a central faculty, if not the foremost of them.[42] As the Andalusian Sufi metaphysician Muḥyī al-Dīn Ibn al-

ʿArabī (d. 638/1240) states, "He who does not know the status of imagination has no knowledge whatsoever."[43] In his view, the imagination is multiple things at once: (1) the entire cosmos, (2) an intermediate imaginal world (*ʿalam al-mithāl*) between this corporeal world and the realm of the Divine, (3) the human soul itself, and (4) a faculty that allows human beings to bring together the spiritual and corporeal worlds.[44] While each level of meaning is dramatically different from the others, what they have in common is a fundamentally in-between quality or liminality.[45] Like a threshold situated between two rooms, the imagination represents a space where one both crosses boundaries and connects them at the same time.

As expansive as Ibn al-ʿArabī's understanding of the imagination is, my concern lies with his understanding of the imagination as a human faculty and as the human soul. Chittick provides a summation of both levels of meaning:

> In the narrowest sense of the term, imagination refers to a specific faculty of the soul that brings together sensory things, which have shapes and forms, and consciousness, which has no shape and form. . . . In a slightly more extended sense, imagination refers to the realm of the soul, a level of being and consciousness that is situated between spirit and body.[46]

On the first count, the imagination is a human faculty that works in concert with others like the senses, reason, and memory as I described at the outset of the chapter. It allows a person to envision and encounter the matters of the unseen—like angels, the heavens, and God—in ways that reason and other faculties cannot. Put another way, reason is "the faculty of understanding God," while the imagination is "the faculty of seeing God."[47] On the second count, Ibn al-ʿArabī believes that the imagination can also be equated with the human soul. The imagination brings together the spiritual and corporeal—image and materiality—just as the soul is the union of the life-giving spirit with the earthly body.

While not all scholars conceived of the imagination in as encompassing terms as Ibn al-ʿArabī, they generally recognized the incredible potential of the religiously attuned imagination for deepening the life of faith. Inspired by the precedent set by God's revelation—the Qur'an and the prophetic tradition—Muslim preachers, sages, artists, and artisans developed and deployed the religious imagination in incredibly diverse, creative, and lasting ways. Some two centuries after the death of the Prophet Muhammad, the moral theologian al-Ḥārith al-Muḥāsibī (d. 243/857) composed *The Book of the Imagination*, in which he invites his readers to imagine the moment of their death and all that follows afterward.[48] Through a guided narrative, al-Muḥāsibī brings to life, so to speak, the terribleness of hell and the beauty of heaven. The message is made all the more poignant because of the personal tone that he adopts: "Imagine yourself. . . ." The audience is repeatedly asked to "Imagine yourself in death, cast down never to rise again until the [final] gathering before your Lord."[49] "Imagine your place in the narrowness of your grave."[50] "Imagine your heart in the gardens [of Paradise]."[51] "Imagine yourself when your Lord bestows blessings upon you."[52] Through al-Muḥāsibī's powerfully woven words, his readers are drawn into the dramatic journey that awaits every soul after death. Many other scholars and preachers would follow suit with similarly evocative works of their own.[53]

In respectful emulation of the language of the Qur'an and the Prophet's choice words, the devout cultivated a rich visual lexicon of the grave, the end times, final judgment, and otherworldly recompense over the course of many centuries.[54] Whether fostered in the tales of the popular storytellers, the emotive homiletics of the preachers, or the tomes and lectures of erudite sages, the shared religious imaginary of the Muslim community grew over time.[55] The religious imagination, then, is socially constituted in nature, as anthropologist Zareena Grewal identifies: "Although the imagination is often thought of in highly individualized terms . . . it is also a social formation that is shared and sustained by a collective."[56] While the exercise of the imagination seems to be an entirely personal affair, the act is rooted, nonetheless, in a broader social imaginary historically developed by a community. Imagining draws upon a socially constituted constellation of symbols, memories, ideals, relationships, and prejudices that extends beyond the immediacy of one's time and place. And like constructions of rationality, there are different social constructions of the imagination. According to Christian theologian Gordon Kaufman, "All thinking about God and all devotion to God take place within a cultural and linguistic context in which the notion of God has already been highly developed through the imaginative work of many preceding generations."[57] The Muslim community of faith, then, is a community that develops, draws from, and continues to refine its own tradition of theological imagining.

The Muslim imaginative tradition, of course, did more than simply array the wonders and terrors of death and the end times before the eyes of the faithful. Its architects raised vaulted chambers and constructed encircling domes over their houses of worship in order to deliver worshipers to the celestial heights of the Divine. Its theologians and mystics compellingly conveyed the depths and subtleties of faith through poetic meter and verse. Indeed, the power to summon images, evoke emotions, and induce contemplation has been exercised for pious ends through a variety of poetic forms. One of the most important examples is the "Ode of the Mantle," or *Qasīdat al-Burda*, which was originally written by the mystic al-Būṣīrī (d. ca. 694/1294) as an intercessory prayer. Through its rhythmic verses, the poem brings to life the virtues and character of the Prophet Muhammad. The hymn has proven to be so captivating that it is still committed to memory, copied upon innumerable pages and walls, and movingly sung out of loving reverence and devotion to this day.

The religious imagination is also powerfully on display in the intellectual industry of the scholars. Beyond exacting treatises, many took recourse to metaphorical tales and thought-provoking images. For instance, the Andalusian philosopher Ibn Ṭufayl (d. 581/1185–1186) weaves the tale of a child named Ḥayy b. Yaqẓān (literally "Living, son of Wakefulness") who is raised by a gazelle on a remote island free of all human contact.[58] As the captivating story reveals, the protagonist is able to discover and experience metaphysical truths through the keen application of the intellect alone.[59] Sufi spiritual masters, for their part, had cultivated their own repertoire of images and stories. Memorable mention is made of the enamored moth that flies unhesitatingly into the flame as a metaphor for the all-consuming nature of divine love. Similarly, the image of a mirror in need of polishing was employed to represent the heart in need of self-purification.[60] Representing a more robust imaginative undertaking is the metaphorical narrative composed by the Persian mystical poet Farīd al-Dīn ʿAṭṭār (d. 627/1230). In this poetic tale, which is meant to signify the spiritual aspirant's inward discovery of the Divine through the annihilation of the self, ʿAṭṭār describes the long and perilous journey of thirty birds in search of their king who only realize at the journey's end that their hard-sought goal had always lain within.[61] As scholar of Islam Cyrus Zargar writes of these traditions of ethical teaching, Muslim philosophers and Sufi mystics "used storytelling of many varieties to convey normative standards of virtue," recognizing that "narratives seem distinctly able to reveal values, situations, decisions, character, and the relationship between them all."[62]

As for the commentators of the Qur'an, they gathered unto themselves a vast and impressive array of opinions and interpretations in their prodigious efforts to open up the multitude of meanings bundled into the words of the Qur'an.[63] When confronted with the fathomless depth of God's word, the human imagination was unfurled and cast widely in hopes of capturing some iota of the divinely disclosed reality. Perhaps no Qur'anic phenomenon better demonstrates the imaginative industriousness of the exegetes than "the disconnected letters" of the Qur'an.[64] At the beginning of only twenty-nine chapters of the Qur'an are stand-alone Arabic letters with no apparent plain-sense meaning or immediately discernable pattern to them. The Prophet Muhammad never seems to have provided an explanation during his lifetime, nor does the Qur'an seem to shed further light on them elsewhere in the Scripture. In response, Muslim exegetes offered a breathtaking range of interpretive possibilities for each of these letters. Early interpreters speculated that the letters represented different names for the Qur'an, chapter titles, abbreviated names or attributes of God, divine oaths, and so on.[65] Others focused on how some of the letters were graphically written, seeing in their shape the celestial inkwell from which God drew the ink to inscribe creation into existence, a reverent servant of God standing upright and alone in utter devotion before the Divine, or a mythic mountain or sapphire encompassing the entire earth.[66] Even the individual letters of the Qur'an have provided the impetus for the exercise of the religious imagination. While the voices of the imaginative Muslim tradition understood and deployed the imagination in substantially different ways, as the preceding examples attest, the imagination was and remains a vibrant element of the Muslim community's engagement with God and the world.

THE MEASURE OF THE RELIGIOUS IMAGINATION

> Is not the imagination, by common consent, a faculty of free invention, therefore something not governed by rules, something wild and untamed?
> —Paul Ricoeur, *Figuring the Sacred*[67]

> The man who has no imagination
> Stands on the earth.
> He has no wings,
> He cannot fly.
> —Muhammad Ali[68]

The twentieth-century South Asian philosopher Muhammad Iqbal describes the human person "in his innermost being" as "a creative activity, an ascending spirit who, in his own onward march, rises from one state of being to another."[69] When Iqbal first penned these words, he reveals immediately afterward his Qur'anic inspiration: *But, Nay! I swear by the sunset's redness and by the night and its gatherings and by the moon when at her full, that from state to state shall ye be surely carried onward* (Q. 84:16–19).[70] In this back-and-forth between revelation and the author, Iqbal is identifying creativity as a constitutive element of human beings that is intended to transform and elevate them. As attested by the rest of *The Reconstruction of Religious Thought*, from which these lines come, this analysis was part of Iqbal's broader interest in developing "a vision of the spirit of Islam" that could transcend erroneous and ossified conceptions of the faith.[71] He was, in his own way, foregrounding the imagination for the work of modern Muslim theology.

How the imagination figures into Iqbal's religious thought, however, is more apparent in his poetry. Among the most memorable examples is a pair of poems composed four years apart. In 1909, in a poem entitled "The Complaint," or "*Shikwā*," Iqbal gave voice to a pervasive feeling of despair that had emerged from out of the colonial subjugation and sense of civilizational eclipse that were spreading across the Muslim world, especially in his own British-ruled India. In verse after verse of eloquently emotive words, a pious complainant laments to God the continual decline of the modern Muslim community in spite of its triumphant past and vibrant tradition. At the heart of Iqbal's imagined complaint, however, is a more incisive message—an indictment of God. How could this state of affairs overtake the community of faith, the interlocutor pleads, when they worship and serve God Almighty so fastidiously and passionately?

> And we filled the Holy Kaaba with our foreheads humbly bent,
> Clutching to our fervent bosoms the Koran in ecstasy,
> Yet the charge is laid against us we have played the faithless part;
> If disloyal we have proved, has Thou deserved to win our heart?[72]

Taking advantage of the in-between space that poetry carves out, Iqbal dares to imagine a betrayal by the Divine. It was not until 1913 that Iqbal published the poem's counterpart, "The Response to the Complaint," or "*Jawāb-i shikwā*," in which God answers with a scathing and humbling rejoinder.

> Who once filled the Holy Kaaba with their foreheads lowly bent,
> Clutching to their fervent bosoms the Koran in ecstasy?
> Who were they? They were your fathers; as for now, why, what are you,
> Squatting snug, serenely waiting for tomorrow to come true?[73]

As these words witheringly clarify, it is not God who has failed but the present generation—a sentiment that Iqbal echoes in other poems and writings. Iqbal's theology, whether delivered with *poesis* or philosophical acuteness, was aimed at diagnosing the modern Muslim predicament and providing a constructive alternative. He was attempting to formulate a new theological vision through different avenues of the religious imagination.

It is in this spirit that I believe the religious imagination to be critical to the task of theology today. First, I understand the imagination as a distinctive faculty that must necessarily be brought into concert with reason and our other faculties for the present task of modern theology. What I mean by the imagination, however, is not merely a product or function of the mind. It is something more diffuse and integrative within our being than generally recognized. As the Canadian humanist philosopher John Ralston Saul writes, "So there is an image in our imagination, but only as part of something else—a rhythm of the body. The imagination is caught up in many things—intellect, perception, our body as a whole, our relationship to others, what we create, to rooms, to atmospheres."[74] The act of imagination, then, is not merely a mental procedure but rather an embodied activity. It is the exercise of our being in toto, similar to how Ibn al-ʿArabī understood the imagination to be the human self itself, in that it arises from the union of spirit and body.

As for the function of the imagination, it is our ability to envision—to form within our minds—that which is not immediately before us. It allows us to think beyond what we immediately receive through our sense perceptions and to perceive what might not be apparent. Moreover, creativity, inspiration, and invention all emerge from out of its exercise because, when paired with passion, faith, or determination, the imagination can enable us. Saul ascribes to imagination two distinctive qualities: inconclusiveness and inclusiveness.[75] With respect to the former, there is an element of insatiability. Whereas reason seeks to draw conclusions and bring things to a close, the imagination seeks to fling open all the doors. It continually entertains new possibilities. When confronted with a dilemma or difficulty, we tirelessly exercise our imagination alongside our other faculties to find solutions. When wielded well, the imagination reveals to us new ways of thinking and expression and can change how we see things. It can pivot us toward unexpected vistas and unforeseen perspectives. It prompts us to think outside the conventional norm.

With respect to inclusiveness, the imagination seeks to draw together seemingly disparate elements in hopes of discovering unanticipated connections, similarities, and patterns or generating new relationships and understandings. As Chittick describes, "Imagination and images function by bringing together two sides—in contrast to reason and abstraction, which separate and establish difference."[76] In the case of empathy, the imagination plays a crucial role in that it enables us to see ourselves in someone else's place. We imagine what it is like to be them—to feel what they feel and suffer what they suffer—so that we might appreciate and better understand their experiences and circumstances. The imagination, then, places us at the threshold of empathy, or at least it *can*. As Saul cautions, empathy is not always ensured.[77] We can just as readily demonize the other as we humanize them. Both are acts of the imagination, although to dehumanize someone takes little imagination overall. We need not imagine much of an inner life to rob someone of their humanity. Indeed, to dehumanize someone—to imagine it—is more properly a form of unthinking. In contrast, to humanize the other, especially when the differences appear great, requires an active and fertile imagination.

There is wildness to the imagination as well. As the above-cited words of the French philosopher Paul Ricoeur indicate, the imagination can be "something wild and untamed."[78] The very openness of the imagination that makes it generative is also the source of its audacity and unpredictability. The imagination does not incline to caution but turns us—at times it dares us—to venture into the unknown. It can and does push us beyond the comfortable confines of convention. In the act of imagining, we allow ourselves to entertain all sorts of possibilities from the staid, tried, and true to the radical, fantastic, and precipitous. When left uninhibited, the imagination can turn the undesirable desirable or the wicked virtuous. When paired with hubris—that ever-present human inclination—the imagination can actually lead us terribly astray. Yet despite the dangers, the imagination is worth maintaining and fostering. After all, both the Qur'an and Prophet, as indicated earlier, sought to strengthen and beautify faith through the right exercise of the imagination. When the imagination is tempered with wisdom instead, it can lead us to envision ourselves, our world, and our faith in powerfully new ways.

Indeed, the imagination's inclusiveness and inconclusiveness serve faith well. If we allow ourselves to imagine the other in a meaningful way, we will find ourselves transformed. Empathetic imagining affects us foremost. As Saul states, "Transcending the self is about imagining the other; not to weaken the self, but to be capable of reaching beyond it."[79] We are, in a way, refining the self through this act of imagining the other. We are honing our ability to access the richness of reality that lives and thrives outside of our immediate selves. And what greater reality is there in which to draw closer in relationship than the Divine?

Nor should the inconclusiveness of the imagination be seen as a detriment that must necessarily spiral downward into inaction and skepticism. Its insatiability, rather, can push us to keep imagining, through a continual series of faithful possibilities, of what lies ahead. After all, it is the imagination—when mediated through revelation—that makes conceivable the possibility of life after death, the Unseen, the Hereafter, and ultimately the Divine. It is by the imagination that we are able to "worship God as though we see Him." To have faith, then, is a wildly radical act. To pray is even more so because of the engagement that prayer entails. The religious imagination makes the power and efficacy of faith and prayer conceivable. As Ricoeur states, "The imagination can be considered as the power of giving form to human experience or . . . as the power of redescribing reality."[80] In speaking of God and to God, theology is perpetually engaged in the act of "redescribing reality." It sets God as both its center and circumference. And today in the midst of our modern times, we must work to *reinscribe* God into a world that presumes the Divine to be so dispensable.

NOTES

1. Al-Nawawī, *An-Nawawī's Forty Hadith: An Anthology of the Sayings of the Prophet Muhammad*, trans. Ezzeddin Ibrahim and Denys Johnson-Davies (Cambridge: Islamic Texts Society, 1997), 31. All citations to al-Nawawī's forty hadith collection are to the Arabic text in the book. The English translations provided are my own.

2. Abū al-Ḥusayn Muslim b. al-Ḥajjāj al-Qushayrī al-Naysabūrī, *Ṣaḥīḥ Muslim*, ed. Muḥammad Fu'ād 'Abd al-Bāqī, 5 vols. (Cairo: Dār Iḥyā' al-Kutub al-'Arabiyya, 1955–1956), 1:37–38, chapter 1 *kitāb al-īmān*, no. 1; al-Nawawī, *Forty Hadith*, 28–33; al-Bukhārī, *Ṣaḥīh*, 1:19, *kitāb al-īmān*, no. 50. The narrative of the prophetic report is preserved in the two most prominent Sunnī hadith collections. I am using the account preserved by Muslim b. al-Ḥajjāj (d. 261/875) in *Saḥīḥ Muslim* as it was related by 'Umar b. al-Khaṭṭāb (d. 23/644), a leading companion of the Prophet and the second Caliph of the Muslim community after the death of the Prophet. It is the first hadith in the chapter "*Kitāb al-īmān*," which is the first chapter after the introduction. The renowned scholar al-Nawawī (d. 676/1277) famously features Muslim's account as the second hadith in his concise compilation of forty-two hadiths. Al-Bukhārī (d. 256/870) also preserves the account in *Ṣaḥīḥ al-Bukhārī*, but through the narration of a different companion of the Prophet, Abū Hurayra (d. ca. 58/678).

3. The Prophet answers each question before the visitor continues with his next inquiry. While the exchange will end with a discussion of the signs of the Final Hour (*al-sā'a*), my focus will be on *iḥsān* given my interest in the religious imagination.

4. Al-Nawawī, *Forty Hadith*, 29–31.

5. Al-Nawawī, *Forty Hadith*, 31.

6. Sachiko Murata and William Chittick translate *ihṣān* as "doing what is beautiful," which I find compelling. I have opted for "spiritual excellence"

primarily for its succinctness. Sachiko Murata and William C. Chittick, *The Vision of Islam* (St. Paul, MN: Paragon House, 1994), xxv.

7. Michel Chodkiewicz, *An Ocean without Shore: Ibn Arabi, the Book, and the Law*, trans. David Streight (Albany: State University of New York Press, 1993), 32. As noted by Chodkiewicz, the Sufi sage Ibn al-ʿArabī (d. 638/1240) also explicitly recognized the role of the imaginative faculty (*khayāl*) underlying this prophetic report.

8. As discussed in chapter 1, it is not inconsequential that the Qur'an refers to the human being as an *ʿabd*, meaning a servant, slave, or bondsman, which shares the same root as *ʿibāda* or worship. The Arabic word for "worship" in the cited prophetic report, *taʿbuda*, is directly related to *ʿibāda*.

9. Al-Nawawī, *Forty Hadith*, 33.

10. While Ibn al-ʿArabī does emphasize the role of the imagination in understanding the Prophet's words, as stated above in note 7, his overall interpretation rests on a significantly different reading of the Prophet's words. His reading is as follows: "Worship God as if you see Him, for if you do not see Him, He sees you." The phrase *fa-in lam takun tarāhu*, "for though you do not see Him," is alternatively read as "for if you do not see Him," which implies more strongly the possibility of beholding God in this world. William C. Chittick, *The Sufi Path of Knowledge: Ibn al-ʿArabi's Metaphysics of Imagination* (Albany: State University of New York, 1989), 439; Ibn al-ʿArabī, *The Meccan Revelations*, vol. 1, *Selected Texts of al-Futūhāt al-Makkiya*, ed. Michel Chodkiewicz, trans. William C. Chittick and James W. Morris (New York: Pir Press, 2002), 292–93 fn. 108; Murata and Chittick, *Vision of Islam*, xxv, 267.

11. Another transmission recounts: "They gathered round him, and he said, 'If I were to tell you that horsemen were coming out at the foot of the mountain, would you believe me?' They replied, 'We have never known you to tell a lie.' Then he said, 'I am "a warner to you in the face of a terrible doom."'" Al-Ṭabarī, *The History of al-Ṭabarī*, 6:89.

12. Al-Tirmidhī, *al-Jāmiʿ al-kabīr*, 4:185, *bāb* 43, hadith 2376.

13. Al-Bukhārī, *Ṣaḥīḥ*, 8:93, *kitāb al-riqāq*, no. 6438.

14. Al-Bukhārī, *Ṣaḥīḥ*, 3:129, *kitāb al-maẓālim*, no. 2446.

15. Al-Nawawī, *Forty Hadith*, 43.

16. Soroush, *Expansion of Prophetic Experience*, 193.

17. John Walbridge, *God and Logic in Islam: The Caliphate of Reason* (New York: Cambridge University Press, 2011), 15.

18. Numerous epistemological discussions by classical Muslim theologians use the term *ʿaql* ("intellect") or *naẓar* ("reason") in reference to the rational faculty. For example, see Abū Manṣūr al-Māturīdī, *Kitāb al-Tawḥīd*, ed. Bekir Topaloğlu and Muhammad Aruçi (Ankara: İSAM, Türkiye Diyanet Vakfı, İslâm Araştırmaları Merkezi, 2005), 5–7, 15–17; Abū Bakr b. al-Ṭayyib al-Bāqillānī,

Al-Inṣāf fī mā yujab i'tiqāduhu wa-lā yajūzu al-jahl bi-hi, ed. Muḥammad Zāhid b. al-Ḥasan al-Kawtharī (Cairo: Maktabat al-Khānjī, 2001), 14–15; al-Juwaynī, *Kitāb al-Irshād ilā qawāṭi' al-adilla fī uṣūl al-i'tiqād*, ed. Muḥammad Yusūf Mūsā and 'Alī 'Abd al-Mu'nim 'Abd al-Ḥamīd (Cairo: Maktabat al-Khanjī, 2002), 3–11; al-Juwayni, *A Guide to Conclusive Proofs for the Principles of Belief: Kitāb al-irshād ilā qawāṭi' al-adilla fī uṣūl al-i'tiqād*, trans. Paul E. Walker (Reading, UK: Garnet, 2000), 3–7; al-Taftazani, *A Commentary on the Creed of Islam: Sa'd al-Dīn al-Taftazānī's Commentary on the Creed of Najm al-Dīn al-Nasafī*, trans. Earl Edgar Elder (New York: Columbia University Press, 1950), 15–27.

19. See Binyamin Abrahamov, *Islamic Theology: Traditionalism and Rationalism* (Edinburgh: Edinburgh University Press, 1998); Griffel, *Al-Ghazālī's Philosophical Theology*, 111–22; Sophia Vasalou, *Ibn Taymiyya's Theological Ethics* (Oxford: Oxford University Press, 2016), 229–41. Abrahamov provides a general overview of the rationalist–traditionalist spectrum for the early centuries of Islamic thought. As for specific thinkers, Griffel has carefully examined how Abū Ḥāmid al-Ghazālī understood the relationship of reason and revelation. Vasalou has done likewise for the renowned religious scholar of Damascus Ibn Taymiyya (d. 728/1328).

20. With respect to the Mu'tazila, Ziai states that their "rationalist position was sometimes called the 'Primacy of Reason' (*aṣālat al-'aql*)." In fact, when making this statement, Ziai is referencing both the Mu'tazila and the Ismā'īlīs, a sect of Shī'ism. Hossein Ziai, "Islamic Philosophy (*falsafa*)," in *Cambridge Companion to Classical Islamic Theology*, 55. Vasalou notes the Mu'tazila are typically characterized as having "an approach that gives supremacy to reason." Sophia Vasalou, *Moral Agents and Their Deserts: The Character of Mu'tazilite Ethics* (Princeton, NJ: Princeton University Press, 2008), 1.

21. Abrahamov, *Islamic Theology*, 32–36. As explained by Martin, Woodward, and Atmaja, "confidence in the rational and knowable nature of physical reality is based on theodicy: God would not deceive His creatures by creating an irrational universe." Richard C. Martin, Mark R. Woodward, and Dwi S. Atmaja, *Defenders of Reason in Islam: Mu'tazilism from Medieval School to Modern Symbol* (Oxford: Oneworld, 1997), 11–12. For a careful account of Mu'tazilī views of rationally knowable obligations and prohibitions, see Vasalou, *Moral Agents*, 33–66.

22. Majid Fakhry, *A History of Islamic Philosophy, Second Edition* (New York: Columbia University Press, 1983), 140–44. Chittick renders the original *nafs nāṭiqa* as "rationally speaking soul," which connects the intellect more firmly to the Qur'anic idea referenced in (Q. 2:31) that God granted human beings with special knowledge of the names of things. William C. Chittick, *The Heart of Islamic Philosophy: The Quest for Self-Knowledge in the Teachings of*

Afḍal al-Dīn Kāshānī (New York: Oxford University Press, 2001), 50. The notion that the human being possesses a "higher, rational soul (*al-nafs al-nāṭiqah*)" persists within Islamic theology today as demonstrated by the work of the Malaysian philosopher Syed Muhammad Naquib al-Attas. What he means by the rational soul, however, is more explicitly grounded in Qur'anic revelation, particularly the notion of a Primordial Covenant alluded to in (Q. 7:127). Al-Attas, *Islam and Secularism*, 139–43.

23. Aristotle, *Nicomachean Ethics*, I.13, in *The Complete Works of Aristotle: The Revised Oxford Translation*, ed. Jonathan Barnes, 2 vols. (Princeton, NJ: Princeton University Press, 1995), 2:1741–42.

24. According to the Māturīdī theologian al-Bayāḍī (d. 1078/1678), "This potentiality or preparedness is called Reason in potency (*'aql bi-al-quwwah*) or inborn Reason (*'aql gharīzī*). Then this Reason develops little by little by the creative activity of God until it reaches perfection. Reason thus perfected is called 'acquired Reason' (*'aql mustafād*)." Quoted in Toshihiko Izutsu, *The Concept of Belief in Islamic Theology: A Semantic Analysis of Īmān and Islām* (Kuala Lumpur: Islamic Book Trust, 2006), 139.

25. Mohammad Azadpur, *Reason Unbound: On Spiritual Practice in Islamic Peripatetic Philosophy* (Albany: State University of New York Press, 2011). Building on the work of Pierre Hadot, Azadpur argues convincingly for this reading of Muslim Peripatetic philosophers.

26. Walbridge, *God and Logic in Islam*, 17.

27. Jackson, *Boundaries of Theological Tolerance*, 24. While I am identifying particular schools of thought, Jackson here is speaking of Muslim rationalism broadly.

28. Jackson uses the phrase "constructions of reason" in specific reference to Muslim rationalist and traditionalist conceptions of reason. Jackson, *Islam and the Problem of Black Suffering*, 40.

29. Jackson, *Islam and the Problem of Black Suffering*, 10.

30. Alasdair MacIntyre, *Whose Justice? Which Rationality?* (Notre Dame, IN: University of Notre Dame Press, 1988). Similarly, MacIntyre, working with Western Christian traditions, has drawn into question the supposed universality of reason. See also Max Horkheimer, *Eclipse of Reason* (New York: Seabury Press, 1947); Walbridge, *God and Logic in Islam*, 15–29, 107–20.

31. I will return to al-Ghazālī's experience in chapter 6.

32. Abū Ḥāmid Muḥammad b. Muḥammad al-Ghazālī, "*Al-Munqidh min al-ḍalāl*," in *Majmū'at rasā'il al-imām al-Ghazālī* (Beirut: Dār al-Fikr, 2003), 539, 552–53; al-Ghazālī, *Deliverance from Error: Five Key Texts including His Spiritual Autobiography, al-Munqidh min al-Dalal,* trans. R. J. McCarthy (Louisville, KY: Fons Vitae, 1980), 57, 78; al-Ghazālī, *Al-Ghazali's Path to*

Sufism: His Deliverance from Error—al-Munqidh min al-Dalal, trans. R. J. McCarthy (Louisville, KY: Fons Vitae, 2000), 23, 52.

33. Syed Muhammad Naquib al-Attas, *The Concept of Education in Islam: A Framework for an Islamic Philosophy of Education* (Kuala Lumpur: International Institute of Islamic Thought and Civilization, 1999), 13–15; Syed Muhammad Naquib al-Attas, *On Quiddity and Essence: An Outline of the Basic Structure of Reality in Islamic Metaphysics* (Kuala Lumpur: International Institute of Islamic Thought and Civilization, 1990), 3–13; Thérèse-Anne Druart, "Al-Razi's Conception of the Soul: Psychological Background to His Ethics," *Medieval Philosophy and Theology* 5, no. 2 (1996): 245–63; Peter Adamson, "Abū Bakr al-Rāzī on Animals," *Archiv für Geschichte der Philosophie* 94, no. 3 (2012): 249–73. The desire to single out a unique quality as the defining differentia is itself problematic. Syed Muhammad Naquib al-Attas offers a different but still compelling critique of the Aristotelian formulation "rational animal" as well as Western conceptions of reason. Concerning the possible rationality of animals, see the debate between Druart and Adamson over the thought of Abū Bakr al-Rāzī.

34. Ernst Cassirer, *An Essay on Man: An Introduction to a Philosophy of Human Culture* (New Haven, CT: Yale University Press, 1944).

35. MacIntyre writes, "Man is in his actions and practice, as well as his fictions, essentially a story-telling animal." MacIntyre, *After Virtue*, 216. Reformed theologian James K. A. Smith restates MacIntyre, writing, "We are narrative animals whose very orientation to the world is fundamentally shaped by stories." James K. A. Smith, *Imagining the Kingdom: How Worship Works* (Grand Rapids, MI: Baker Academic, 2013), 108.

36. Eliade, *Sacred and the Profane*, 14–15, 116–18, 138, 203.

37. Wilfred Cantwell Smith, *Faith and Belief* (Princeton, NJ: Princeton University Press, 1979), 3.

38. Smith, *Imagining the Kingdom*, 109, 126–27.

39. Charles Taylor, *The Language Animal: The Full Shape of the Human Linguistic Capacity* (Cambridge, MA: Harvard University Press, 2016). While many other theorizations can be named, I believe it worthwhile to mention one more here, namely Charles Taylor's proposition to think of language as constitutive of the human being.

40. D. B. MacDonald, "*Wahm* in Arabic and Its Cognates," *Journal of the Royal Asiatic Society* 4 (October 1922): 509–11; Sa'd al-Dīn al-Taftazānī, *Sharḥ 'aqā'id al-Nasafiyya*, ed. Aḥmad Ḥijāzī al-Saqqā (Cairo: Maktabat al-Kulliyāt al-Azhāriyya, 1987), 15–16; Taftazani, *Commentary on the Creed of Islam*, 17–18; al-Ghazālī, *The Niche of Lights*, trans. David Buchman (Provo, UT: Brigham Young University Press, 1998), 35–36, 39–40; Harry Austryn Wolfson, "The Internal Senses in Latin, Arabic, and Hebrew Philosophic

Texts," *Harvard Theological Review* 28, no. 2 (April, 1935): 77–79. Those who explicitly spoke of the imagination typically referred to it as *khayāl*, *takhayyul*, *mutakhayyala*, *wahm*, or *tawahhum*. In the discipline of logic (*ʿilm al-manṭiq*), religious scholars describe a type of proposition called *wahmiyyāt* that is determined by *wahm*, a faculty intrinsic to our being, its source being our *fiṭra* or innate constitution. In this context, *wahm* is akin to "instinctive perception" in that it can ascertain the reality of sensible objects but fails to attain certainty with respect to that which lies beyond the senses. Reason, rather, must intervene to rein it in. Many of the same scholars identified another proposition type, the *mukhayyalāt*, which are the product of *khayāl* or "imagination." Such propositions are formed via "attractive or repulsive metaphors and comparisons" and more properly the concern of poetics than logic. The Ashʿarī theologian al-Taftazānī ultimately subsumes *wahm*, as the estimative faculty, under the conceptual rubric of *ʿaql* ("intellect"). Muslim philosophers like al-Fārābī (d. 339/950) and Ibn Sīna believed the imagination plays an important role for prophets. As Walbridge describes, "Unlike the philosopher, the prophet also possesses a particularly strong imaginative faculty, which enables him to express the intelligibles in imaginative forms understandable to all levels of men." Walbridge, *God and Logic in Islam*, 7. Azadpur maintains that for Ibn Sīna, "the intellect disciplines the imagination in order that it can receive the influences of the Active Intellect and the celestial souls." Azadpur, *Reason Unbound*, 71. Al-Ghazālī provides a similar usage for imagination as *khayāl* in *The Niche of Lights*. The enigmatic philosophers known as the Brethren of Purity (*Ikhwān al-Ṣafā*) describe the imagination (*mutakhayyila*) as one of the five internal senses, the others being cogitation (*mufakkira*), memory (*ḥāfiza*), the speaking faculty (*nāṭiqa*), and the productive faculty (*ṣāniʿa*). The Shīʿī metaphysician Mullā Ṣadrā Shīrāzī (d. 1050/1640) developed a fourfold schema of perception in which the imagination figures prominently. According to Chittick, Ṣadrā identifies the second level of perception as "imagination (*khayāl*, *takhayyul*), which is the perception of a sensory thing" regardless of whether or not it is immediately present, while the third level he identifies as *wahm*, meaning *estimatio* or "sense intuition," which indicates "the perception of intelligible meaning while attributing the meaning to a particular, sensory thing." William C. Chittick, *In Search of the Lost Heart: Explorations in Islamic Thought*, ed. Mohammed Rustom, Atif Khalil, and Kazuyo Murata (Albany: State University of New York Press, 2012), 223. The term *mithāl* can also mean "imagination" and was used as such by Ibn al-ʿArabī. I exclude it here, however, because I am presently concerned with identifying the imagination as an important human faculty for theology. As Chittick explains, "Ibn al-ʿArabī employs the term *mithāl*, 'image,' as a synonym for imagination. The basic difference between the manner in which he uses the terms is that *khayāl* refers both to the mental faculty known as imagination and the objective world 'out there' known as imagination, whereas *mithāl* is never used for the faculty." Chittick, *Sufi Path of Knowledge*, 117.

41. Sherman Jackson, *Sufism for Non-Sufis? Ibn ʿAṭāʾ Allāh al-Sakandarī's Tāj al-ʿArūs* (Oxford: Oxford University Press, 2012), 28–29.

42. Moosa, *Ghazālī and the Poetics of the Imagination*, 29–30, 34, 39, 45–49, 271; Christian Jambet, *The Act of Being: The Philosophy of Revelation in Mullā Sadrā*, trans. Jeff Fort (New York: Zone Books, 2006), 283–345; Chodkiewicz, *Ocean without Shore*, 1–18; Alexander D. Knysh, *Ibn ʿArabi in the Late Islamic Tradition: The Making of a Polemical Image in Medieval Islam* (Albany: State University of New York Press, 1999). Arguably, Ibn al-ʿArabī undertook the most profound and extensive theological engagement with the imagination. This is not to say that important contributions were not made by other scholars. For example, Ebrahim Moosa identifies and analyzes the "Ghazālian imagination" at work in al-Ghazālī's influential body of work. Al-Ghazālī challenged the scholarly conventions of his time. Rather than writing in disciplinary silos, where each field of religious knowledge was compartmentalized into a discrete discourse, al-Ghazālī transgressed boundaries, working in what Moosa identifies as a metaphorical *dihlīz*, "that space between the door and the house"—a threshold always suspended in-between. In the face of perceived peril and decline, al-Ghazālī labored to usher in a "resuscitation" of the faith through the tradition's many fields of religious learning. As Moosa explains, "The life-form and ethics that Ghazālī conceived is mingled with spirituality and piety." Al-Ghazālī wrote in both Arabic and Persian, interwove poetics alongside scholastics, and drew the different fields of religious knowledge into close conversation—the inclusiveness of the imagination at work—to create a new, integrative religious vision that resulted in his magnum opus *The Revival of the Religious Sciences*. Jambet analyzes the place of the imagination in the thought of the Mullā Ṣadrā, wherein he traces influences through earlier thinkers like Ibn Sīnā and the Illuminationist philosopher al-Suhrawardī. As for Ibn al-ʿArabī, his enduring legacy is evident in the enduring efforts either to sustain and elaborate on his ideas or to vociferously refute them as documented by Knysh. While a number of important modern studies have examined his understanding of the imagination, see especially Henry Corbin, *Alone with the Alone: Creative Imagination in the Sūfism of Ibn ʿArabī* (Princeton, NJ: Princeton University Press, 1997); Chittick, *Sufi Path of Knowledge*; William C. Chittick, *Imaginal Worlds: Ibn al-ʿArabī and the Problem of Religious Diversity* (Albany: State University of New York Press, 1994).

43. Quoted in Chittick, *Imaginal Worlds*, 12.

44. Chittick, *Imaginal Worlds*, 70–72; Chittick, *Sufi Path of Knowledge*, 117. With regard to the first meaning, the cosmos itself, Ibn al-ʿArabī is ad-

dressing the question of existence. While creation appears to possess existence, God is the only real existent, for existence is a divine attribute that God alone possesses in perfection. Creation, rather, lies between God's absolute existence and nonexistence. All of the created cosmos, then, is rendered as an ambiguous in-between or what Ibn al-ʿArabī terms as the imagination at its utmost limit, *al-khayāl al-muṭlaq*. At this macrocosmic level, the imagination is a figuration of existent reality. Scaling downward, the imagination was also understood to represent an intermediate imaginal domain that bridges the angelic domain of the Divine with the corporeal world of physical existence.

45. The basis for this conception lies with the Qur'anic symbol of the *barzakh*, which literally means a "separation" or "something that intervenes." In the Qur'an, *barzakh* is used to mean either a barrier between this life and the Hereafter (Q. 23:100) or an isthmus between two seas (Q. 25:53, Q. 55:20). The term came to be used to refer to an intermediate boundary world between life in this world and life in the eternal Hereafter. For Ibn al-ʿArabī, the idea of *barzakh* is just as much a bridge as it is a barrier.

46. Chittick, *Imaginal Worlds*, 54–55.

47. Chittick, *Science of the Cosmos*, 71. The Arabic terms used are *ʿaql* for reason and *khayāl* for imagination.

48. Al-Ḥārith al-Muḥāsibī, *Kitāb al-Tawahhum*, ed. A. J. Arberry (Cairo: Maṭbaʿat al-Taʾlīf wa'l-Tarjama wa'l-Nashr, 1937).

49. Al-Muḥāsibī, *Kitāb al-Tawahhum*, 1.

50. Al-Muḥāsibī, *Kitāb al-Tawahhum*, 3.

51. Al-Muḥāsibī, *Kitāb al-Tawahhum*, 40.

52. Al-Muḥāsibī, *Kitāb al-Tawahhum*, 56. For more on al-Muḥāsibī's *Kitāb al-Tawahhum*, see Christian Lange, *Justice, Punishment, and the Medieval Muslim Imagination* (Cambridge: Cambridge University Press, 2008), 112; Rustomji, *Garden and the Fire*, 107–8.

53. Other texts composed on the same subject include Kaʿb al-Aḥbār's (d. ca. 32/652–653) *Kitāb al-Ākhira* (Book of the Hereafter); Abū Marwān ʿAbd al-Malik b. Ḥabīb al-Sulamī's (d. 238/853) *Kitāb Waṣf al-firdaws* (Book of the Depiction of Paradise); Ibn Abī'l-Dunyā's (d. 280/892) *Kitāb al-Mawt* (Book of Death), *Kitāb al-Qubūr* (Book of Graves) and *Ṣifāt al-nār* (Qualities of the Hellfire); Abū'l-Layth al-Samarqandī's (d. ca. 393/1002) *Kitāb al-Ḥaqāʾiq wa'l-daqāʾiq* (Book of Realities and Intricacies); Abū Nuʿāym al-Iṣfahānī's (d. 430/1038) *Ṣifāt al-janna* (Qualities of Paradise); ʿAbd al-Raḥīm b. Aḥmad al-Qāḍī's (fl. fifth/eleventh century) *Daqāʾiq al-akhbār fī dhikr al-janna wa'l-nār* (Intricacies of the Reports on the Remembrance of the Garden and the Fire); *Al-Durra al-fākhira*, attributed to Abū Ḥāmid al-Ghazālī (d. 505/1111), as well as the section "Dhikr al-mawt wa-mā baʿdahu" ("The Remembrance of Death and Afterward") from his *Iḥyā ʿulūm al-dīn*; Diyāʾ al-Dīn Muḥammad b. ʿAbd

al-Wāḥid al-Maqdisī's (d. 643/1245) *Ṣifāt al-janna* (Qualities of the Garden) and *Dhikr al-nār* (Remembrance of the Hellfire); al-Qurṭubī's (d. 671/1273) *Al-Tadhkira* (The Memorial); Ibn al-Qayyim al-Jawzyiyya's (d. 751/1350) *Kitāb al-Rūḥ* (Book of the Spirit); Ibn Rajab al-Ḥanbalī's (d. 795/1392) *Ahwāl al-qubūr* (Terrors of the Grave); Jalāl al-Dīn al-Suyūṭī's (d. 911/1505) *Sharḥ al-sudūr bi-sharḥ al-mawtā wa'l-qubūr* (The Opening of Hearts by the Opening of Death and the Grave); and ʿAbd Allāh b. ʿAlawī al-Ḥaddād's (d. 1132/1720) *Sabīl al-iddikār wa'l-i ʿtibār bimā yamurru bi-'l-insān wa-yanqaḍī lahu min al-a ʿmar*, which has been translated as *The Lives of Man*. Modern works include Aḥmad Fā'iz's *Al-Yawm al-ākhir fī ẓilāl al-Qur'ān* (The Last Day in the Shadow of the Qur'an), Muṣṭafā al-Ṭayr's *Hādī al-arwāḥ*, Saʿīd Ṭah al-Kurdī's *Al-Mawt fī khidmat al-ḥayāt* (Death in Service of Life), and Sayyid Quṭb's (d. 1966) *Mashāhid al-qiyāma fī'l-Qur'ān* (Testimonies to the Resurrection in the Qur'an). The enumeration of this literature can be found in ʿAbd Allāh b. ʿAlawī al-Ḥaddād, *The Lives of Man: A Sufi Master Explains the Human States; Before Life, in the World, and after Death*, trans. Mostafa al-Badawi (Louisville, KY: Fons Vitae, 1991), 92–93; Smith and Haddad, *Islamic Understanding of Death*, 63–146; Rustomji, *Garden and the Fire*, 98–100, 117.

54. On the imagery of heaven and hell in the Islamic tradition, see again Smith and Haddad, *Islamic Understanding of Death*; Rustomji, *Garden and the Fire*; and Lange, *Paradise and Hell in Islamic Traditions*.

55. See Berkey, *Popular Preaching and Religious Authority*; Rustomji, *Garden and the Fire*, 101–5. Despite participating in a shared religious discourse, the relationship of the popular storytellers (*quṣṣāṣ*) and preachers (*wu ʿʿāẓ*) with the religious scholars (*ʿulamā'*)—if such an easy distinction can be made—was often tense since they were effectively competing for religious authority.

56. I believe it worth noting that Grewal's analysis, which is based on her study of the social imaginaries of Muslim Americans studying in the Middle East, also includes a spatial dimension in addition to the social one. The quoted passage in full reads, "Although the imagination is often thought of in highly individualized terms, we must also remember that relationships to places are not lived in solitary moments but most often in the company of others; the religious imagination is personally meaningful, but it is also a social formation that is shared and sustained by a collective." Zareena Grewal, *Islam Is a Foreign Country: American Muslims and the Global Crisis of Authority* (New York: New York University Press, 2014), 54. Jackson makes a similar point later in the context of Sufism, stating, "Self-reflection, human experience and religious imagination . . . are not limited to the individual but extend to the insights, discoveries, and tried and tested successes and failures of the Community as a whole." Jackson, *Sufism for Non-Sufis?*, 29.

57. Gordon D. Kaufman, *The Theological Imagination: Constructing the Concept of God* (Philadelphia: Westminster Press, 1981), 23.

58. Ibn Ṭufayl, *Ibn Ṭufayl's Ḥayy ibn Yaqẓān: A Philosophical Tale*, trans. Lenn Evan Goodman (Los Angeles: Gee Tee Bee, 1983); Cyrus Ali Zargar, *The Polished Mirror: Storytelling and the Pursuit of Virtue in Islamic Philosophy and Sufism* (London: Oneworld, 2017), 107–24. Zargar has provided an insightful narrative-oriented analysis of the text.

59. Nahyan Fancy, *Science and Religion in Mamluk Egypt: Ibn al-Nafīs, Pulmonary Transit and Bodily Resurrection* (New York: Routledge, 2013), 39–50; Zargar, *Polished Mirror*, 62–67; Nader El-Bizri, *The Phenomenological Quest between Avicenna and Heidegger* (Binghamton, NY: Global Publications, 2000), 149–53. So compelling was Ibn Tufayl's narrative device that a century later the Mamluk physician and scholar Ibn al-Nafīs (d. 687/1288) retold the tale through the fictional Fāḍil b. Nāṭiq (literally "Virtuous, son of Rational Speaking") in order to correct what he perceived to be one of the tale's heterodox conclusions, namely the marginalization of revelation. Ibn Sīnā also wrote his own narrative of Ḥayy b. Yaqẓān. A well-known thought experiment is also ascribed to Ibn Sīna in which he asks his reader to imagine one who is created fully formed and suspended in the air, but completely without sense perceptions. Zargar provides a concise but thorough reading of Ibn Sīna's account of Ḥayy b. Yaqẓān, while El-Bizri does likewise for the thought experiment.

60. Zargar, *Polished Mirror*, 18. As Zargar notes, Muslim and Jewish philosophers also made good use of the polished mirror metaphor.

61. Farīd al-Dīn ʿAṭṭār, *The Conference of the Birds*, trans. Afkham Darbandi and Dick Davis (New York: Penguin, 1984); John Renard, ed. and trans., *Knowledge of God in Classical Sufism: Foundations of Islamic Mystical Theology* (Mahwah, NJ: Paulist Press, 2004), 26; Zargar, *Polished Mirror*, 237–59. The group of birds in search of the king of birds is built around the Persian word play of "thirty birds" or *sī murgh* and the reported king of birds, the Simurgh. While the tale of the thirty birds is primarily known through ʿAṭṭār's poetic tale, the premise first appears in a work entitled *Risālat al-ṭayr*, which is attributed to Aḥmad al-Ghazālī (d. 520/1126), the brother to Abū Ḥāmid al-Ghazālī. Zargar has also insightfully analyzed ʿAṭṭār's contribution from the perspective of ethical formation.

62. Zargar, *Polished Mirror*, 22–23.

63. Walid A. Saleh, *The Formation of the Classical Tafsīr Tradition: The Qur'ān Commentary of al-Thaʿlabī (d. 427/1035)* (Leiden: Brill, 2004), 14–16. Saleh describes the nature of the exegetical enterprise as genealogical in that commentators had to engage with the interpretative tradition that preceded them.

64. Martin Nguyen, "Exegesis of the *ḥurūf al-muqaṭṭaʿa*: Polyvalency in Sunnī Traditions of Qur'anic Interpretation," *Journal of Qur'anic Studies* 14, no. 2 (2012): 1–28. In the classical texts, "the disconnected letters" are called *al-ḥurūf al-muqaṭṭaʿa*. I have previously examined how the Sunnī exegetical tradition has historically approached these letters. While my study may provide some sense of the tradition's imaginativeness, much work remains to be done in order to fully appreciate other Muslim approaches such as those proposed by Ibāḍī, Imāmī, Ismāʿīlī, and Muʿtazilī exegetical traditions.

65. Al-Ṭabarī, *Jāmiʿ al-bayān ʿan taʾwīl al-Qurʾān al-maʿrūf tafsīr al-Ṭabarī*, ed. Maḥmūd Shākir, 30 vols. (Beirut: Dār Iḥyāʾ al-Turāth al-ʿArabī, 2001), 1:101–2. This relatively early selection of opinions attributed to the companion Ibn ʿAbbās is found in al-Ṭabarī's commentary on verse (Q. 2:1).

66. Al-Ṭabarī, *Jāmiʿ al-bayān*, 29:19–21; Abū Isḥāq Aḥmad b. Muḥammad al-Thaʿlabī, *Al-Kashf wa-l-bayān ʿan tafsīr al-Qurʾān*, ed. Abū Muḥammad b. ʿĀshūr and Naẓīr al-Sāʿīdī, 10 vols. (Beirut: Dār Iḥyāʾ al-Turāth alʿArabī, 2002), 10:5; al-Wāḥidī, *Al-Tafsīr al-basīṭ*, ed. Muḥammad ibn Ṣāliḥ b. ʿAbd Allāh al-Fawzān, 25 vols. (Saudi Arabia: Jāmiʿat al-Imām Muḥammad ibn Saʿūd al-Islāmiyya, 1430/[2009]), 22:69–70; Ibn ʿAjība, *Al-Baḥr al-madīd fī tafsīr al-Qurʾān al-majīd*, ed. ʿUmar Aḥmad al-Rāwī, 8 vols. (Beirut: Dār al-Kutub al-ʿIlmiyya, 1999), 6:221–22; al-Shawkānī, *Fatḥ al-qadīr: Al-Jāmiʿ bayna fannī al-riwāya wa-l-dirāya min ʿilm al-tafsīr*, ed. ʿAbd al-Raḥmān ʿUmayra, 6 vols. (Cairo: Dār al-Wafāʾ, 1994), 5:265; Abū al-Qāsim ʿAbd al-Karīm b. Hawāzin al-Qushayrī, *Laṭāʾif al-ishārāt: Tafsīr ṣūfī kāmil li-l-Qurʾān al-karīm*, ed. Ibrāhīm Basyūnī, 6 vols. (Cairo: Dār al-Kitāb al-ʿArabī, 1968), 1:65–66; Ibn Qutayba, ʿAbd Allāh b. Muslim, *Taʾwīl mushkil al-Qurʾān*, ed. al-Sayyid Aḥmad Ṣaqr, 2nd ed. (Cairo: Dār al-Turāth, 1393/1973), 299; Yāqūt ibn ʿAbd Allāh al-Ḥamawī, *Muʿjam al-buldān*, 5 vols. (Beirut: Dār al-Ṣādir, 1397/1977), 4:298.

67. Paul Ricoeur, *Figuring the Sacred: Religion, Narrative, and Imagination*, ed. Mark I. Wallace, trans. David Pellauer (Minneapolis: Fortress Press, 1995), 144.

68. Quoted in Victor Brockis, *Muhammad Ali: In Fighter's Heaven* (London: Hutchinson London, 1998), 36.

69. Iqbal, *Reconstruction*, 10.

70. The Qur'an translation provided here is the one that originally appeared in the text. Iqbal, *Reconstruction*, 10.

71. Iqbal, *Reconstruction*, 114.

72. Muhammad Iqbal, *Complaint and Answer of Iqbal*, trans. A. J. Arberry (Lahore: Sh. Muhammad Ashraf, 1997), 10.

73. Iqbal, *Complaint and Answer*, 30.

74. John Ralston Saul, *On Equilibrium: Six Qualities of the New Humanism* (New York: Four Walls Eight Windows, 2004), 143.

75. Saul, *On Equilibrium*, 116.

76. Chittick, *Imaginal Worlds*, 75.

77. Saul, *On Equilibrium*, 117. Christian theologian and ethicist Stanley Hauerwas has made a similar case but goes further to delineate limitations. Specifically, he discusses the case of intellectual disability and how our imagination can fail us. Stanley Hauerwas, "Should Suffering Be Eliminated? What the Retarded Have to Teach Us (1984)," in *The Hauerwas Reader*, ed. John Berkman and Michael Cartwright (Durham, NC: Duke University Press, 2001), 569–74.

78. Ricoeur, *Figuring the Sacred*, 144.

79. Saul, *On Equilibrium*, 127.

80. Ricoeur, *Figuring the Sacred*, 144.

5

REVELATION AND RESPONSE

THE QUR'AN AS REVELATION

> *The disbelievers also say, "Why was the Qur'an not sent down to him all at once?" We sent it in this way to strengthen your heart; We have recited it to you in a measured pace.*
> —Qur'an 25:32

God speaks. God has spoken to us since before our beginnings. God speaks to us now. God shall speak to us even beyond the ending of all things. Even though we may fail to hear the Divine, God addresses us still, for His divine address does not cease or falter. God's speech is eternal. Herein lies the aspect of revelation with which we are engaged and to which we are responding. While God's revelation permeates creation and is signified throughout nature and our human selves, the face of revelation with which I am concerned here is the Qur'an as God's revelation.

When I describe the Qur'an as revelation, however, I am taking the Qur'an as more than a text to be cognitively understood, philologically dissected, and interpretatively bent to human will. As the Anglican bishop and scholar of Islam Kenneth Cragg acknowledges, "The Qur'ān is a fusion, unique in history, of personal charisma, literary fascination, corporate possession, and imperative religion."[1] If we reduce the Qur'an to a text, we immediately limit and constrain our ability to engage fully with its breadth and depth. Of course, the Qur'an is read, studied, parsed, and interpreted, but it also lives in the lives of its interlocutors in manifold other ways. It is carefully intoned and continuously recited. It is committed to memory and inscribed upon hearts. It is carefully illuminated and meticulously adorned. It is etched and engraved into edifices. It is formed and fashioned to fill the spaces in which the faithful and faith seeking abide. It fills the aural soundscape and marks the visual landscape. It renders sacred spaces that are otherwise mundane. Its physical presence can alter one's behavior. It comes to rest upon the highest of shelves. It is carried and handled with ritual reverence. The devout kiss it, imbibe it, and consume it. It is worn around necks and sewn into garments. It names the newly born. The Qur'an becomes a refuge from suffering. The Qur'an is a cure for afflictions. Its intonation delivers supplications. It shapes, directs, and transforms those who turn to it. It comforts and consoles. It challenges and confronts. It accompanies and at times haunts those who encounter it. The Qur'an engages our bodies, our human faculties, and our malleable sensibilities in myriad ways. Its reach is extensive, and its influence is existential. What the Qur'an's pervasiveness and insistence in human life points to is an idea that the Qur'an itself places before humanity. *We tell you the best of stories in revealing* [*awḥaynā*] *this Qur'an to you* (Q. 12:3); *Do not rush to recite before its revelation* [*waḥyuhu*] *is fully complete* (Q. 20.114); *So We have revealed* [*awḥaynā*] *an Arabic Qur'an to you* (Q. 42:7). More than a text, the Qur'an is *waḥy*—revelation.

By revelation, however, I am not only referring to its first order of meaning that scholars of religion have worked to identify, that is, "Revelations are communications believed to come from a divine being."[2] I do not question that this register of meaning is significant. Indeed, the Jesuit scholar of the Qur'an Daniel Madigan goes further to define *waḥy* specifically as "a kind of communication that remains impenetrable, and perhaps exotic to a third person observing it, yet it remains full of meaning for the one receiving it."[3] The "one receiving it," of course, is the Prophet Muhammad, who received God's message as it was progressively unfolded to him over the course of twenty-three years. The Qur'anic verses cited above can be interpreted on an immediate level as pointing to this historical process. These definitions are important for anchoring revelation to the historical circumstances of its supposed origination.

The Qur'an as revelation, however, can also be interpreted more broadly from a theological perspective. The Qur'an is more than a text disclosed to the Prophet in his Arabian context. As the array of experiences that I enumerated above disclose, the Qur'an is an ongoing act of divine disclosure that continues to engage the community of the faithful across time, space, and contexts. The same above-cited Qur'anic verses concerning *waḥy* can also be interpreted on another level as addressing the Qur'an's many and endless interlocutors outside of the Prophet Muhammad's immediate historic moment. The Qur'an is as much speaking to us as it is speaking to the Prophet Muhammad.

In other verses, the Qur'an calls itself *kalām Allāh* (Q. 2:75, Q. 9:6, Q. 48:15), literally "God's speech" or "the word of God." The Qur'an represents the most direct form of God's communication to humanity in that it descends as "speech." God makes it manifest in a human language against the phenomenological structures of our perceived existence. After all, the Qur'an is experienced first and foremost as a "recitation" or "lecture," which is the literal meaning of the word *qur'ān* itself. The Qur'an, then, is not just a textual phenomenon but embodies more comprehensively a speech act possessing both existential force, such that it is in the world, and an experiential structure, such that it transforms those who engage with it.

Connected to this last point, there is also an intrinsic relational dimension to the Qur'an. Revelation is fundamentally dialectic in nature. Humankind is God's intended recipient. The Qur'an addresses our nature, our community, our past, our future, and our present situatedness in this world. When the Qur'an refers to itself as a reminder (*dhikr*), a guidance (*hudā*), a criterion (*furqān*), and a scripture (*kitāb*), a dialectical element is implied in every instance.[4] The Qur'an is a weighty matter to be received. It is a reminder to be heeded. It is a guidance to be followed. It is a criterion for judgment. It is a scripture to be read and preserved. It is a recitation to be uttered and heard. A dialogical relationship is implicit in each of its names.

God speaks in the Qur'an with munificent and overwhelming abundance. As even a cursory engagement with the Qur'an reveals, it is rich with arguments and indications, warnings and disclosures, and enticements and terrible warnings. Portents of things to come are disclosed with purpose. The errors of past peoples are shared so that those in the present will pay heed. Even the silences that emerge in the breaks and pauses of the Qur'an's recited disclosure are addressed to us. Indeed, it is in those profound and deliberate silences that we are invited to pause, reflect, and respond. It is into this integral back-and-forth of revelation that we are existentially drawn.

IN THE MOMENT OF REVELATION

Recite! In the name of your Lord who created, created the human being from a clinging form. Recite! Your Lord is the most bountiful.
—Qur'an 96:1–3

An archetype for the relational nature of the Qur'an as revelation is found in the very first occasion of its earthly descent. There is a prophetic report in the hadith collection of al-Bukhārī (d. 256/870) that recounts this event:

Yaḥyā b. Bukayr transmitted to us saying: al-Layth transmitted to us on the authority of ʿUqayl: on the authority of Ibn Shihāb: on the authority of ʿUrwa b. Zubayr: on the authority of ʿĀʾisha, Mother of the Believers, may God be pleased with her, who said:

The beginning of revelation for the Messenger of God, may God's prayers and peace be upon him, came as the true dreams of sleep and when a dream came to him it came like the breaking of dawn. Then he was made to love seclusion and used to go into seclusion in the cave of Ḥirāʾ where he would perform devotions—that is worship—for a number of nights until he felt inclined to return to his family. He would take provision for [his retreats]. Then he would return to Khadīja to take more provisions to do likewise again until the Real came to him while he was in the cave of Ḥirāʾ.[5]

The angel came to him and said, "*Recite!*" [The Prophet] said, "I am not a reciter." [The Prophet] said: He seized me and squeezed me until all the strength went out of me and then released me and said, "*Recite!*" I said, "I am not a reciter." Then he seized me and squeezed me a second time until all the strength went out of me and then released me and said, "*Recite!*" I said, "I am not a reciter." Then he seized me and squeezed me a third time and then released me, and then he said, "*Recite! In the name of your Lord who created, created the human being from a clinging form. Recite! Your Lord is the most bountiful* (Q. 96:1–3)."[6]

The quintessence of the God–human relationship is conveyed in the preceding account. As related by the narrative, the Prophet Muhammad had secluded himself in the cave of Ḥirāʾ for a series of nights in the month of Ramadan. And it was in the quiet of one of these nights that God, "the Real," proclaimed—through the angelic intermediary Gabriel—the beginning of the Qur'anic revelation: *Recite!* (Q. 96:1).[7] Thrice is the command *recite* given and thrice is a response meekly uttered, "I am not a reciter," or in other accounts, "I cannot recite" or "What do I recite?"[8] God speaks and the Prophet Muhammad attempts to respond. Moreover, we might imagine that on this momentous occasion the Prophet, in his utter humanness, stands for all of humanity. His response is our response, as both aspiration and reality. In each of these divine commands to recite, we can imagine different dimensions of revelation: (1) as the unrelenting and uncompromising command in demand of a response, (2) as the irruption of the divine word into human history, and (3) as a bestowal from on high.

The Unrelenting and Uncompromising Command in Demand of Response

> *O humankind! Worship your Lord who created you and those who were before you so that you might be reverent.*
> —Qur'an 2:21[9]

The call and attempt at response expressed in the narrative is a recurrent feature of revelation. According to the primordial covenant, when preexistent humanity is gathered before the Creator, God says: *"Am I not your Lord?" and they said, "Yes, we bear witness"* (Q. 7:172). Or consider the Qur'anic verse where God says to the still-forming heavens and the earth, *"Come forth, willingly or not," and they said, "We come willingly"* (Q. 41:11). In many other places the Qur'an states, *"Be," and it is* [*Kun fa-yakūn*] (Q. 2:117, Q. 3:47, Q. 3:59, Q. 6:73, Q. 16:40, Q. 19:35, Q. 36:82, Q. 40:68). With this single utterance from God, "Be [*Kun*]," creation springs into being. God speaks and creation existentially responds. Our very existence is but a response to the divine imperative.

When revelation is made manifest, it exerts a gravitational force upon those who hear it. Like the Prophet Muhammad, humankind is drawn into its dialectical orbit. The absoluteness of God's utterance lays claim to those addressed and draws forth from them a response. Whether commanded to recite, to testify, or to exist, a response is precipitated. The back-and-forth initiated by revelation is not an exchange of equals but a command from the Creator to creation. It is incredibly difficult for a human being to respond given the immeasurable difference between interlocutors. A person's ability to respond is all the more difficult because revelation does not reconcile itself to human conceptions of the world. Rather, it demands the opposite. Revelation asserts the absolute centrality of God while simultaneously displacing all else. It decenters humanity in its createdness and recenters it on the Creator.

Consider too the nature of a created being's response. Recall the impotence of the Prophet's "I am not a reciter" and "I cannot recite," and the scrambling *Yes, we bear witness* of preexistent humanity to acknowledge God's lordship. Imagine the meagerness of human existence when faced with the creative omnipotence of God the Creator, our Lord and Sustainer. Humankind responds in whatever way it can muster. Each of us responds in spite of the immense gulf that divides us from God. And however that response is made, it is a response that must be done with humility. *Recite!—Come forth—Be!* When God speaks with such existential primacy, how else could we respond? *O you who have faith! Revere God and speak rightly* (Q. 33:70).

The Irruption of the Divine Word into Human History

> *If We had sent down this Qur'an upon a mountain, you would have seen it humbled and rent asunder from fear of God.*
> —Qur'an 59:21

> *By the press of time, truly humankind is in loss.*
> —Qur'an 103:1–2

> *The trustworthy Spirit brought it down upon your heart, so that you might be among the warners—in a clear Arabic tongue.*
> —Qur'an 26:193–95

The dialectic of revelation represents only one facet of how we can understand the Qur'an as God's revelation. We may also imagine it as an irruption if we turn to the Qur'an's historic unfolding. It breaks into the world, it overwhelms human measures of time, and it transforms the language in which it appears. The Qur'an radically challenges and overturns human conceptions of the world, time, and language. And once it is in the world, the Qur'an does not leave it. The irruption is ongoing; God's revelation is eternal.

With respect to the world, the Qur'an enters human life with shattering decisiveness. On the first night of revelation, when the Prophet Muhammad is called by God, each command to *recite* is accompanied by a crushing intensity, "He seized me and squeezed me until all the strength went out of me."[10] Elsewhere, the Prophet describes it with even greater severity: "He pressed me tight and almost stifled me, until I thought I would die."[11] Or he would say, "I hear sounds like metal being beaten. Then I listen and often I think I will die."[12] Another tradition reports, "The Messenger of God used to move his lips from pain as soon as the revelation began."[13] As these transmitted accounts indicate, revelation is not a light burden to bear. With the word of God comes a share of suffering in this world. That the Prophet Muhammad continued to respond to the Qur'anic revelation, despite the physical pain that it brought, is telling. Theology, if it is indeed our human response to revelation, should likewise go forth with a share of suffering in this world. Our response to revelation ought to persist through the adversities that we witness and endure. In fact, the arrival of God's eternal word—the truth to power that it speaks—awakens humanity more keenly to the ongoing suffering that pervades existence. It reveals the brokenness of the world and the darkness that envelops it. Revelation—God's clarion call to creation—resounds all around us unimpeded and inescapable. As the Prophet Muhammad testifies, "Sometimes it comes as the ringing of a bell; this kind is the most painful."[14]

The ringing of revelation reverberates through the thrice-commanded *Recite!* Each iteration is like the striking of the hammer upon the sound bow of a bell. Although each blow may land upon a single point in a single instant—the specific historical moment—the sounding of the bell reverberates across the broad fields of history.[15] Here is the word of God in its historicity and its eternity. Although revelation strikes on that first night of revelation's descent, the word of God continues ever onward without loss of clarity or force.

With respect to time, the irruption of revelation can be imagined along epistemological lines. The entrance of God's speech into the world radically challenges what human beings imagine that they know about the world. It overturns human perceptions of the familiar. The descent of the Qur'an into the world is a marked disruption to the habitual norm or perceived natural order that humanity observes and experiences in the everyday. Revelation pulls humanity from its complacency within history and proclaims that there is only one God, life after death, a final judgment to come, and an awaiting, eternal Hereafter. The end is coming, the Qur'an repeatedly reveals, but the precise moment of its arrival is intentionally left undisclosed. The human sense of time, however understood, is challenged by the amorphous measure proclaimed in revelation. God is reminding us that there are limits to what we humans can know.

Similarly, revelation can also be said to domesticate time. As God states in the sacred report ascribed to the Divine, "God, mighty and glorious is He, said, 'Humanity inveighs against time [*dahr*] though I am time. Night and day are in My hand.'"[16] Time is nothing more than a created thing under God's dominion. As the religious scholar al-Nawawī (d. 676/1277) clarifies, the sacred report is figurative explaining "as for *dahr* ('time'), which is time (*zamān*), it cannot do anything [in itself]. Rather it is a created thing from among God's creation. The meaning of 'God is time' is that He is the causer of events and occurrences and that He is the Creator of all existent things."[17] Human conceptions of time are swept aside. History is dismissed as merely a human construct strung across an arbitrary measure of time. Time, meanwhile, belongs to the Creator.

The Qur'an demonstrates this emphatically in its own handling of temporality. As Cragg has found, the Qur'an presents vexingly and perhaps paradoxically both a "presence and absence of chronology."[18] Time is often obfuscated or compressed in service of the message being proclaimed. The prophetology of the sacred past and the eschatology of the unrevealed future intentionally displace and confound the traces of human record keeping. At the same time, history remains an intrinsic and central dimension to revelation in that revelation can only be encountered and experienced in those same historical traces.

The divide between human conceptions of time and the Qur'an seems all the more poignant for Muslims living in modernity. With modern societies moving ever toward both a mastery of time and the emptying of time, revelation responds with the language of timelessness and eternity. God promises an end time and the possibility of life eternal ever afterward. Human time, in all its hubris and vacuousness, is brought to naught with the oncoming of revelation, for God alone has mastery over time. The speech of God challenges and overwhelms all temporal expectations and the careful crafting of human calculations. The clock faces of our most intricate artifices of time are effaced. Our prognostications are brought to naught. Any notion of *our time* is washed away by the oncoming of revelation. *By the press of time, truly humankind is in loss* (Q. 103:1–2). Time belongs to God and no other. The Divine alone knows the length of each life and the precise moment of its passing. He alone knows when each soul will come into this world at birth, and He alone knows when each soul will depart from it at death.

With respect to language, the eternal word is sent down and made manifest in a human tongue, the Arabic of the seventh-century Hejaz. Arriving in the cultural wellspring of pre-Islamic Arabia, the Qur'an assumes the expressive form of highest regard for that time and place, the oral poetic tradition. But God does not simply adopt the form of a human language. Revelation, when it descends, both breaks it and perfects it simultaneously. As Seyyed Hossein Nasr poetically captures,

> The text of the Quran reveals human language crushed by the power of the Divine Word. It is as if human language were scattered into a thousand fragments like a wave scattered into drops against the rocks at sea. One feels through the shattering effect left upon the language of the Quran the power of the Divine whence it originated. The Quran displays human language with all the weakness inherent in it becoming suddenly the recipient of the Divine Word and displaying its frailty before a power which is infinitely greater than man can imagine.[19]

The Qur'an proceeds in its gradual revelation to redefine the Arabic language itself. In the words of the American philosopher Norman O. Brown, the dynamism of the Arabic language was "absolutely audaciously exploited and developed in the Qur'ān" through the very "destruction of human language."[20] According to the Syrian poet Adonis, the Qur'an opened "new horizons" for Arabic poetics.[21] It set a new course for the language's sophisticated development. The Qur'an was the impetus for the refinement and fixing of the Arabic script. It became the model par excellence from which the rules of syntax and morphology were derived. The Qur'an generates the Arabic language as much as it was made manifest within it.

Indeed, the Arabic Qur'an as the speech of God perpetually represents the pinnacle of linguistic expression in the eyes of the faithful. As the Qur'an states, *Say, "Even if all humankind and jinn came together to produce a semblance of this Qur'an, they could not produce anything like it, however much they helped each other"* (Q. 17:88). Though humans struggle and scramble to respond in kind, they are fated to fall short of revelation's eloquence, complexity, and completeness.

Yet long have Muslims tried to respond with sufficiency. If the lives dedicated to the Qur'an are any indication, if the ever-accumulating volumes of commentary and interpretation are any testament, the depths of the Qur'an cannot be exhausted by centuries of human effort. It continues to speak, provoke, and challenge. It turns back humanity's many attempts to make it their own. No matter how convoluted or contorted the hermeneutics, no violence can be done to the Qur'an because the Qur'an is no human text. It is the eternal speech of God, which is not subject to subjugation. Rather, it transforms and directs its human interlocutors. It makes *us* its own. With perpetual constancy, it conveys decisively on the one hand, while asserting a boundless openness, on the other, so that humankind might be guided. Indeed, the Qur'an, as an outpouring of revelation, possesses a quality of inexhaustibility. *If all the trees on earth were pens and the sea, with seven more seas besides, [were ink,] the words of God would still not be exhausted. Truly God is the Almighty, the All-Wise* (Q. 31:27). *Say, "If the sea were ink for the words of my Lord, the sea would be exhausted before the words of my Lord would be exhausted, even if We brought its like to replenish it"* (Q. 18:109). Here is the Qur'an unbound by language yet undeniably of language at the same time. God's speech is revealed in a manner that is inimitable and categorical on the one hand, while also comprehensible and accessible on the other. *Truly We have sent it down as an Arabic Qur'an so that you may understand* (Q. 12:2).

No understanding of the Holy Book is possible until it is actually revealed to the believer just as it was revealed to the Prophet.
—Nūr Muḥammad, from *The Reconstruction of Religious Thought in Islam*[22]

Timing, my sister, timing. We do what we must do; the timing is Allah's.
—Farid Esack, *On Being a Muslim*[23]

The Qur'ān was not only a new way of seeing things and new reading of mankind and the world, but also a new way of writing. As well as representing a break with the *Jāhiliyya* on an epistemological level, it represented a break on the level of forms of expression. The Quranic text was a radical and complete departure: it formed the basis of the switch from an oral to a written culture—from a culture of intuition and improvisation to one of study and contemplation, and from a point of view which made contact with the pagan surface of existence to one which reached into its metaphysical depths.
—Adonis, *An Introduction to Arab Poetics*[24]

A Bestowal from on High

Truly We have sent down the reminder and truly shall We preserve it.
—Qur'an 15:9

This immense and necessary rupture in earthly existence is not confined to a historical period. God has spoken and is ever speaking. The first *Recite!* irrupting into the Prophet's life continues to address humankind just as it continued to address him through the rest of his days. As the Iranian philosopher Abdulkarim Soroush observes, "It was not as if the Prophet experienced revelation once and ascended to the heavens once, to then rest on those laurels and spend from that treasure for the rest of his life. No, the blessings of revelation rained down upon him constantly, giving him ever greater strength and flourishing."[25] Although the prophetic period of Qur'anic revelation and the age of prophecy itself came to an end with the passing of the Prophet Muhammad, the eternal speech of God continues to communicate to humanity.

It speaks still in the here and now. The hammer, so to speak, still strikes.

Yet, as hard and clamorous as the hammer fall of revelation may be, we may also rightly envision it as being sent down out of God's beneficence and compassion. The very overwhelmingness of revelation ought to be seen as the onrush of God's love, for God declares in a sacred tradition, "Verily, My mercy prevails over My wrath."[26] God speaks with a fullness and perfection that is undeserved, and yet the Divine persists in speaking nonetheless. The outpouring of the Qur'an into the world is God's compassionate rejoinder to human obstinacy and temperamentality and humankind's primordial and perpetual forgetfulness. We are the recipients of an unmatchable reciprocity. Let us bow and be humbled.

Our most modest, sincere, and devout replies perpetually fall short of the Almighty's compassionate outpouring. Yet this matters not to the Almighty as the Qur'an makes clear: *O humankind! You are the ones in need of God; God is the All-Sufficient, the All-Praiseworthy* (Q. 35:15). Whatever response we muster, however humble or meek, God the Merciful shall hear and receive it. Such is how God's love unfolds. In another sacred report, God assures,

> I fulfill My servant's expectation of Me, and I am with him when he remembers Me. If he remembers Me in his heart, I remember him in My heart; and if he remembers Me in public, I remember him before a public [far] better than that. And if he draws nearer to Me by a handsbreath, I draw nearer to him by an armslength; and if he draws nearer to Me by an armslength, I draw nearer to him by a fathom; and if he comes to Me walking, I come to him running.[27]

God is patient, enduring, and ever responsive, and His reply shall exceed whatever the faithful and faith seeking may offer in turn. The Qur'an that He bestows upon humanity is given as a pure gift. Such are the ways that we can imagine the Qur'an as revelation: as God's speech, as part of a dialogic relationship, as a forcible irruption into the world and individual consciousness, as an eternal assertion of timelessness, as a breaker and maker of human language, and as an onrush of effusive and unrelenting love.

TOWARD A THEOLOGY OF PROSTRATION

> *When My servants ask you about Me, truly am I near. I respond to the prayer of the supplicant who calls upon Me, so let them respond to Me and have faith in Me so that they might be rightly guided.*
> —Qur'an 2:186

This figurative exploration of the Qur'an as revelation is far from exhaustive. Others will differ or disagree over how the Qur'an might be envisioned, and indeed we ought to imagine many other possibilities.[28] Nevertheless, I believe what I have presented here goes some way in demonstrating that how we conceive of the Qur'an can provide us with different starting points and trajectories to pursue a wide array of imaginative theological undertakings. While the Qur'an is undoubtedly a text, the Qur'an's textuality constitutes only one part of a greater whole, a whole that the person of faith living today cannot afford to ignore. It behooves us to understand the Qur'an in a more phenomenologically extensive way.

In sum, to approach the Qur'an as revelation is to experience it as completely, fully, and humbly as humanly possible, knowing all the while that its fullness can never be experienced exhaustively. The approach of theology is always asymptotic, never reaching completion. Nonetheless, the aspiration abides. When God has given so much, we must try. For the faithful who live in the wake of revelation—those who are alive to it—theology is where they come to grips with what humanity has lost and what humanity must do. It is through the diffuse and varied work of theology that human beings gather themselves and attempt to respond again and again to God's call and command.

Here, prostrating oneself before the immensity of revelation, is where the human interlocutor—the soul in search of faith—begins to muster her response to God. Bowed at the base of the crater of revelation is where all theology begins. But how do servants of God—human beings who are so utterly fallible, dependent, and contingent—rise to respond? How can we stand in reply? Herein lies my key proposition, the heart of this imaginative theology: To respond to revelation is not to rise with hubris but to fall upon one's hands and knees before God. The answer is to prostrate oneself. A faithful theology of response must be a theology of prostration. How each person embodies this posture of humility is manifold, as manifold as the ways by which we engage the

Qur'an in the world. Indeed, to bow before revelation is not the end but a creative beginning. It marks a point and posture from which living theologies ought to emerge.

Theology need not always be constituted as a complex system of religious thought or a carefully constructed array of convictions requiring endless tending and defending. There are times when prayer is our most appropriate response. More than that, there are times when prayer is our best recourse. Prayer both habituates us to humility and amplifies our sincerity. It physically and mentally orients us rightly for our humble response to the Divine. After all, is it not in the folds of prayer that we have been asked to worship God as though we see Him? Prayer is a rhythm around which we can form a life of faith and righteousness.

> How then do we heal the hearts of those who suffer, with no courts to give them their day, and no advocates to chronicle their grievances and demand they be redressed? We cannot. And we must recognize our own inability to do that; we must weep, not only for them, but more for ourselves, that we are so impotent. For God alone has the power to heal their hearts; God alone has the power to redress their wrongs; and God alone has the power to punish their oppressors.
> —Hamza Yusuf, *The Prayer of the Oppressed*[29]

NOTES

1. Kenneth Cragg, *The Event of the Qur'ān: Islam in Its Scripture* (Oxford: Oneworld, 1994), 13.
2. Rodney Stark, "A Theory of Revelations," *Journal for the Scientific Study of Religion* 38, no. 2 (1999): 289.
3. Daniel Madigan, *The Qur'ân's Self-Image: Writing and Authority in Islam's Scripture* (Princeton, NJ: Princeton University Press, 2001), 144.
4. Take, for example, the following verses of the Qur'an: *For it is a reminder [dhikr] for you and for your people* (Q. 43:44); *It was in the month of Ramadan that the Qur'an was revealed as a guidance [hudā] for humankind* (Q. 2:185); *Exalted is He who has sent down the criterion [furqān] to His servant* (Q. 25:1); *That is the Scripture [kitāb] in which there is no doubt* (Q. 2:2).
5. The phrase *jā'ahu al-ḥaqq*, which I have translated as "the Real came to him" could also be translated as "the truth came to him" since *al-ḥaqq* can

mean "truth" generically speaking. I have gone with the above translation because *al-ḥaqq* is also a name of God, "the Real."

6. Al-Bukhārī, *Ṣaḥīḥ*, 1:7, *Bad' al-waḥy*.

7. Al-Bukhārī, *Ṣaḥīḥ*, 1:7.

8. The Arabic for "I am not a reciter" is *mā anā bi-qāri'*, while *mā aqra'u* can be read as either "I cannot recite" or "What do I recite?" The account provided by al-Ṭābarī in his voluminous historical chronicle contains the Arabic *mā aqra'u*. Al-Ṭabarī, *Tārīkh*, 309.

9. This verse is the first command to be encountered in the Qur'an if it is read from the beginning of the scripture.

10. Al-Bukhārī, *Ṣaḥīḥ*, 1:7, *bad' al-waḥy*.

11. Al-Ṭabarī, *The History of al-Ṭabarī*, 6:71.

12. Translation from A. J. Wensinck and A. Rippin, "Waḥy," *Encyclopaedia of Islam*, new ed. (Leiden: Brill, 1986–2004), 11:55; Aḥmad b. Ḥanbal, *Al-Musnad*, ed. Aḥmad Muḥammad Shākir, 8 vols. (Cairo: Dār al-Ḥadīth, 1995), 6:484, ḥadīth 7071.

13. Translation with slight modification from Wensinck and Rippin, "Waḥy," 11:54–55; al-Bukhārī, *Ṣaḥīḥ*, 9:154, *tawḥīd*.

14. Translation from Wensinck and Rippin, "Waḥy," 11:54; al-Bukhārī, *Ṣaḥīḥ*, 1:6, *bad' al-waḥy*; Muslim, *Ṣaḥīḥ*, 4:1816–17, *Kitāb faḍā'il*, no. 87; Muslim b. al-Ḥajjāj and Yaḥyā b. Sharaf al-Nawawī, *Ṣaḥīḥ Muslim bi-sharḥ al-Nawawī*, 18 vols. (Cairo: al-Maṭba'at al-Miṣriyya bi-l-Azhar, 1347–1349/1929–1930), 15:88; al-Tirmidhī, *Al-Jāmi' al-kabīr*, 6:25, *Abwāb al-manāqib*.

15. I offer this image as an inversion of the poignant observation made by Adonis, the pen name of the Arab poet and critic 'Alī Aḥmad Sa'īd: "And if it [the Qur'an] is sacred, being the language through which Islam was revealed, this sacredness is in some sense localized and historical." Adonis, *An Introduction to Arab Poetics*, trans. Catherine Cobham (London: Saqi Books, 1990), 42.

16. The sacred report in question is understood as a *ḥadīth qudsī*, a special kind of report in which the Prophet Muhammad is relating the words of God. Muslim and al-Nawawī, *Ṣaḥīḥ Muslim bi-sharḥ al-Nawawī*, 15:2; Graham, *Divine Word and Prophetic Word*, 212, saying 89.

17. Muslim and al-Nawawī, *Ṣaḥīḥ Muslim bi-sharḥ al-Nawawī*, 15:2.

18. Cragg, *Event of the Qur'ān*, 112.

19. Seyyed Hossein Nasr, *Ideals and Realities of Islam*, rev. ed. (Chicago: Kazi Publications, 2000), 36.

20. Norman O. Brown, *The Challenge of Islam: The Prophetic Tradition, Lectures, 1981* (Santa Cruz, CA: New Pacific Press, 2009), 47, 50.

21. Adonis, *Introduction to Arab Poetics*, 37.

22. Iqbal, *Reconstruction*, 143. The text attributes the saying to "a Muslim Sufi," which the editorial endnote reveals to be Muhammad Iqbal's father, Nūr Muḥammad. Mustansir Mir, *Iqbal* (London: I. B. Tauris, 2006), 1.

23. Farid Esack, *On Being a Muslim: Finding a Religious Path in the World Today* (Oxford: Oneworld, 2009), 27.

24. Adonis, *Introduction to Arab Poetics*, 37.

25. Soroush, *Expansion of Prophetic Experience*, 10.

26. Graham, *Divine Word and Prophetic Word*, 184, saying 59.

27. Graham, *Divine Word and Prophetic World*, 127, saying 12.

28. For example, Navid Kermani has approached revelation from the perspective of aesthetics, concluding provocatively, "The Qur'an cannot be called a piece of art, not because it is something completely different from art, but because it is so artistic, it could not be man-made art." Navid Kermani, "Revelation in Its Aesthetic Dimension: Some Notes about Apostles and Artists in Islamic and Christian Culture," in *The Qur'an as Text*, ed. Stefan Wild (Leiden: E. J. Brill, 1996), 223. See also Navid Kermani, *God Is Beautiful: The Aesthetic Experience of the Quran*, trans. Tony Crawford (Cambridge: Polity, 2015).

29. These words are from the introduction that precedes Yusuf's English translation of a prayer known in Arabic as "Al-Duʿāʾ al-Nāṣirī," so called for its author, Ibn Nāṣir al-Darʿī (d. 1085/1674), a Moroccan scholar of admirable piety and learning. Hamza Yusuf, trans., *Imam Muḥammad b. Nāṣir al-Darʿī's the Prayer of the Oppressed: The Sword of Victory's Lot over Every Tyranny and Plot* (Danville, CA: Sandala, 2010), 20.

6

FAITH IN THE TRADITION

A LIFE OF FAITH

> If writing these words yields no other outcome save to make you doubt your inherited beliefs, compelling you to inquire, then it is worth it—leave alone profiting you. Doubt transports [you] to the truth. Who does not doubt fails to inquire. Who does not inquire fails to gain insight. Without insight, you remain blind and perplexed. So we seek God's protection from such an outcome.
> —Al-Ghazālī, *Mīzān al-ʿamal*[1]

Faith is an expression of how a human being lives with respect to revelation. It constitutes the core of theology, for it is through faith that a person discovers the language best suited to answer the reverberating call of God. In truth, all human beings carry some measure of faith because God has created within each of them the *fiṭra*, a natural disposition to believe in the Creator. The Prophet Muhammad related that "every infant is born endowed with the natural disposition,"[2] while the Qur'an states, *So set your face to the religion as one of pure faith, in accordance with the natural disposition that God has instilled in humankind* (Q. 30:30). Faith, or rather the possibility of faith, is a common human quality. Nevertheless, the experience of faith differs dramatically from life to life. Indeed, that experience unquestionably changes over time. This dimension of change with respect to faith is the central concern of this chapter. Across time and place, Muslims have understood faith in many different ways.

The eminent sage and theologian Abū Ḥāmid al-Ghazālī shares his journey of faith through periods of doubt and discovery in his famous autobiography *The Deliverer from Error*. Early in his account, he describes his initial disillusionment as a youth with unquestioning adherence to socially transmitted beliefs or *taqlīd*.[3] He observed that many people simply conformed to the social expectations and beliefs to which they were exposed. The children of Christians grew up to be Christians, the children of Jews grew up to be Jews, and the children of Muslims grew up to be Muslims. There was something unsettling to him that so many seemed to adopt the faith of their forebearers without question. If each soul has been created with a natural disposition to believe in the Creator, then why did so many continue to adhere to other religious paths? How was it that human discernment could be so divided between unquestioning adherence to socially transmitted beliefs (*taqlīd*) on the one hand and the natural disposition instilled by God (*fiṭra*) on the other? To answer this question, al-Ghazālī reasoned, he could no longer rely on the expertise of others. He would have to tackle this issue on his own, and so he did.

The young al-Ghazālī began by questioning the very basis of what he knew. He questioned what his sense perceptions conveyed to him. He questioned the faculties of his intellect. He even ventured to imagine ways of apprehension that lie beyond the limits of rationality. He thought of the mystics and what they claimed to witness with their hearts. He thought of death and the realities of the Hereafter, recalling the words of the Prophet: "People are asleep and when they die, they awaken."[4] As he wrestled and wrangled with these difficult questions, downward he spiraled until he found himself lost in skepticism. For nearly two months his doubts plagued him mercilessly, though he continued to mouth outwardly the beliefs expected of him. To the world he appeared a devout person of faith, but inwardly he was plagued with disquiet and despair. Eventually, he was brought out of this pitiful state, but not by his own doing. As he describes the experience, "God most High cast a light into my breast and that light is the key to most knowledge."[5] His deliverance came by the grace of God, not the machinations of his mind.

Al-Ghazālī's early tribulation, however, was not the end of his seeking but only the beginning. As he matured and advanced in his learning, he continued to explore critically the substance of faith and reality.

Later in his life, when he was at the seeming pinnacle of his career, he was struck by another crisis of faith. This crisis was more pernicious than before, escalating with each passing day until "the matter ceased to be one of choice and became one of compulsion. God caused my tongue to dry up. . . . My tongue would not utter a single word nor could I accomplish anything at all."[6] So severe was his internal turmoil that al-Ghazālī found himself incapacitated completely. This respected man of words was made mute. He had been brought low, and all of his learning did little to mend him. In time he realized that his condition could only be alleviated by wayfaring far from home. Thus he departed, leaving behind his family and career in order to walk and pray in faith. He journeyed for several years, resolving not to return until his soul was burnished to shine brighter than before.[7] When finally al-Ghazālī did return, he returned with a sagacity and spiritual maturity that eclipsed his prior state. It was after this lengthy time away that he came to pen his most profound works of faith, *The Alchemy of Happiness* and *The Revival of the Religious Sciences*.

Al-Ghazālī's lifelong experience is a paradigm for the life of faith. Writing many years later, he describes his experience with the following words:

> There is no hope of returning to unquestioned belief after leaving it because a condition of the uncritical follower is that he does not realize that he is being uncritical. For once he realizes that, then the glass of his unquestioned belief is shattered. The fragments cannot be mended; they cannot be pieced back together and remade. It must be melted in the fire and made anew into another form altogether.[8]

When an uncritical faith is lost, one must forge something stronger, a *critical* faith. He likens faith to a glass in that it is an object of refinement that reflects the exquisiteness of its craftsmanship. Nonetheless, it is also delicate and not easily subjected to undue pressure or mishandling. It is precisely this aspect of fragility that al-Ghazālī is attributing to unquestioned belief. Such a glass may be pleasing to the eye, but it cannot endure the turbulence of an inquiring soul. Under pressure a faith founded on unquestioned belief—an uncritical faith—will break. The damage is irreparable. The fragments of what once was cannot be reassembled. Instead, if faith is to be found again, if the glass is to be remade, its shape and form must change. It must be thrust into the fire all over again. That is no easy task because it requires us to stride into the heat of the forge and to labor away. Moreover, as the life of al-Ghazālī demonstrates, one may have to stand before the maw of the furnace many times over in a single lifetime. Faith requires continual renewal.

I have spent some time going over al-Ghazālī's journey of faith for two reasons. First, his story brings to light the range and complexity of faith. While for some faith is nothing more than precariously held unquestioned beliefs that are inherited unthinkingly, for others faith is that which is diligently wrought over and over again during the span of a lifetime, gaining in strength and beauty with every visitation. Faith, then, is not merely a cache of doctrines or ideas. Nor is it a prize that reflects religious zeal. Faith, rather, dynamically embodies the human being's ever-changing relationship with the Creator and His creation. It weakens and strengthens with difficulties and triumphs. It is continually subject to challenge, no matter one's age or experience. Nevertheless, faith never loses its potential to be made stronger and better, as long as it is tended to with care and patient perseverance.

Second, al-Ghazālī's life of critical inquiry and searching is a microcosm for the life of the wider tradition. The tradition has had to face and overcome numerous challenges to questions of faith, just as al-Ghazālī had to during his lifetime. Faced with a seemingly endless series of incisive questions, critiques, and crises, both al-Ghazālī and the tradition adapted and shifted accordingly in order to find firmer footing and sounder ground. When necessary, they found new paths to follow altogether.

THE MEASURE OF FAITH

> Difference of opinion in the community is a token of divine mercy.
> —Abū Ḥanīfa, *Al-Fiqh al-akbar*[9]

From the very beginning, Muslims have asked time and again, "What is faith?" and "Who are among the faithful?"[10] While the outward inquiry has remained the same, the circumstances and context of the inquiry have changed from place to place and from era to era. This point is worth underscoring. The tradition has always changed and developed in response to the perennial stream of questions that we face. It continues to do so. The tradition is negotiated continually because our position in the current of history is shifting perpetually.

What follows is a venture into historical theology. More precisely, the following section provides a theological reading of the history of Muslim scholastic theology on the question of faith. My aim is twofold. First, I am interested in how the participants of the classical tradition of theology understood faith. As will be demonstrated, their responses were varied and not always complementary. Indeed, the definition of faith within the classical tradition changed with time, place, and circumstance. At times the debates were heated, if not divisive. Second, I want to illustrate clearly that the theological tradition itself developed and changed as a consequence of these differences of opinion. By tracing the question of faith historically, the human dimensions of the tradition become more evident. To invoke my earlier imagining of the Kaʿba as a figuration of tradition, what we are doing, in effect, is examining the handiwork of the many who have labored to preserve and replace the stones of the Kaʿba throughout the centuries for the sake of the Divine.

During the lifetime of the Prophet, questions of faith were certainly present within the nascent Muslim community, but those who wrestled with such questions benefited from the immediacy of revelation, which was still being revealed, and the attention and counsel of the Prophet himself. Both seekers and skeptics could approach the Messenger of God and receive in response direct prophetic guidance. We should not imagine, however, that questions of faith were any easier because of this. The stakes during the Prophet Muhammad's lifetime were incredibly high. Whether facing persecution in Mecca or armed conflict in Medina, the question of faith was a live and dangerous issue. Do we follow this man who claims to be a messenger of God? Is the message that he brings truly the speech of God? Shall we imperil our lives and the bonds of family for this radical new community? Do we have the courage to be among *those who have faith* (Q. 2:25, passim)—*faithful men and faithful women* (Q. 33:35)?

These questions continued and multiplied in the postprophetic era. The first critical juncture arrived during the reign of ʿAlī b. Abī Ṭālib (d. 40/661), the fourth Caliph to lead the Muslim community after the death of the Prophet. The community of faith was spreading into domains far beyond the Arabian peninsula. With so many new souls joining the faith, some Muslims feared that the purity and integrity of the religion was not being upheld. Does the committal of a grave sin mark a complete loss of faith? Who shall we count among the faithful? Who is worthy to lead the community of faith? A zealous faction, known as the Khawārij ("seceders"), answered these questions with puritanical decisiveness. Faith and deeds are one. To transgress the decrees of God is to forfeit one's membership in the community of faith. In the eyes of the Khawārij, few demonstrated the fastidiousness of faith that was demanded; fewer still could lead such a community. In fact, their fanatical fervor boiled over one early morning in the month of Ramadan of 40/661. Having perceived the Caliph ʿAlī of failing to uphold God's will, several members of the Khawārij attacked the Caliph as he entered the congregational mosque of Kufa to perform the predawn prayer. As the blade that fatally wounded ʿAlī struck, one of the assailants shouted, "Authority [*al-ḥukm*] belongs to God, ʿAlī, not to you or your accomplices!"[11] This uncompromising view of faith led to the assassination of a man who was not only the rightly guided leader of the Muslim community but also the cousin and son-in-law of the Prophet Muhammad. The Khawārij, for their part, seceded from the larger community and would war continuously against it in the centuries to follow.

In the decades following ʿAlī's death, the Muslim community became embroiled in conflict, civil war, insurrection, and widespread discontent. The Umayyad dynasty came to occupy the seat of leadership, establishing a caliphate of hubris. Opposition to them grew with each violation of the public trust that they committed, the greatest of which occurred in 61/680, when Umayyad forces martyred a prominent voice and symbol of opposition, al-Ḥusayn, the son of ʿAlī and the grandson of the Prophet Muhammad. Shortly thereafter, ʿAbd Allāh b. al-Zubayr (d. 73/692), another companion of the Prophet Muhammad, established a counter-caliphate in Mecca that would last for nearly a decade. As mentioned in chapter 3, it was during this same period that harm would be done to the Kaʿba as well. Indeed, many other rivals would challenge and confront the Umayyads over their leadership of the Muslim community.[12] Political and religious disunion had become the norm and not the exception in the first post-prophetic century.

Out of this chaotic whirlwind arose a group of religious scholars, including the eminent jurist Abū Ḥanīfa (d. 150/767), who sought to quell the rampant divisiveness within the Muslim community. They came to be known as the Murjiʾa for the doctrine of "suspension" or *irjāʾ* that they advocated.[13] When faced with a rapidly growing community of faith that was also increasingly diverse in character and creed, the Murjiʾa "suspended" judgment as to whether a Muslim lost his or her status of faith through the committal of any transgression. Whereas the Khawārij had answered this same question with expulsion, the Murjiʾa sought to maintain an ethos of inclusion. They reasoned that judgment ought to be deferred to God since no other human being could know what truly lies in the heart of another. As Abū Ḥanīfa professed, "We do not consider anyone to be an infidel on account of sin; nor do we deny his faith."[14] The position of the Murjiʾa was also partially motivated by the difficult realities faced by the newly converted out on the frontiers of Islamdom. When Abū Ḥanīfa was asked "about the status of a Muslim in the territory of polytheism [*arḍ al-shirk*] who assents to Islam as a whole but has no knowledge of the Qurʾan or any of the religious duties of Islam," he affirmed that such a person was still a person of faith.[15]

While the Murjiʾa were effective in refuting the Khawārij, their positions were not always amenable to other scholars in the tradition.[16] One voice that was especially critical of the Murjiʾa was that of the famed hadith scholar Aḥmad b. Ḥanbal (d. 241/855). Like the Murjiʾa, he sought to unite rather than divide the community. He shunned, however, the speculative reasoning of his theological peers and instead appealed to the most basic common denominators of belief. He believed that the Qur'an and rigorously authenticated hadiths could serve as the core of correct belief.

In a short creed attributed to him, Aḥmad b. Ḥanbal states, "Faith is speech and action (or works). It increases and decreases. It decreases where works are few, and increases where they are many."[17] Several important differences stand out. Firstly, faith and works are related. Throughout the Qur'an, the believers are referred to through the combination of the two: *those who have faith and do righteous deeds* (Q. 2:25, passim). In contrast to the Khawārij, Aḥmad b. Ḥanbal argued that works were a reflection of faith, not its litmus test. Secondly, faith was not a singular status for all, as the Murjiʾa maintained. Rather, faith could be strong or weak and grow or diminish. *The true faithful are those whose hearts become fearful when God is mentioned, and who increase in faith when His signs are recited to them, and who place their trust in their Lord* (Q. 8:2); *He it is who sent down tranquility into the hearts of the faithful so that they might increase their faith with faith* (Q. 48:4). Moreover, Aḥmad b. Ḥanbal posed, do the Murji'a imagine that the faith of an everyday person was somehow comparable to the faith of angels and prophets? Or to the faith of the Arabs of the Prophet's early community?

While Aḥmad b. Ḥanbal took recourse to scripturalism, the contemporaneous theological school of the Muʿtazila turned to scholasticism.[18] The Muʿtazila developed this approach in response to polemics originating from outside the Muslim community. Muslim rule had quickly spread to lands where robust communities of Christians, Jews, Zoroastrians, and others had long been present. Many of the leading religious voices of these communities met Islam with harsh criticism. A case in point is John Damascene (d. 132/749), a Christian monk and theologian who was born in Damascus after the early Muslims had conquered it. His father, Sergius, had served in the Muslim Umayyad court and had encouraged his son to become acquainted with the scripture of their new rulers. John Damascene's familiarity with the Qur'an and Muslims is evident in his work *The Fount of Knowledge*, a penetrating tome of Christian theology. Therein he discusses Islam, but relegates it to the section on Christian heresy.[19] As was typical of the time, John did not see Islam as a separate religion but as a heretical deviation from the Christian truth.

It was futile for Muslim theologians to respond to this sort of criticism with verses of the Qur'an and reports from the Prophet Muhammad. These sources, while revered by Muslims, held no authority for non-Muslim critics. Instead, the Muʿtazila turned to reason as the common touchstone for the defense of the faith, apologetics, and the critique of others, polemics.[20] While this position was not easily reconcilable with the view of others, like Aḥmad b. Ḥanbal, who granted divine revelation, Qur'an and hadith, greater priority than human reasoning, it nonetheless established an enduring model that future schools of theology would adopt and adapt even as they challenged it.[21]

The most well-known case is the theologian Abū al-Ḥasan al-Ashʿarī (d. 324/935-6), who began among the Muʿtazila in Baghdad but left them to articulate an influential and long-enduring reconciliation of rationalist theology and scripturalism for the Sunnī tradition.[22] Although al-Ashʿarī left Muʿtazilism, he retained his valuation of the human intellect with some modification.[23] The methods of scholastic theology were important and versatile, but priority had to be granted to revelation and the tenets of faith that issued from such an arrangement. This became a guiding principle for the Ashʿarī school of theology that developed out of al-Ashʿarī's teachings.[24] Like Aḥmad b. Ḥanbal, the theologians of the Ashʿarī school believed that the faith of the everyday Muslims could both increase and decrease. The ranks to which one could rise or fall reflected degrees of faith's perfection. The Ashʿarīs, however, did not rely on scriptural attestations alone. Like the Muʿtazila, the Ashʿarīs used evidentiary proofs and rational arguments to demonstrate that their positions were sound, while continually affirming the primacy of revelation over reason. By the late fifth/eleventh century, Ashʿarism gained enduring traction within the Sunnī theological mainstream. As a result, the community of faith gained a robust rational apparatus with which to contend with outside criticism and to articulate a coherent and sustaining religious framework.

Ashʿarism was not the only rationalist approach to successfully join the Sunnī theological tradition. Contemporaneous with Abū al-Ḥasan al-Ashʿarī was the theologian Abū Manṣūr al-Māturīdī (d. 333/944), the namesake of the Māturīdī school of theology. Like al-Ashʿarī, al-Māturīdī developed his system of thought as a refutation of Muʿtazilism, but his results were markedly different. While al-Ashʿarī lived in Baghdad, al-Māturīdī was in the Central Asian city of Samarkand out on the caliphal periphery. While united in purpose, the two theologians were oblivious to one another's efforts. Moreover, al-Māturīdī and his followers were also the inheritors of the Murjiʾa that had spread into Central Asia hand in hand with the teachings of Abū Ḥanīfa. As would be expected, Māturīdī theology aligns with Murjiʾism in several ways. Like the Murjiʾa, the Māturīdī school separates faith and works, affirming that faith entails confession of the tongue and conviction in the heart alone.[25] The Māturīdīs also deny that faith increases and decreases, instead maintaining that the essence (*dhāt*) of faith is immutable.[26] Acts of obedience might change, but they are categorically separate from faith. Just as Abū Ḥanīfa had articulated his opinions with a view toward the new converts of his day, so too were the Māturīdīs dealing with the converted nomadic Turkic peoples in the lands east of the Oxus River. The Māturīdī school clearly struck a chord in the region, as it was largely adopted by the Turkic peoples, who took it with them as they expanded beyond the lands of Transoxania. Māturīdism spread into Khotan and Ghazna and then eventually westward into Khurasan, Iraq, and Anatolia with the rise of the Saljūq Turks.

As impressive as the spread of the Māturidī school was, it unfolded over the course of centuries and was held with suspicion as it moved westward. Several Ashʿarīs wrote critiques of the Māturīdīs, using their late historical arrival as evidence against them.[27] Unsurprisingly, the scripturalist theologians disliked the method of scholastic theology used by the Māturīdīs, Ashʿarīs, and Muʿtazilīs alike. It took centuries of heated discussion for a tolerant balance to be forged by all those involved. By the eighth/fourteenth century, the Ashʿarī and Māturīdī schools had lived long enough side by side that many of the most contentious debates had ebbed in fervor.[28] This is not to say that the particularisms did not persist, for they most certainly did, but a largely civil and scholarly détente had been reached. The story of Māturīdism's rise, uneasy as it was, serves to illustrate further the theological tradition's state of constant growth and development.

FAITH IN THE CHANGING TRADITION

> I began to wonder about the inevitability of a "Black Muslim Theology"—or, to extend the analogy beyond the African-American community, a "Muslim American Theology," or a "Muslim Feminist Theology," or even a "Muslim Womanist Theology"—and how these might relate to traditional Islamic theologies from the Muslim world.
> —Sherman Jackson, *On the Boundaries of Theological Tolerance in Islam*[29]

Indeed, the tradition emerges—or rather it is constructed—from out of historical contestations. Every voice within the tradition has faced criticism. Each voice has had to overcome its share of challenges. Aḥmad b. Ḥanbal suffered persecution during the infamous inquisition or *miḥna* ("ordeal") when the debate over the Qur'an's nature, whether it was created or uncreated, was politicized by the Abbasid Caliph al-Maʾmūn (r. 198–218/813–833). The Caliph demanded that government-appointed scholars confess that the Qur'an was indeed created. While some acquiesced, others resisted vigorously. When Aḥmad b. Ḥanbal refused to bow and bend his views to that of the Caliph, he suffered imprisonment and flogging. Ashʿarism faced its own ordeal early in its development. When the Saljūq Turks of Central Asia swept into Khurasan in the early fifth/eleventh century, they deemed the nascent Ashʿarī school to be unfamiliar and unfaithful. The Saljūqs decreed the name of Abū al-Ḥasan al-Ashʿarī to be cursed from the pulpits alongside the Shīʿa. Ashʿarism was officially condemned. Many Ashʿarī scholars were barred from preaching and teaching, and several were outright arrested. Fighting broke out in the city of Nishapur as a result.[30] Even al-Ghazālī had his share of tensions during his lifetime. He labored to bring Sufism into the heart of the Sunnī mainstream, refuted the arguments of Muslim philosophers, and articulated harsh critiques against the Nizārī Ismāʿīlīs, who were actively resisting the Saljūq regime in power. Challenges were faced on many fronts.

These trials of history are not the exception but the rule. It is within the furnace of history that the tradition grows. We should not suffer the illusion that the tradition has always been as it has been without issue or dispute. Voices that we now consider an important part of the tradition were not always seen as such. Each had to struggle for its place. Not every voice was successful in its endeavor. Every group discussed above ardently believed that it was upholding the tradition in its own way. Each beheld the tradition from a different perspective. The Khawārij saw a tradition on the brink of sinful collapse and responded with an uncompromising rule of life. The Murjiʾa beheld the same tradition, but saw a tide of exclusionary intolerance overtaking it instead. Their response was to suspend judgment so that the community of faith might be for the many rather than for the few. Scripturalist and rationalist theologians alike were equally invested in maintaining the tradition's fidelity to revelation, but they understood how this fidelity was best preserved in fundamentally different ways. As this account illustrates, these competing schools of thought did not always look kindly upon each other. Detailed refutations, scathing censures, ad hominem attacks, and exhaustive and exhausting heresiographies have been penned. Scattered throughout the historical chronicles are reports of vendettas, riots, imprisonments, uprisings, and campaigns of persecution, many of which were carried out in the name of tradition, faith, or both.

Finally, I must caution that the preceding narrative is only a partial view of the tradition in two respects. First, the theological views discussed here hardly represent all the voices that have sought to find a place within the tradition. The early ascetics, the sages of Sufism, and the Muslim philosophers, among many others, could just have readily joined the story to reveal other facets of faith in the changing tradition. What of the voices of women?[31] As the Muslim American ethicist and legal scholar Kecia Ali has critiqued, "'Textual Islam' has historically been the province of a male elite, and does not accurately represent the understandings of Islam embedded in the experiences of many Muslims, especially women."[32] What of the material, literary, and cultural contributions produced by Muslim artisans, poets, and litterateurs? What of the innumerably many Muslim souls who may have been untrained in the fields of religious learning yet were just as deeply animated by faith? All these voices have also contributed in their own way although they may not always be recognized, much to our detriment. For the time being, it suffices to recognize that many others have labored just as vigorously to offer their responses. The preceding account is only a part of a larger story to be told, and the tradition is always greater than some subset of perspectives. Second, the question of faith provides us with only a glimpse of the many challenges that have captivated the tradition's attention. In some respects, the focus on "faith" could have been otherwise. Any number of other questions could have been taken up to come to the same set of conclusions, to which I shall now turn.[33]

The tradition's eventual acceptance of Ashʿarism, Māturīdism, and various threads of scripturalism was not an a priori given but an accomplishment negotiated over time. The balance struck between these schools was not always enjoyed but was achieved after decades and centuries of exhaustive discussion, arduous debate, and public contestation. Compromises eventually emerged from out of the cacophony. The tradition is a series of agreements that are always tenuous, contextual, and temporary in nature. The détentes, compromises, and balances made in one time and place must be reaffirmed or renegotiated for another. However a tradition is constructed or reconstructed, an element of change is inescapable.

The tradition that is received today is not the same tradition as experienced and understood in times past. It has always been dynamically adapted to the needs of its community, whatever the time and wherever the place. There was a time when the bold protestations of Aḥmad b. Ḥanbal had not yet been precipitated. There was a time when the Ashʿarī school was misunderstood to the point of public condemnation. There was a time when the Māturīdī school was unknown or relegated to the obscurity of the margins. With time, each of these perspectives came into the fold of the tradition prompted by changing historical circumstances. The present moment, as profoundly modern as it may be, is no different. We shall pass on and adapt the tradition just as our predecessors have done. The challenge is that we each hear and receive God's word in our own ways. How we understand revelation differs from person to person. Nonetheless, as Abū Ḥanīfa has written, "Difference of opinion in the community is a token of divine mercy."[34] Tradition is where these differences are continually negotiated.

The malleability of tradition, then, is neither a defect nor a deficiency. Rather, there is divine wisdom behind it. The pliancy of our tradition is precisely what is needed for its survival, if not fluorescence. However tenuous, contentious, and cacophonous the human construction of the tradition may appear, all of it unfolds in accordance with the will of God. Time belongs to the Creator, as revelation reminds; all things are foreordained. No gain, loss, or revolution transpires outside of God's omniscient and omnipotent determination. The tradition is precisely as the Divine determines it to be, changes, challenges, and all, even if the how of it remains obscured to human perception.

The balances and détentes that the tradition presently enjoys may very well be radically changed again—by the will of God. Just as God's providence has brought the tradition to where it is now, so too will His providence shepherd it onward to new articulations and expressions. This does not mean, however, we should fall silent or complacent in expectation of the change to come. We must remain active, engaged, and open to where God's revelation is directing us so that our response can fall in accord with God's will. And if tradition is indeed about community and history, then we must also account for the many new voices that join the fray. To what new horizon is God leading the tradition of this growing community of faith? Change pervades tradition. Change has come, by the will of God, and change is coming, if God wills.

A LIFE OF CHANGE

> Malcolm X's faith was marginal not only in America as a whole but in the African-American community itself. . . . The idea that a person from the black underclass, with no university or seminary education, could teach the people of America something about their God and country was and still is today almost unthinkable for the vast majority of whites and blacks. What could a former convict and dope pusher teach us about things holy and divine?
> —James Cone, *Martin and Malcolm and America*[35]

> Allah always gives you signs, when you are with Him, that He is with you.
> —Malcolm X, *The Autobiography of Malcolm X*[36]

As the narrative of faith in the tradition demonstrates, variations in context precipitated different theological responses to the questions of faith. The questions themselves changed in emphasis and trajectory over time. Who is among the faithful? What does one make of grave sinners? Does faith increase and decrease? Are there varieties of faith? What was at stake on the periphery was not the same as what was at stake at the center. Whether looking at Baghdad, Cordoba, or Samarqand, or Kuala Lumpur, New York, or Johannesburg, every place has its own set of circumstances and particularities that shapes the nature of our theological inquiry. While our theologies might aspire to transcend the particularities of our historical circumstance, our theologies are unavoidably colored by the specificities in which we live. What, then, is the present context? Where might faith in God today be made to stand? How ought the human response to God look when issued from an English-speaking horizon inflected by the language of the Qur'an? I opened this chapter by retracing al-Ghazālī's life of faith, which was born out of the turmoil of his century in a land quite distant from our own. To end this chapter, I turn to the brilliant and fiery life of el-Hajj Malik el-Shabazz, Malcolm X, one much closer to home.

Malcolm X was a man of many names who wrestled with faith in a way most revealing for our lives today.[37] His awakening to faith did not begin with a conscious search for God. It began with a desire for escape during the time of Malcolm's incarceration. Imprisoned for the legal crime of burglary and the social transgression of a black man sleeping with a white woman, Malcolm found himself a denizen in the darkness of the lowest depths. His condition was not simply one that was without faith. His mind was set against it. "I considered myself beyond Atheism—I was Satan."[38] What could be worse than the ingratitude of a misbeliever? Why, nothing less than the archetype of tragic disobedience himself, Satan, who, according to the Qur'an, had once been known as Iblīs. This was the fallen Malcolm, who had once been Malcolm Little. He had hustled and tempted, whispered and lied, rebelled and defied, until at last he was ensnared by his own devilish vices. "I was just deaf, dumb, and blind."[39] It was in this most feeble and powerless of states that Malcolm *was* Satan, a figuration of powerlessness whose only quarter is gained through the weaknesses of others.[40] Malcolm had given the devil within all the quarter that it needed such that Malcolm himself was cast out, cornered, and condemned.

It was in his dank corner of concrete that Malcolm began to turn. A fellow inmate named Bimbi revealed to him the power of language. "He was the first man I had ever seen command total respect," Malcolm said, "with his words."[41] Motivated by Bimbi's captivating boldness, Malcolm began to tame his rebellious soul. Malcolm studied language, both English and Latin. He labored over his penmanship. He read voraciously tome after tome of whatever was available to him within the walls of the prison. Malcolm knew that in knowledge lay his empowerment. His efforts would culminate at last in that seemingly most mundane of efforts, his meticulous copying and studying of the English dictionary. Yet it was precisely through this labor that Malcolm would achieve his mastery. Through the word, Malcolm would attain to faith and the freedom it offered.

His path to salvation began with letters from his brothers Philbert and Reginald. In one letter, Reginald cryptically disclosed, "Malcolm, don't eat any more pork, and don't smoke any more cigarettes. I'll show you how to get out of prison."[42] Although Malcolm did not understand the reasoning behind the message, the promise of release drove him to act accordingly. In retrospect, Malcolm recognized something profound in his acquiescence. "Later I would learn, when I had read and studied Islam a good deal, that, unconsciously, my first pre-Islamic submission had been manifested. I had experienced, for the first time, the Muslim teaching, 'If you will take one step toward Allah—Allah will take two steps toward you.'"[43] The first steps of faith are often taken without realizing it. Unbeknownst to him, Malcolm had committed himself to something greater than himself.

In the months and years that followed, the letters would continue to arrive. With each received page, Malcolm learned more and more of Islam. "Over and over, I read, and heard, 'The key to a Muslim is submission, and attunement of one toward Allah.'"[44] The Islam disclosed to Malcolm was charismatic and revolutionary, but its end, however, was not otherworldly salvation. The Islam he received was concerned with life and death in this world. It sought the resurrection of minds from the mass graves of slavery. It told a radically different story of the way of the world. It told that story in black and white. As Malcolm describes,

> History had been "whitened" in the white man's history books, and that the black man had been "brainwashed for hundreds of years." Original man was black, in the continent called Africa where the human race had emerged on the planet Earth. The black man, original man, built great empires and civilizations and cultures while the white man was still living on all fours in caves. "The devil white man," down through history, out of his devilish nature, had pillaged, murdered, raped and exploited every race of man not white. . . . The devil white man cut these black people off from all knowledge of their own kind, and cut them off from any knowledge of their own language, religion, and past culture, until the black man in America was the earth's only race of people who had absolutely no knowledge of his true identity. . . . And where the religion of every other people on earth taught its believers of a God with whom they could identify, a God who at least looked like one of their own kind, the slavemaster injected his Christian religion into this "Negro." This "Negro" was taught to worship an alien God having the same blond hair, pale skin, and blue eyes as the slavemaster. This religion taught the "Negro" that black was a curse. It taught him to hate everything black, including himself. . . . This white man's Christian religion further deceived and brainwashed this "Negro" to always turn the other cheek, and grin, and scrape, and bow, and be humble, and to sing, and to pray, and to take whatever was dished out by the devilish white man; and to look for his pie in the sky, and for his heaven in the hereafter, while right here on earth the slavemaster white man enjoyed *his* heaven.[45]

All that was white, Christian, and Western was mercilessly critiqued to the point of negation. Offered in its place was Islam, a black religion of authenticity that hailed from the Holy World of the East. This Islam recognized the global white supremacy that was at work (and is still at work) and strove to confront it with its own bold voice. In this Islam, faith and righteousness were united as a lived principle. At the same time, this Islam, as Malcolm would later learn, was not the same path disclosed by the Qur'an and the Prophet Muhammad. This Islam also spoke powerfully through the Bible and the words of its living teacher, the Messenger of the Lost-Found Nation in the Wilderness of North America, the Honorable Elijah Muhammad. The Nation of Islam was the path out of the wilderness, and Elijah Muhammad was the guide to lead the lost along it.

The Islam of the Nation unearthed a history that was mythic in power and arresting in rhetoric. In it the stigma of blackness was overturned. Blackness was no blemish but the beginning of us all. Greatness lay in the past and greatness could be had again, not in the far off future or in heaven above, but in the immediacy of the here and now. Souls rendered dead by a system of oppression so pervasive that none could escape were now offered life once more. Even one who was Satan, the troubled Malcolm, could be made to live among the resurrected. All one had to offer in return was discipline, devotion, and unwavering faith. All these Malcolm gave freely and wholeheartedly.

The words preached to Malcolm, which sustained and delivered him from death and devilry, were divisive in nature. For my present concern, the truth or falsehood of those words is not as important as the divine wisdom behind them. However problematic those words may have been, they were precisely the words Malcolm needed to hear for his time and place. It was a necessary step for Malcolm to find his way from out of the depths. The words may not have been Qur'anic, but the unfolding that they precipitated was by the determination of the Divine through and through.

As Malcolm moved toward release, his own voice began to crystallize. He transformed from one of the preached to a preacher. He not only received letters but began to write them, inviting others to join him in his rise. He spoke to those he once knew on the outside and those he met on the inside. Malcolm was finding the words with which he would respond: racism, justice, Islam, Allah.

Like al-Ghazālī, Malcolm's life of faith faced moments of crisis as well. The first transpired early on while he was still imprisoned. Malcolm learned that his brother Reginald had been suspended from the Nation of Islam for immoral behavior. The very blood of his blood who had introduced him to Islam had now departed from the path. Reginald had been a vital conversation partner when Malcolm had been exploring his new faith, but now, Malcolm lamented, "Reginald began to speak ill of Elijah Muhammad."[46] Malcolm's nascent and fragile faith was being tested. His brother had been cast out from precisely where Malcolm was fervently trying to get in. Malcolm wrote and prayed in his turmoil seeking an answer. Then one day he had a vision:

> It was the next night, as I lay on my bed, I suddenly, with a start, became aware of a man sitting beside me in my chair. He had on a dark suit. I remember. I could see him as plainly as I see anyone I look at. He wasn't black, and he wasn't white. He was light-brown-skinned, an Asiatic cast of countenance, and he had oily black hair. I looked right into his face. I didn't get frightened. I knew I wasn't dreaming. I couldn't move, I didn't speak, and he didn't. I couldn't place him racially—other than that I knew was a non-European. I had no idea whatsoever who he was. He was just there. Then, suddenly as he had come, he was gone.[47]

It is a wordless, ephemeral encounter, but one of immense import to Malcolm. During it Malcolm was frozen. He is only able to gaze into the stranger's face, but that was enough to convey what needed to be conveyed: Reginald was in the wrong; keep true to your faith. Soon thereafter, Elijah Muhammad wrote plainly in response to Malcolm that the truth is the truth without qualification or condition. Malcolm's faith, for a time, was restored.

This remarkable vision, however, warrants further consideration. Malcolm would later state, "I would later come to believe that my prevision was of Master W. D. Fard, the Messiah, the one whom Elijah Muhammad said had appointed him."[48] Writing many years later, Malcolm does not dismiss his vision as a delusion. There is something real about it all. The words he uses in retrospect say as much: "I remember . . . I knew I wasn't dreaming."[49] He does not understand his prevision as a remnant lingering from his days with the Nation of Islam. He never renounces it. Rather, the vision represents a critical and inseparable part of his narrative of faith, and this is something to keep in mind.[50] Although Malcolm would eventually break with the Nation for "real" or "true" Islam, he deferentially recognized a continuity linking the Islam of the Nation to the Islam to which he would later turn. As DeCaro notes, Malcolm would "blur the distinction between the Nation and Sunni Islam" even as he looked back from his post-Hajj period.[51] Malcolm attributes his discovery of Islam, unqualified in any way, to his time in prison, rather than the months leading up to his pilgrimage. Malcolm would state, "I believe, today, that it was written, it was meant, for Reginald to be used for one purpose only: as a bait, as a minnow to reach into that ocean of blackness where I was, to save me. I cannot understand it any other way."[52] Just as the tradition includes the struggles of the Khawārij, Murji'a, Mu'tazila, and so many others, so too does it also include the struggles of the Nation and its like.

The continuity of Malcolm's faith also finds expression in his life after prison. After a time, Malcolm was paroled and released. He joined the members of his family who were then living in Detroit, and with them he would come to meet Elijah Muhammad face-to-face at long last. Traveling to Chicago, Malcolm sat in the audience listening to his teacher speak. Until this moment, their only contact was through their extensive correspondence by letters. It is in the midst of this event that Elijah Muhammad called out to Malcolm to rise and be recognized. It is then that the Honorable Elijah Muhammad uttered, "I believe that he [Brother Malcolm] is going to remain faithful."[53] Malcolm did not dismiss these words when he recounted this part of his autobiography many years later. Instead, Malcolm immediately followed Mr. Muhammad's words with a reflection: "And Allah blessed me to remain true, firm and strong in my faith in Islam, despite many severe trials to my faith."[54] (Indeed, the greatest trial, as we will see, would be Mr. Muhammad himself.) The shape of Malcolm's faith may have changed several times over during the course of his life, but his faith itself abides through it all.

Malcolm was a voice for his people calling them away from their former lives to the path of the Nation. From street corner to street corner and temple to temple, he progressed. In a short time he found himself within the fold of Elijah Muhammad's own home and family. Malcolm X had arrived, and with that came the manipulative scrutiny of the press and the facile criticisms of so many "Bishop Chickenwings."

In the face of these blustering winds, a great fire was kindled. Minister Malcolm now spoke relentlessly, eloquently, and angrily. "I'd have *scathing* in my voice; I *felt* it."[55] Facing the storm, Malcolm became the Nation's "most respected apologist or theologian."[56] He argued tirelessly that the Islam of the Nation was the Islam of the global community. He worked ceaselessly to connect his brothers and sisters in the wilderness with those who lived in Asia and Africa. Malcolm's voice and visage reached far and wide. The Honorable Elijah Muhammad stood behind him at each step, but he warned Malcolm, "You will grow to be hated when you become well known. Because usually people get jealous of public figures," to which Malcolm would write, "Nothing that Mr. Muhammad ever said to me was more prophetic."[57] As Malcolm's star was ascending, a new crisis was cresting over the horizon.

Through those bright and bold years with the Nation, Elijah Muhammad had been Malcolm's Messenger, teacher, supporter, confident, and spiritual father. An Islam without the Honorable Elijah Muhammad was unimaginable to Malcolm. The Honorable Elijah Muhammad had delivered him out of the depths. What could be greater? An answer was not expected, but one came nonetheless in a powerful and unanticipated epiphany.

> A chance event brought crashing home to me that there was something—one thing—greater than my reverence for Mr. Muhammad. It was the awesomeness of my reason to revere him. I was the invited speaker at the Harvard Law School Forum. I happened to glance through a window. Abruptly, I realized that I was looking in the direction of the apartment house that was my old burglary gang's hideout. It rocked me like a tidal wave. Scenes from my once depraved life lashed through my mind. *Living* like an animal; *thinking* like an animal! Awareness came surging up in me—how deeply the religion of Islam had reached down into the mud to lift me up, to save me from being what I inevitably would have been: a dead criminal in a grave, or, if still alive, a flint-hard, bitter, thirty-seven-year-old convict in some penitentiary, or insane asylum. Or, at best, I would have been an old, fading Detroit Red, hustling, stealing enough for food and narcotics, and myself being stalked as prey by cruelly ambitious young hustlers such as Detroit Red had been. But Allah had blessed me to learn about the religion of Islam, which had enabled me to lift myself up from the muck and the mire of this rotting world.[58]

Malcolm realized that it was Islam that had truly lifted him up. It was Islam to which Malcolm ultimately owed his salvation. “Standing there by that Harvard window, I silently vowed to Allah that I never would forget that any wings I wore had been put on by the religion of Islam.”[59] This moment of recognition was a necessary and decreed precondition for the next challenge that Malcolm would face. The challenge did not emerge from the harsh critics from without but issued from within, from the very center itself. The trangressions of the Honorable Elijah Muhammad had come to Malcolm's attention, and they could no longer be ignored. “Around 1963, if anyone had noticed, I spoke less and less of religion. I taught social doctrine to Muslims, and current events, and politics. I stayed wholly off the subject of morality. And the reason for this was that my faith had been shaken in a way that I can never fully describe. For I discovered Muslims had been betrayed by Elijah Muhammad himself.”[60] Former secretaries had brought paternity suits against the Honorable Elijah Muhammad. In Malcolm's eyes, immorality towered over Mr. Muhammad. Defying the communal injunction against speaking with outcast members of the Nation, Malcolm investigated. What he learned from these women was more than acts of immorality. He discovered that he himself had been betrayed. “I learned from these former secretaries of Mr. Muhammad that while he was praising me to my face, he was tearing me apart behind my back. That deeply hurt me.”[61] The effect was stunning. “The thing to me worse than death was the betrayal. I could conceive death. I couldn't conceive betrayal.”[62]

Malcolm's outspokenness in the aftermath of President Kennedy's assassination became the pretense for the Nation of Islam's break with him. Mr. Muhammad took away Malcolm's words; Malcolm was silenced. “An announcement was made throughout the Nation of Islam that I would be reinstated within ninety days, '*if he submits.*' This made me suspicious—for the first time. I had completely submitted. But, deliberately, Muslims were being given the impression that I had rebelled.”[63] He who had once been Satan to be raised from the darkness was now being accused by his own salvific community of being a rebellious Satan once again. Falsely accused, Malcolm was being cast down and thrown out. “I knew when I was being set up.”[64] The betrayal did not end there. Former associates sowed discord themselves, saying, “If you knew what the Minister [Malcolm] did, you'd go out and kill him yourself."[65] Malcolm was being subjected to a reversal of the most dramatic sort. Death had come to Malcolm's door.

In one sense, Malcolm *was* dying. The world he knew was falling to ruin. The reversal was apocalyptic. "I felt as though something in nature had failed, like the sun, or the stars. It was that incredible a phenomenon to me—something too stupendous to conceive."[66] The death and dying that followed, however, was not physical (not yet) but mental in nature. This death harkens back to the mental death wrought upon African Americans by decades and centuries of slavery and oppression. Malcolm now faced a second mental extinguishment. "I was numb. . . . My head felt like it was bleeding inside. I felt like my brain was damaged."[67] Malcolm was out of the Nation. He was anathema. He was dead to them, never to return.

Malcolm may have been out of the Nation, but not out of Islam. The call of justice and righteousness that had first ignited his faith still blazed brightly within him. It blazed even more stunningly now. It was to this white-hot fire—the forge within—that Malcolm would now turn to reshape his faith. Another radical transformation was underway.

FAITH IN THE FORGE

> My whole life had been a chronology of—*changes*.
> —Malcolm X, *The Autobiography of Malcolm X*[68]

What followed next for Malcolm was a period of uncertainty and searching. His unquestioned belief in the Honorable Elijah Muhammad—the very vessel of his unquestioned belief—had shattered at last. "I had blind faith in him. . . . My faith in Elijah Muhammad was more blind and more uncompromising than any faith that any man has ever had for another man."[69] A return to that faith was impossible. The damage was irreparable. Malcolm had to find his own footing. The criterion of his faith could no longer rest upon the Nation or the ministry of the Honorable Elijah Muhammad. Instead, Malcolm realized, he had to begin with himself. "I do not pretend to be a divine man, but I do believe in divine guidance, divine power, and in the fulfillment of divine prophecy. I am not educated, nor am I an expert in any particular field—but I am sincere, and my sincerity is my credentials."[70] From this starting point, Malcolm began to search for the new shape of his faith, just as al-Ghazālī's earlier words made clear:

> There is no hope of returning to unquestioned belief after leaving it because a condition of the uncritical follower is that he does not realize that he is being uncritical. For once he realizes that, then the glass of his unquestioned belief is shattered. The fragments cannot be mended; they cannot be pieced back together and remade. It must be melted in the fire and made anew into another form altogether.[71]

It was now time for Malcolm to look past Elijah Muhammad, his former mentor, and interpret for himself the religion of God that had always blazed beneath. Malcolm knew what had to be done: stoke the fires and make one's faith anew—make oneself anew—in another form altogether.

Although Malcolm might not have realized it when it was happening, the many encounters of his life had been leading him up to this point. Throughout his career as a minister, Muslims from outside of the Nation had confronted him and encouraged him to learn of "true Islam," to which Malcolm had instinctively recoiled. "Automatically, as a follower of Elijah Muhammad, I had bridled whenever this was said. But in the privacy of my own thoughts after several of these experiences, I did question myself: if one was sincere in professing a religion, why should he balk at broadening his knowledge of that religion?"[72] Elijah Muhammad's own son, Wallace Muhammad (later to be known as Imam Warith Deen Muhammad and the future herald of an entire community of transformation), had come to a similar point of critical realization and encouraged Malcolm to do likewise. He told Malcolm, "Yes, certainly, a Muslim should seek to learn all that he could about Islam."[73] To this end, Malcolm knew he had to venture to the beating heart of the religion itself. As Malcolm describes, "There was one further major preparation that I knew I needed. I'd had it in my mind for a long time—as a servant of Allah."[74] Turning to his half-sister Ella Collins, who preceded him in his journey of faith, he told her, "I want to make the pilgrimage to Mecca."[75] Malcolm's eyes were set upon the Kaʿba, the house of God where the prophets and faithful had walked, struggled, and prayed since time immemorial. He sought to experience the communion of Islam in the vicinity of the holy. With great love and sacrifice, Ella

Collins took the money she had saved for her own pilgrimage of faith and gave it to Malcolm so that he could undertake his.

On this journey, Malcolm would rise again, brought back to life and guided by the persistence and tenacity of his faith. He departed knowing full well the newness of life that awaited him. When he left, he left not as Malcolm X but as Malik el-Shabazz, a new name for the promise of a renewed faith.[76] The transformation, however, was not easy. The loss of the Honorable Elijah Muhammad as his interpreter of faith was just the first step. Only during those deeply self-reflective moments of the Ḥajj pilgrimage did Malcolm fully come to terms with the fault of his former faith, the shattered shards of his unquestioned belief.

> In Mecca, too, I had played back for myself the twelve years I had spent with Elijah Muhammad as if it were a motion picture. I guess it would be impossible for anyone ever to realize fully how complete was my belief in Elijah Muhammad. I believed in him not only as a leader in the ordinary *human* sense, but also I believed in him as a *divine* leader. I believed he had no human weaknesses or faults, and that, therefore, he could make no mistakes and that he could do no wrong. There on a Holy World hilltop, I realized how very dangerous it is for people to hold any human being in such esteem, especially to consider anyone some sort of "divinely guided" and "protected" person.[77]

The pilgrimage, however, was not only an opportunity for critical self-reflection. Malcolm had to experience all over again that weakest of states, which he had first crawled out of in prison when he "was just deaf, dumb, and blind."[78] Before, in prison, he had had to submit to the order and rule of the Honorable Elijah Muhammad in order to be saved. Now Malcolm had to learn what it was to submit—truly to submit—to God. The Holy World, in all its foreign sanctity, would see to this.

On the Ḥajj, Malcolm was a stranger in the land. In the presence of the Kaʿba—in "my ignorant, crippled condition in the Holy Land"—Malcolm experienced what it was to be voiceless, vulnerable, and at the mercy of the Almighty.[79] His words, which he had carefully cultivated throughout the course of his life and which had carried him so far, lost all their power. Arabic was the language of first order here, not English. "Never before in my life had I felt so deaf and dumb as during the times when no interpreter was with me to tell me what was being said around me, or about me, or even to me."[80] Malcolm was indeed deaf, dumb, and blind all over again. It was needed. Only when all else was muted was he able to look within and come to grips with his faith. "There is no greater serenity of mind . . . than when one can shut the hectic noise and pace of the materialistic outside world, and seek inner peace within oneself."[81] The profundity of isolation allowed Malcolm to examine his faith, his relationship with God, with sincerity and clarity. With no one else to guide him, Malcolm had to ask himself, how would he respond to his Lord?

The gradual and painstaking process of remaking his faith granted Malcolm new perspective. "My thinking had been opened up wide in Mecca."[82] By turning inward and struggling therein, Malcolm gained new eyes, new ears, and a renewed heart with which to behold and understand the world. His understanding broadened. "Everything about the pilgrimage atmosphere accented the Oneness of Man under One God."[83] Old divisions and discernments were reevaluated. The struggle for justice had to be reimagined and reenvisioned. The cause of the black American community remained a priority, but now Malcolm insisted that it "must also be the concern and moral responsibility of the entire Muslim World—if you hope to make the principles of the Quran a *Living Reality*."[84] A different Malcolm was stepping out of the fire. "I'm speaking now from what I think, from what I have seen, from what I have analyzed, and the conclusions that I have reached."[85] He was no longer just Malcolm X, but el-Hajj Malik el-Shabazz, a servant of God reborn. "A part of me, I left behind in the Holy City of Mecca. And, in turn, I took away with me—forever—a part of Mecca."[86]

Mecca, however, was not the only place in which Malcolm sojourned in search of faith. His crucible was much wider; God's work was more intricate and far reaching. Like al-Ghazālī before him, Malcolm left behind family and friends for a time to seek renewal in the far-off reaches of the world. In addition to Mecca, Medina, and Jedda, Malcolm's journey of faith took him to Frankfurt, Cairo, and Beirut. It took him to Lagos, Accra, Monrovia, Dakar, Casablanca, and Algiers. In all of these places and many others—in "the Holy World" and in Africa—did Malcolm labor in the forge of faith.[87] At each station, he developed further his new vision of what was to come and what must be done. The Nation for him was no more, but he no longer needed it. His community of faith had grown incredibly greater. "I'm for truth, no matter who tells it. I'm for justice, no matter who it is for or against. I'm a human being first and foremost, and as such I'm for whoever and whatever benefits humanity *as a whole*."[88]

Faith and righteousness had always gone hand in hand for Malcolm, but his reforged faith demanded a reconfiguration of how the struggle for righteousness ought to unfold. Law and the exertion of force could not lead the way.

> Mankind's history has proved from one era to another that the true criterion of leadership is spiritual. Men are attracted by spirit. By power, men are *forced*. Love is engendered by spirit. By power, anxieties are created. I am in agreement one hundred per cent with those racists who say that no government laws ever can *force* brotherhood. The only true world solution today is governments guided by true religion—of the spirit.[89]

Malcolm saw immense potential in the power of rightly oriented faith. It is a striking contrast with the thinking of his earlier days. Islam now bequeathed to Malcolm a new framework and trajectory. "I have so much faith in *Allah*, and in *right*, and in my people, that I believed I can come back and start from scratch if it is necessary and as long as I mean right *Allah* will bless me with success and our people will help me in this fight."[90]

We should not mistake Malcolm's understanding of Islam with a facile adoption of some pristine, timeless religion. The faith that Malcolm forged was not simply a distillation of a Meccan or Medinan Islam. His Islam was thoroughly American in context and orientation, but one open to the wider world at hand. He was deeply conscious of the kindred struggles fought by many others outside of the American North and South. The justice he sought was more than the deprecating domesticity of civil rights. He argued for the affirmation of human rights on the international stage. He sought fraternity and solidarity across the Atlantic in the promise of Pan-Africanism and the Muslim International.[91] Malcolm's response to God—his theology—was to live and struggle alongside the oppressed, his own community foremost of all (but not exclusively so), even at the cost of his own fragile and fallible life. His response to revelation was to proceed with faith and humility pulsing at his core and his utter mortality hanging ever before his eyes. This was the Malcolm who emerged out of the forge. "And if I can die having brought any light, having exposed any meaningful truth that will help destroy the racist cancer that is malignant in the body of America—then, all of the credit is due to Allah. Only the mistakes have been mine."[92] This is the Malcolm of our tradition. It is a life given for those of us who live now. It was not given lightly, but given to bring us light.

The faith of Malcolm X, el-Hajj Malik el-Shabazz, reveals to us many things. It discloses to us that in our times faith can and does take many forms. It teaches us that faith can careen to the precipice and still find its center in the end. It impresses upon us that even Satan can be redeemed when all others think him lost. It demonstrates to us that faith ought to be wedded to righteousness and in that bond grow stronger in the sight of God. It shows us that *our* faith can be shaped in ways as bold and unanticipated as the faith of Malcolm.

In Malcolm and *through* him we can imagine a world of possibilities for our here and now. We can begin to imagine theologies that stand where revelation strikes. We can begin to articulate theologies that speak to the ills that make our hearts constrict and our bodies crumble and fold. What theologies might emerge when we see in Malcolm a paradigm of faith for the living present? What theologies might we develop when we connect him to our storied tradition? The nature of faith is turbulent and surprising. When God speaks, we have come to see how men like Malcolm, al-Ghazālī, and others have responded. It is time at last to turn to ourselves and imagine how we shall begin to answer the call of revelation. It is time to consider *our* theology. Yet, as I have said before, it is not an occasion to which we rise, but rather one to which we must fall.

NOTES

1. Quoted in Moosa, *Ghazālī and the Poetics of Imagination*, 257.
2. Al-Ghazālī, *Deliverance from Error*, 55; al-Ghazālī, *Path to Sufism*, 19; al-Ghazālī, "*Al-Munqidh min al-ḍalāl*," 538. The English translation preserves the Arabic word *fiṭra* where I have used "natural disposition." The hadith is mentioned in al-Bukhārī, *Ṣaḥīh*, 6:114, *kitāb al-tafsīr*.
3. Al-Ghazālī, "*Al-Munqidh min al-ḍalāl*," 538ff. *Taqlīd* is a difficult word to translate given the contentious differences in understanding surrounding it. The term prominently figures in both the legal and theological discourses. In

the legal context, *taqlīd* is best understood as "legal conformism" or stare decisis (literally "stand by things decided"), which is the legal doctrine of precedent. See Ahmed El Shamsy, "Rethinking *Taqlīd* in the Early Shāfiʿī School," *Journal of the American Oriental Society* 128, no. 1 (2008): 1; Sherman Jackson, "*Taqlīd*, Legal Scaffolding and the Scope of Legal Injunctions in Post-Formative Theory: *Muṭlaq* and *ʿĀmm* in the Jurisprudence of Shihāb al-Dīn al-Qarāfī," *Islamic Law and Society* 3, no. 2 (1996): 165. *Taqlīd* carries an entirely different register, however, for matters of theology. As ʿAbdullāh b. Ḥamīd ʿAlī explains, "*Taqlīd* in *fiqh* is compulsory for all who do not fulfill the conditions of absolute *ijtihād* (scholarly endeavors; competence to infer expert legal rulings). The view of most scholars is that *taqlīd* is impermissible in the area of creed (*ʿaqīda*), and specifically in those matters that relate to the character of God. In this regard we find the statement attributed to ʿAbd Allāh ibn Masʿūd, 'Let no one subject his religion to the blind imitation of a person. If he believes, he will believe. And if he disbelieves, he will [also] disbelieve.'" ʿAbd al-Raḥmān Ibn al-Jawzī, *The Attributes of God (Dafʿ Shuhab al-Tashbīh bi-Akaff al-Tanzīh)*, trans. ʿAbdullāh b. Ḥamīd ʿAlī (Bristol: Amal Press, 2006), 49, n. 6. For the present discussion, translators of al-Ghazālī's *Al-Munqidh* have proposed "servile conformism," "naive and derivative belief," or "naive and second-hand belief," all of which I find lacking. I translate *taqlīd* instead as "unquestioned belief" or "unquestioning adherence to socially transmitted beliefs" and the related *muqallid* (literally "one who does *taqlīd*") as "uncritical follower" in accordance with the context and argument of al-Ghazālī's text. Al-Ghazālī, *Path to Sufism*, 18, 25; Abū Ḥāmid al-Ghazālī, *The Faith and Practice of al-Ghazālī*, trans. W. Montgomery Watt (Chicago: Kazi Publications, 1982), 19, 27.

4. Al-Ghazālī, "*Al-Munqidh min al-ḍalāl*," 539.

5. Al-Ghazālī, "*Al-Munqidh min al-ḍalāl*," 539.

6. Al-Ghazālī, *Faith and Practice*, 57; al-Ghazālī, "*Al-Munqidh min al-ḍalāl*," 553.

7. Garden, *First Islamic Reviver*, 56–59; Griffel, *Al-Ghazālī's Philosophical Theology*, 40–49. Garden and Griffel have provided more exacting accounts of al-Ghazālī's life. Garden develops a compelling synthesis of political and personal concerns for understanding al-Ghazālī's departure. Griffel's analysis is more concerned with analyzing the consistencies and differences in al-Ghazālī's thought that appear after his departure from Baghdad than on the motives for the sudden change in the course of his life.

8. Al-Ghazālī, "*Al-Munqidh min al-ḍalāl*," 540.

9. This statement is found in *Fiqh al-Akbar I*, which presents the opinions of Abū Ḥanīfa. The line is quoted in A. J. Wensinck, *The Muslim Creed: Its*

Genesis and Historical Development (New Delhi: Oriental Books Reprint Corporation, 1979), 104.

10. As first mentioned in chapter 4, I am translating the Arabic word *īmān* as faith. The term is central to the message of revelation. The Qur'an, for example, states, *The Messenger had faith in what was revealed to him from His Lord, and [so have] the faithful. All of them have faith in God, His angels, His scriptures, and His messengers* (Q. 2:285). Prophetic reports undertake the topic of *īmān* as well. Recall the hadith of Gabriel in which it is related, "Tell me about *īmān*. . . . It is that you have faith in God, His angels, His scriptures, His messengers, and the Last Day and that you have faith in foreordainment, its good and its evil." In fact, the entire collection of forty-two hadiths compiled by al-Nawawī is thematically oriented around the question of faith. Al-Nawawī, *Forty Hadith*, 31.

11. Al-Ṭabarī, *The History of al-Ṭabarī*, vol. 17, *The First Civil War*, trans. G. R. Hawting (Albany: State University of New York Press, 1996), 218.

12. In Kufa in 66/685, al-Mukhtār b. Abī ʿUbayd (d. 67/687) led a rebellion with apocalyptic overtones. At the turn of the eighth century, the Iraqi noble Ibn al-Ashʿath led a military revolt for grievances against the Umayyad governor of Iraq, al-Ḥajjāj. In the frontier regions of Khurasan and Transoxiana in 116/734, al-Ḥārith b. Surayj (d. 746) led yet another uprising against the Umayyads. In the meantime, the Khawārij menace continued to spread.

13. A justification of the doctrine of *irjāʾ* is provided in Abū Muqātil Ḥafṣ b. Salam al-Samarqandī's (d. 208/823) *Kitāb al-ʿĀlim waʾl-mutaʿallim*, which presents itself as an exchange between a teacher and his student. The teacher in question is none other than Abū Ḥanīfa, who attributes the origin of *irjāʾ* with the angels. For an explanation, he points to the Qur'anic episode in which the angels ask God why He would place the human being as a *khalīfa* over the earth when they *will cause corruption and shed blood* (Q. 2:30), to which God responds, *Truly I know what you do not know* (Q. 2:30), and proceeds to teach Adam all the names (*al-asmāʾ kullahā*). God then commands the angels to inform Him of the names, to which they reply, *May You be glorified! We have no knowledge except what You have taught us. Truly You are the All-Knowing, the All-Wise* (Q. 2:32). The angels' humble deference to the knowledge of God serves as the archetype for *irjāʾ*. Then, Abū Ḥanīfa poses, "He [God] did not allow His Messenger to speak to, oppose, or defame anyone without certainty of knowledge. So how can people oppose and decry one another?" Abū Ḥanīfa, *Kitāb al-ʿĀlim wa-l-mutaʿallim: riwāyat Abī Muqātil ʿan Abī Ḥanīfa rāḍiya Allāh ʿanhumā wa-yalīhi Risālat Abī Ḥanīfa ilā ʿUthmān al-Battī thumma al-Fiqh al-absaṭ riwāyat Abī Muṭīʿ ʿan Abī Ḥanīfa raḥimahum Allāh*, ed. Muḥammad Zāhid al-Kawtharī (Cairo: Maṭbaʿat al-Anwār, 1368/[1949]),

22–23. On the question of authorship, see Joseph Schacht, "An Early Murci'ite Treatise: The *Kitāb al-ʿĀlim wal-Mutaʿallim*," *Oriens* 17 (1964): 96–100.

14. One of the leading exponents of the Murjiʿa was the famed legal scholar Abū Ḥanīfa. In his theological composition *Al-Fiqh al-akbar I*, he clearly states, "We do not consider anyone to be an infidel on account of sin; nor do we deny his faith." Wensinck, *Muslim Creed*, 103–4. I have modified the translation.

15. Wilfred Madelung, *Religious Trends in Early Islamic Iran* (Albany: Bibliotheca Persica, 1988), 19.

16. For instance, the great hadith scholar al-Bukhārī (d. 256/870) criticized Abū Ḥanīfa and the Murjiʾa in the following century. Concerning their separation of faith and works, Gibrīl Ḥaddād reports that "Imām al-Bukhārī took issue with Abū Ḥanīfa over it and devoted pages of his *Ṣaḥīḥ* trying to refute him," which explains al-Bukhārī's statement, "I met more than one thousand men from the Ḥijāz, Iraq, Syria, Egypt, Khurāsān. . . . I never saw a single one of them differ on the following: 'Religion consists in words and deeds.'" Gibrīl Fouād Ḥaddād, *The Four Imams and Their Schools: Abū Ḥanīfa—Mālik—al-Shāfiʿī—Aḥmad* (London: Muslim Academic Trust, 2007), 42. Similarly, the legal scholar, historian, and Qur'an commentator al-Ṭabarī defined faith in a way counter to Murjiʾī concerns: "It is speech and works, it increases and decreases." Al-Ṭabarī defended his position as being corroborated by the reports of the companions of the Prophet. Dominique Sourdel, "Une Profession de Foi de l'Historien al-Ṭabarī," *Revue des Études Islamiques* 36, no. 2 (1968): 197.

17. Cited in William Montgomery Watt, trans., *Islamic Creeds: A Selection* (Edinburgh: Edinburgh University Press, 1994), 32. The creed from which the statement is taken appears in *Ṭabaqāt al-Ḥanābila* under the entry for Abū Jaʿfar Muḥammad b. ʿAwf, who reports that Aḥmad b. Ḥanbal dictated the creed to him. Abū al-Ḥusayn Muḥammad b. Abī Yaʿlā al-Baghdādī al-Ḥanbalī, *Ṭabaqāt al-ḥanābila*, ed. ʿAbd al-Raḥmān b. Sulaymān al-ʿUthaymīn, 3 vols. (Riyadh: al-Mamlaka al-ʿArabiyya al-Saʿūdiyya al-Amāna al-ʿĀmma li-l-Iḥtifāl bi-Murūr Miʾat ʿĀmʿalā Taʾsīs al-Mamlaka, 1999), 2:343.

18. See Martin, Woodward, and Atmaja, *Defenders of Reason*, 106–7. This group of scholars had engaged with the same theological challenges faced by Abū Ḥanīfa and the Murjiʾa, namely the zealotry of the Khawārij. Whereas the Khawārij claimed that sinners forfeited their faith and Muslim identity upon committing a grave sin, the Muʿtazila responded that there was an intermediate position, *manzila bayna manzilatayn* ("a position between the two positions"), in which the malefactor was neither a person of faith nor an outright infidel. This spared offenders expulsion from the community of faith yet still placed them in a separate class.

19. John Damascene names the followers of Islam Ishmaelites and spends considerable time refuting it. He writes, "There is also the superstition of the Ishmaelites which to this day prevails and keeps people in error, being a forerunner of the Antichrist. . . . A false prophet named Mohammed has appeared in their midst. This man, after having chanced upon the Old and New Testaments and likewise, it seems, having conversed with an Arian monk, devised his own heresy." John of Damascus, *Writings: The Fountain of Knowledge*, trans. Frederic H. Chase Jr. (Washington, DC: Catholic University of America Press, 1970), 153.

20. Dimitri Gutas, *Greek Thought, Arabic Culture: The Graeco-Arabic Translation Movement in Baghdad and Early ʿAbbāsid Society (2nd–4th/8th–10th Centuries)* (New York: Routledge, 1998). The recourse to reason was also influenced in part by the Arabic translation movement of classical Greek texts in which systems of Greek rational thought were expounded.

21. Ignaz Goldziher, *Introduction to Islamic Theology and Law*, trans. Andras Hamori and Ruth Hamori (Princeton, NJ: Princeton University Press, 1981), 88, 94. In general, the Muʿtazila were more inclined to question the authenticity of hadith.

22. Al-Ashʿarī was not the first to articulate such a system. Men like Ibn Kullāb (d. ca. 239/854), al-Ḥārith al-Muḥāsibī (d. 243/857), and Abū al-ʿAbbās al-Qalānisī (fl. early fouth/tenth century) had thought likewise, but al-Ashʿarī's efforts proved the most diffuse, enduring, and influential. See Gavin Picken, "Ibn Ḥanbal and al-Muḥāsibī: A Study of Early Conflicting Scholarly Methodologies," *Arabica* 55 (2008): 361.

23. Wensinck, *Muslim Creed*, 88–93; Abū al-Ḥasan al-Ashʿarī, *The Theology of al-Ashʿarī: The Arabic Texts of al-Ashʿarī's Kitāb al-Lumaʿ and Risālat Istiḥsān al-Khawḍ fī ʿIlm al-Kalām*, ed. and trans. Richard McCarthy (Beirut: Imprimerie Catholique, 1953), 231–32; George Makdisi, "Ashʿārī and the Ashʿarites in Islamic Religious History II," *Studia Islamica* 18 (1963): 19–39; W. Montgomery Watt, *Early Islam: Collected Articles* (Edinburgh: Edinburgh University Press, 1990), 90; Richard M. Frank, "Elements in the Development of the Teaching of al-Ash'ari," *Le Museon* 54 (1991): 101–90. After abandoning the Muʿtazila, al-Ashʿarī composed *Kitāb al-Ibāna*, in which his doctrinal tenets appeared on the surface of things to resonate with the views of many scripturalist-oriented scholars. This work signaled the direction he was moving in, but it did not fully disclose the rationalist means by which he understood those tenets. A point of disagreement among academic scholars of Islam is the place of the *Kitāb al-Ibāna* in Abū al-Ḥasan al-Ashʿarī's post-Muʿtazilī career. Ignaz Goldziher argues for its lateness reflecting a turn from *kalām*. George Makdisi is similarly inclined but proceeds to make a grander and more radical argument that the Ashʿarī enterprise was a failure on the whole because of its

two-faced nature. Watt understands the *Kitāb al-Ibāna* to be an early work. I am partial to the careful analysis of Richard Frank, who refutes Makdisi's rather Manichaean argument and situates the *Kitāb al-Ibāna* convincingly into al-Ash'arī's larger system of theology.

24. Al-Ash'arī would go on to compose other works in which his doctrinal tenets were argued and defended from a rationalist orientation in addition to a scriptural one. He developed and disseminated his ideas in Baghdad, and then his students carried them beyond, particularly into Khurasan, where Ash'arism eventually took root and flourished. Important scholars of that region, like al-Bāqillānī (d. 403/1013), Imām al-Ḥaramayn al-Juwaynī (d. 478/1085), Abū Ḥāmid al-Ghazālī, and Fakhr al-Dīn al-Rāzī (d. 606/1209), went on to develop the Ash'arī system even further.

25. The word used for "confession of the tongue" is *iqrār bi'l-lisān* and "conviction in the heart" is *i'tiqād bi'l-qalb* or *taṣdīq*. Abū al-Mu'īn Maymūn b. Muḥammad al-Nasafī, *Baḥr al-kalām*, ed. Walī al-Dīn Muḥammad Ṣāliḥ al-Farfūr (Damascus: Maktabat Dār al-Farfūr, 2000), 65, 151; Abū al-Yusr Muḥammad al-Bazdawī, *Uṣūl al-dīn*, ed. Hans Peter Linss (Cairo: al-Maktabat al-Azhariyya li-l-Turāth, 2003), 148–49.

26. Al-Bazdawī, *Uṣūl al-dīn*, 156.

27. Wilferd Madelung, "The Spread of Māturīdism and the Turks," in *Actas do IV Congresso de Estudos Árabes e Islâmicos Coimbra-Lisboa* (Leiden: Brill, 1971) 111; al-Bazdawī, *Uṣūl al-dīn*, passim. The Māturīdīs were perceived as newcomers. The earliest Māturīdī theologians were largely unknown beyond Central Asia. They do not appear to be acknowledged outside of their own circles until the Ash'arī theologian Abū Bakr al-Fūrakī (d. 478/1085) first mentions them in his theological work *Kitāb al-Niẓāmī*, written in 465/1072, over a century after Abū Manṣūr al-Māturīdī's death in 333/944. The Māturīdīs for their part asserted their correctness above all others. For example, the Māturīdī theologian al-Bazdawī (d. 493/1099) refers to his school opinions as the position of the *Ahl al-sunna wa'l-jamā'a* or the Sunni community, implying that the opinions of the other groups that he names separately fall outside of the community. Among those he sets apart are al-Ash'arī, the Mu'tazila, and the *aṣḥāb al-ḥadīth* or doctrinal traditionalists.

28. W. Madelung, "Māturīdiyya," *Encyclopaedia of Islam*, 6:847; A. S. Tritton, *Muslim Theology* (Bristol: Luzac & Company, 1947), 174–76; Taftazani, *Commentary on the Creed of Islam*. The Ash'ārī scholar al-Subkī (d. 769/1368), by his lifetime, argues that the differences between the two schools were only thirteen in number, seven of which were semantic and six substantive, but even the latter were of minor consequence in his opinion. Similarly, the theologian al-Taftazānī (d. 793/1390) wrote a commentary on the Māturīdī *'aqīda* of Najm al-Dīn al-Nasafī (d. 537/1142) in which he weaves back and

forth between Māturīdī and Ashʿarī positions, effectively demonstrating their compatibility, if not complementarity.

29. Jackson, *On the Boundaries of Theological Tolerance*, xii.

30. Nguyen, *Sufi Master and Qur'an Scholar*, 36–42.

31. Hidayatullah, *Feminist Edges of the Qur'an*, 176–77; Nguyen, "Modern Scripturalism and Emergent Theological Trajectories," 64–68. As mentioned earlier, Hidayatullah has provided an insightful survey and theological analysis of several Muslim feminist exegetes writing in English. Using her work, I have argued in a separate article that the Muslim feminist exegetical discourse that has emerged in Western academe represents a significant theological development for both the ongoing Muslim tradition and the Euro-American academic study of the Qur'an. What I identified as one of the discourse's most important theological contributions was the need to reconceptualize the Qur'an. Hidayatullah points to the prospects of conceiving the Qur'an as a discourse instead of a text, which was first argued by Nasr Hamid Abu Zayd. Chapter 5 and the mentioned article represent my response to this compelling provocation.

32. Ali, *Sexual Ethics and Islam*, xix–xx. Ali is expanding on a critique initially raised by Leila Ahmed in her memoir *A Border Passage*. While recognizing the problems inherent to the historical scholarly traditions of "textual Islam," Ali acknowledges that "the Muslim intellectual and, especially, legal tradition provides significant ground for engagement on matters of ethics." The Muslim American feminist exegete of the Qur'an Amina Wadud has similarly critiqued how "women were nearly completely excluded from the foundational discourse that established the paradigmatic basis for what it means to be Muslim, they were often relegated to the role of subject without agency." Wadud, *Qur'an and Woman*, xi. It is my sincere hope that my continual refrain to the textual tradition throughout this book works toward facilitating a similar "ground for engagement" for matters of theology.

33. Arguably, more blood and ink have been spilled over the nature of the Qur'an, prophethood (*nubuwwa*), and religious leadership (*imāma*) than over the nuances of faith and its social implications.

34. The statement is found in *Fiqh al-Akbar I*, which presents the opinions of Abū Ḥanīfa. The text is quoted in Wensinck, *Muslim Creed*, 104.

35. James H. Cone, *Martin and Malcolm and America: A Dream or a Nightmare* (Maryknoll, NY: Orbis, 1991), 151.

36. Malcolm X and Haley, *Autobiography*, 324.

37. The studies of Malcolm X are many. I am not interested, however, in retreading or critiquing these various analyses. Not all of them are concerned with the religious dimensions of his life; even less are concerned with theology. Those that do include the monograph-length works of James Cone and Louis DeCaro Jr.: Cone, *Martin and Malcolm and America*; Louis A. DeCaro Jr., *On*

the Side of My People: A Religious Life of Malcolm X (New York: New York University Press, 1996); Louis A. DeCaro Jr., *Malcolm and the Cross: The Nation of Islam, Malcolm X, and Christianity* (New York: New York University Press, 1998).

38. Malcolm X and Haley, *Autobiography*, 155.
39. Malcolm X and Haley, *Autobiography*, 70.
40. For more on Satan in the Qur'an and the broader Islamic tradition, see Bodman's insightful analysis of the Qur'anic narratives of Iblīs and Satan as well as Awn's earlier work on Satan, which also includes the hadith literature. Whitney S. Bodman, *The Poetics of Iblīs: Narrative Theology in the Qur'an* (Cambridge, MA: Harvard University Press, 2011); Peter Awn, *Satan's Tragedy and Redemption: Iblīs in Sufi Pyschology* (Leiden: Brill, 1983), 18–56.
41. Malcolm X and Haley, *Autobiography*, 155.
42. Malcolm X and Haley, *Autobiography*, 157.
43. Malcolm X and Haley, *Autobiography*, 159.
44. Malcolm X and Haley, *Autobiography*, 163.
45. Malcolm X and Haley, *Autobiography*, 163–64.
46. Malcolm X and Haley, *Autobiography*, 187.
47. Malcolm X and Haley, *Autobiography*, 188.
48. Malcolm X and Haley, *Autobiography*, 190.
49. Malcolm X and Haley, *Autobiography*, 188.
50. What perhaps requires reevaluation is Malcolm's identification of who it is he believes he sees, rather than the vision itself.
51. DeCaro, *On the Side of My People*, 212.
52. Malcolm X and Haley, *Autobiography*, 190.
53. Malcolm X and Haley, *Autobiography*, 199.
54. Malcolm X and Haley, *Autobiography*, 199.
55. Malcolm X and Haley, *Autobiography*, 243.
56. Cone, *Martin and Malcolm and America*, 162–64.
57. Malcolm X and Haley, *Autobiography*, 268.
58. Malcolm X and Haley, *Autobiography*, 290–91.
59. Malcolm X and Haley, *Autobiography*, 291.
60. Malcolm X and Haley, *Autobiography*, 298.
61. Malcolm X and Haley, *Autobiography*, 303.
62. Malcolm X and Haley, *Autobiography*, 310.
63. Malcolm X and Haley, *Autobiography*, 307.
64. Malcolm X and Haley, *Autobiography*, 307.
65. Malcolm X and Haley, *Autobiography*, 307.
66. Malcolm X and Haley, *Autobiography*, 309.
67. Malcolm X and Haley, *Autobiography*, 306–7.
68. Malcolm X and Haley, *Autobiography*, 344.

69. Malcolm X, *February 1965*, 111, "There's a worldwide revolution going on," February 15, 1965, Audubon Ballroom, Harlem; Cone, *Martin and Malcolm and America*, 205.

70. Malcolm X, *Malcolm X Speaks: Selected Speeches and Statements*, ed. George Breitman (New York: Grove Press, 1965), 20; Cone, *Martin and Malcolm and America*, 192.

71. Al-Ghazālī, "*Al-Munqidh min al-ḍalāl*," 540.

72. Malcolm X and Haley, *Autobiography*, 323.

73. Malcolm X and Haley, *Autobiography*, 323.

74. Malcolm X and Haley, *Autobiography*, 321.

75. Malcolm X and Haley, *Autobiography*, 322.

76. Manning Marable, *Malcolm X: A Life of Reinvention* (New York: Viking, 2011), 307.

77. Malcolm X and Haley, *Autobiography*, 371–72.

78. Malcolm X and Haley, *Autobiography*, 70.

79. Malcolm X and Haley, *Autobiography*, 349.

80. Malcolm X and Haley, *Autobiography*, 349.

81. Marable, *Malcolm X*, 311.

82. Malcolm X and Haley, *Autobiography*, 372.

83. Malcolm X and Haley, *Autobiography*, 335.

84. DeCaro, *On the Side of My People*, 239.

85. DeCaro, *On the Side of My People*, 251.

86. Malcolm X and Haley, *Autobiography*, 353.

87. Sohail Daulatzai, *Black Star, Crescent Moon: The Muslim International and Black Freedom beyond America* (Minneapolis: University of Minnesota Press, 2012), 4–7; DeCaro, *On the Side of My People*, 222–23; Grewal, *Islam Is a Foreign Country*, 115–19. The travels of Malcolm are more extensive than detailed by the autobiographical account. He traveled to the "Holy World" and Africa before and after his Ḥajj pilgrimage of 1964. He visited these regions as early as 1959, when he was still a part of the Nation, and again after the Ḥajj in the second half of 1964.

88. Malcolm X and Haley, *Autobiography*, 372.

89. Malcolm X and Haley, *Autobiography*, 375.

90. DeCaro, *On the Side of My People*, 235.

91. Daulatzai, *Black Star, Crescent Moon*, 1–44; Grewal, *Islam Is a Foreign Country*, 80–82, 110–20.

92. Malcolm X and Haley, *Autobiography*, 388.

7

THEOLOGY IN PROSTRATION

PRAYER

> The *ṣalāt* engages people on every level of their existence.
> —William C. Chittick, *In Search of the Lost Heart*[1]

When the revelation of God descends, God engages the human being completely. As a consequence, the human response to God should not be imagined as solely a matter of conviction. It also entails practice or how one lives in the world in the presence of the Divine. An account of theology, then, is as much about praxis as it is about faith. As I have said earlier in this book, theology is as much about falling—falling in prostration—as it is about believing. To respond to revelation is to fall upon one's hands and knees seeking one's total effacement before God. It is to prostrate oneself in prayer. I believe that in the folds of prayer, a faithful and righteous theology of response can begin to unfold. I am ending this book, then, with an exploration of the practical dimensions of theology. What does it mean to fall in prayer? What is offered through prostration?

Prayer is more than a ritual practice. To follow the form of prayer is one thing, but to pray with the totality of one's being—to pray like the prophets—is something else entirely. Prayer is something to be lived in every moment of life because it simultaneously embodies a response to God and signals a commitment to righteous action in the world.

I admit that making the case is a challenge. The very act of prayer today strikes many as out of place or even inappropriate. What use is prayer in times like ours? How can we call people to prayer when those who call for justice are silenced or slain before our eyes? How can we stand in congregation to pray when so many of us are humiliated, violated, hurt, and laid low? How can we bow our bodies to God when so many of us are forced to surrender our bodies to others? How can we prostrate our heads when our face is all we have left to show the world that we deserve dignity? It seems unclear whether we should bow and bend in prayer at all. As tumultuous and terrible as the present era seems, every era of the human past has brimmed with crises. In fact, the time of the Prophet Muhammad was no exception.

From the outset of his prophetic mission, the Prophet Muhammad was met with resistance; the message that he brought, the word of God, was rejected. The tide of the world was turned against him. The Prophet's own people, the blood of his blood, scorned him nearly en masse. The faithful who came to his side were few at first, and the vitriol they received burned intensely. With each passing day, their peril grew. Small gains quickly evaporated in the face of renewed and redoubled hostilities. The Prophet's nascent and fragile community was subjected to privation, abuse, and violence unto death. Mecca was not yet a sanctuary restored to faithfulness in God. It was a minefield. For years the Prophet and the faithful endured these hardships. For years they struggled and staggered on by the grace of God. Nevertheless, the toll was great. Families were broken and lives were lost. This first decade of the Prophet's mission was a dismal time for him and his people. Who could imagine triumph in the face of all these tribulations?

Further losses were in store. After nine years of patient perseverance through suffering and persecution, the Prophet lost his closest companion, his confidant, and his most ardent source of solace. Khadīja, his wife of nearly a quarter century, departed from this world and passed from out of the Prophet's life. Khadīja, who had been the first to have faith, had now returned to her Lord. Then, shortly thereafter—far too soon—the Prophet lost the loving support and counsel of his uncle Abū Ṭālib. Although Abū Ṭālib had not believed in the faith of the Prophet during his lifetime, he had believed in the dignity and righteousness of his nephew such that he extended and expended all of his wealth, strength, and honor to shelter and protect as best he could that fledgling community of God. This was the Year of Sorrow, 619 CE, when the Prophet Muhammad suffered one poignant loss after the other.

The Prophet, bowed down in faith and humility, was brought low. It was at this moment in the depths of sorrow that God would raise him up. *Glorified is He who took His servant by night from the sacred place of prostration to the farthest place of prostration, the vicinities of which We have blessed so that We might show him Our signs* (Q. 17:1).[2] In the middle of the night, God took the Prophet out of Mecca to distant Jerusalem on the miraculous Night Journey. Then, from the remnants of the Temple in Jerusalem, the Prophet was delivered upward on the Heavenly Ascension, from one level of heaven to another until he arrived at its utmost reaches and encountered his Lord. *Truly did he see the greatest of the signs of his Lord* (Q. 53:18).[3] Many things were bequeathed to the Prophet upon those heights in the midst of that night, many things that only God and the Prophet will ever know. One matter is known, however, because it was meant for the Prophet's entire community of faith. The Prophet entered the heavens amid trouble, heartache, and loss and returned to his people with the rites of ritual prayer, *ṣalāh*.[4] When faced with the direst of times, God grants the human being the gift of prayer.

God did not bequeath to the Prophet the rites of prayer as a refuge from or a rejoinder to the trials of this world. Rather, prayer was given first and foremost as a means of responding to the Divine. It is part of the dialectic between God's revelation and human response. Prayer was given to humankind so that it might find the means to answer the unrelenting and uncompromising call of revelation. This is the purpose of prayer in the first order. Nevertheless, we should not mistake this primary orientation as some sort of blithe obliviousness to the world. Prayer is no retreat. Instead, it is a means of confrontation. When the human being responds to revelation with prayerfulness, her voice to the world follows because in prayer one is simultaneously turning to God in faith and against the world in righteousness. In this way are faith and righteousness intimately bound together in prayer. To prostrate is also to protest.

A LIFE OF PRAYER

> The hardest test I ever faced in my life was praying.
> —Malcolm X[5]

Prayer may have been given during the life of the Prophet Muhammad, but its efficacy and meaning only continued to grow with the many lives that followed after him. A particularly powerful experience of prayer shaped the life of one closer to our times. I return us once more to the life of el-Hajj Malik el-Shabazz, Malcolm X. While I have spent some time presenting a theological interpretation of his life of faith, my figuration of him was incomplete. I left out a key component of that life—prayer. In many respects, the changing state of Malcolm's faith is incomprehensible without it.

When Malcolm broke with the Nation of Islam in 1964, he sought to experience the pulsing heart of the religion by journeying to its sacred center. He journeyed to the Kaʿba, the house of God built by prophets and tended by the faithful. His sojourn there was undoubtedly important for the shaping of his faith, but just as important was the journey of the body that he undertook as he learned to humbly bow, bend, and fold in prayer along the way. As Malcolm poignantly testifies, "The hardest test I ever faced in my life was praying."[6] Consider for a moment all the challenges that Malcolm faced—the challenges to his cause, his words, his beliefs, and his life. Of everything that Malcolm suffered and experienced, he singled out prayer as the most difficult of all. He did not utter this confession, however, with respect to the rites of *ṣalāh* that he learned during his pilgrimage to Mecca, as some might suspect. His declaration concerned a time in his life that preceded the pilgrimage by many years. It preceded even his ministry with the Nation of Islam. These words that name prayer "the hardest test I ever faced" were spoken while he languished in prison, when Malcolm had descended to the lowest of lows. This was during a time when he called himself Satan, but wanted the mantle no more. Instead, Malcolm's mind was reeling from the possibility of change—of true transformation—but his body had yet to commit.

In full, Malcolm's confession reads, "The hardest test I ever faced in my life was praying. You understand. My comprehending, my believing the teachings of Mr. [Elijah] Muhammad had only required my mind's saying to me, 'That's right!' or 'I never thought of that.' But bending my knees to pray—that *act*—well, that took me a week."[7] Our condition with respect to faith differs little. We are quick to catch the fervor of ideas. We will speak them, share them, and declare them our heartfelt beliefs, but how slowly do our knees bend, if at all, when the time for action arrives. It is remarkable how atrophied and resistant bodies can become when one is called to do more than simply say, "I believe."

For Malcolm the path of faith lay upon the path of prayer. Faith, as Malcolm knew, requires more than merely mental assent. "I had to force myself to bend my knees."[8] An everyday act that a person performs without a second thought, the bending of the knee, becomes seemingly insurmountable once it is joined to the profoundness of prayer. Faith asks us to commit all that we are so that we might be transformed before our Lord.

Malcolm sought this transformation but knew that the change would not be easy. He had proclaimed himself beyond both faith and belief and claimed the name of Satan, the archetype of pride. As Malcolm explains in his own words,

> I had to force myself to bend my knees. And waves of shame and embarrassment would force me back up. For evil to bend its knees, admitting its guilt, to implore the forgiveness of God, is the hardest thing in the world. It's easy for me to see and to say that now. But then, when I was the personification of evil, I was going through it. Again, again, I would force myself back down into the praying-to-Allah posture.[9]

After a long and perilous struggle, Malcolm found the will to bring himself low. He had at last found that bowed and crouched "praying-to-Allah posture," which embodied that point of intersection deep within him where true transformation could transpire.

This was not the end of prayer, however; it was just the beginning. "When finally I was able to make myself stay down—I didn't know what to say to Allah."[10] Facing his Lord, Malcolm was at a loss for words, yet despair was not what followed. His bodily act of humility set him down upon the path of faith and by bending his knee had already begun to speak to God. His bent form was the first enunciation of his response. His words—those fiery and eloquent words—would come with time. Indeed, once Malcolm had set himself upon this new path, he raced forward. Malcolm describes the years that followed this profound moment as a period of incredible activity. “I never have been more busy in my life.”[11] He was busy reading. He was busy writing. Malcolm was busy discovering his words and through them a new way to live. By his own account, he was a man transformed. “I still marvel at how swiftly my previous life’s thinking pattern slid away from me, like snow off a roof.”[12] In the many years that followed his first true prayer, Malcolm was busy learning how to respond to God from that humble “praying-to-Allah posture.” In fact, in his autobiography he never mentions rising from that prison-born prayer because he never truly rose from that humble, bent position. His whole life afterward, with all of its turbulence, twists, and turns, was lived bowed before God. Through prayer and in prayer, Malcolm was shaping his theology.

PRAYER IN PROSTRATION

> *Have they not seen that whatsoever God has created casts its shadow right and left, prostrating to God while in utter humility? And to God prostrates whatever crawling creatures or angels are in the heavens or on the earth, and they are without arrogance.*
> —Qur’an 16:48–49

In prayer Malcolm was transformed, but the process of that transformation, as his own words reveal, took a lifetime to unfold. That first prayer performed in prison never came to an end but continued on. Indeed, the form of Malcolm’s prayerful position evolved with time. When he fought himself free from the Nation, he found himself in the city of Jedda, the threshold to Mecca, where the critical importance of prayer was brought home to him once more. He needed to learn prayer all over again. To kneel was not enough. He had to learn the rites of *ṣalāh*. This time, Malcolm would have to bring himself lower than he had been before. He needed to prostrate. He described the effort in detail:

> My [pilgrimage] guide moved us over into a corner. With gestures, he indicated that he would demonstrate to me the proper prayer ritual postures. Imagine, being a Muslim minister, a leader in Elijah Muhammad’s Nation of Islam, and not knowing the prayer ritual. I tried to do what he did. I knew I wasn’t doing it right. I could feel the

> other Muslims' eyes on me. Western ankles won't do what Muslim ankles have done for a lifetime. Asians squat when they sit, Westerners sit upright in chairs. When my guide was down in a posture, I tried everything I could to get down as he was, but there I was, sticking up. After about an hour, my guide left, indicating he would return later. I never even thought about sleeping. Watched by the Muslims, I kept practicing prayer posture. I refused to let myself think how ridiculous I must have looked to them. After a while, though, I learned a little trick that would let me get down closer to the floor. But after two or three days, my ankle was going to swell.[13]

Malcolm labored to attain and master a more perfect "praying-to-Allah posture." It did not come easily. It came with its share of suffering. Malcolm's life up until this point, as radically transformative as it had already been, had not prepared his body for this new position and perspective. Vulnerable and exposed, Malcolm worked through the night to bring himself even lower than he had ever been before.

Malcolm's pilgrimage guide returned with the approach of dawn. Together they departed to perform the predawn prayer. "I followed him into the mosque, just a step behind, watching. He did his prostration, his head to the ground. I did mine. '*Bi-smi-llahi-Rahmain-r-Rahim*—' ('In the name of Allah, the Beneficent, the Merciful—') All Muslim prayer began that way. After that, I may not have been mumbling the right thing, but I was mumbling."[14] It is at this moment, as daylight arrived, that Malcolm found his words. These words uttered to God at the deepest depth of prostration were not the most eloquent or articulate. They were not even the "right" ones by Malcolm's account. Those mumbled words were precious nonetheless because Malcolm had at last found the bottom of the crater, that place where he could offer all that he was to God. There in the midst of prostration—at the bottom of creation—Malcolm found his words.

Prostration is a posture that punctuates revelation. In more than a dozen verses of the Qur'an, the very mention of "prostration," as either *sajda* or *sujūd*, prompts the faithful to bow down in worshipful reverence and awe.[15] God but says the word and we fall prostrate. In the rhythm of prayer, prostration marks the climax of the ritual. This climax, however, does not stand at the zenith of the arc of prayer, but lies at its nadir, the lowest point. Prayer carries us there, to the lowest of lows, so that we might perceive the world for what it is and see ourselves as we truly are. It is then and there in the dust, face-to-face with the clay from which we were created, that we find the means to respond to the Creator.

Prayer comes to us as both an obligation and a gift. It is an obligation because it arrives to us through the force of revelation, irrupting in our world in its unrelenting and uncompromising way. God in His glory and might commands our attention and devotion. When the Almighty speaks, we can but tremble and obey. Through God's beauty and mercy, however, we are also invited. In this regard, prayer is a gift. It is not only an act of devotion demanded of us, but also a means of faithful engagement that God offers to us. A horizon of possibilities is opened up when we bow and prostrate. In prayer, we are turning simultaneously to respond to God as well as the world and ourselves. It is time, then, to traverse this horizon of possibilities and see with new eyes how our prayers and prostrations can transform us and the world in which we abide.

THE TIMING OF PRAYER

> In all our deeds, the proper value and respect for time determines success or failure.
> —Malcolm X[16]

Earlier in this theological venture, I delineated the measure of modern time. The various forces that make up the modern world have by either accident or intention altered our sense of time in a radical manner. Sacred time has given way to "empty time." The former has been surrendered so that humankind can measure, parcel, and commodify time for its own earthly ends. Then, with regard to revelation, I described how God reclaims time through the irruption of revelation into the world. However humans imagine time, whether as a resource to manage or as a measure to maximize, revelation wrests time from human grasp directing humanity to gaze instead upon its own mortality. Time belongs to God and no other. Humankind, nonetheless, has a proclivity for forgetfulness. At times, the human being is even willful in turning away, taking comfort instead in the transient offerings of this present life. Herein lies another critical function of prayer. Prayer seeks to turn the worshiper back to God by design. The habituation offered by the rites of prayer seeks to shake the faithful from their earthly reveries so that they might hear and listen again to revelation.

Imagine once more the Kaʿba, the house of God, in Mecca, but this time draw to mind how it stands today in Saudi Arabia. Think of the Kaʿba as it stands astride an expansive and polished plane of stone and marble. Imagine it in its stark black *kiswa*, woven in white silk dyed black and embroidered with intricate calligraphic designs and trim of pure silver and gold.[17] Under the noonday sun, this inner precinct shines in a dazzling white. Then, encircling this sanctum is the ornate multitiered colonnade that allows hundreds of thousands to circumambulate the Kaʿba in the relief of the shade. Imagine now the radiating concentric circles of the faithful who fill the pristine vicinities of the house of God in order to offer their prayers and supplications. Imagine them in their great multitude standing, bowing, and prostrating in unison as an ocean of faith moving as one. Then, as day turns to night, the hollow of the sanctum is made resplendent by a breathtaking array of lights. By the ingenuity of human electric artifice, the night is illumined like the day. Although the sun has long departed past the western horizon, the Kaʿba is made to shine more brilliantly and stunningly now than when under the heat of the high hanging sun.

Now step back and turn but a fraction to have your gaze drawn upward to immense towers floating far above, scraping the sky. There in the middle of this lofty cluster of glass, steel, marble, and concrete stands one building more than twice the height of all the rest. With the Kaʿba resting humbly in the shadows, an immense clock tower reaches high above, projecting from all four of its sides the vacuous face of empty, human time. Whithersoever you stand, the face of that ponderous clock glares down. The hands of the clock face circling endlessly above bear down heavily upon the mind so that none should lose sight of every minute and every hour that is wasted. The clock tower looms gracelessly above like the needle of a sundial, but the shadow it casts does not tell time as measured by celestial sun above, but instead projects the carefully apportioned hubris of man. The meaningless majesty of empty time leers triumphant atop this modern-day tower of Hāmān—a testament to mammon. *And Pharaoh said: O Hāmān! Build for me a tower so that I may reach the ropes—the ropes of the heavens* (Q. 40:36–37).[18]

It is when one stands between the Kaʿba and the *Abrāj al-Bayt*, or the "towers of the house" as the clock tower complex is called, that the temporal tension of the modern world is made most clear. The house of God and that towering timepiece of man each call us, seeking our devotion. Try as one might to turn solely to the Kaʿba, the presence of the clock tower looms ever behind, pulling our eyes wayward. The modern sense of time, which the clock tower exemplifies, is too thoroughly dyed into the fabric of everyday existence to be excised completely. Our recourse, rather, lies in the timing of prayer.

By divine design, the ritual prayer contravenes the rhythms and orders of time imagined by humankind. Before the orb of the sun breaks over the horizon, worshipers are asked to rise and pray. The predawn prayer begins before the morning light is strong enough to aid in rousing. Worshipers, rather, must wake of their own volition while darkness still abides. Prayer also interrupts the hours of daylight. The noon, afternoon, and sunset prayers arrive one after another to pull worshipers away from whatever undertaking with which they may be preoccupied. Prayer turns our attention back to God. As for the evening prayer, even though it may be performed a short time after daylight has faded, the Prophet Muhammad has encouraged the faithful to pray throughout the night, offering the obligatory evening prayer in the first third and supererogatory prayers in the latter parts. The rhythmic regularity of prayer is meant to habituate the human being to a life for God above all other things.

However deeply entranced the human being is by the edifice of manmade time, the spell is broken with every call to prayer. Whatever the hands of the clock might demand, *the Hand of God is over their hands* (Q. 48:10). When the call to prayer is given, the faithful and the faith-seeking turn out of obedience and devotion to the house of God, the divinely established direction of prayer. As bodies incline toward the Kaʿba, backs are turned upon that towering clock hovering behind. To perform the ritual prayer is to restructure and reorient time bit by bit. However human beings order and arrange the rhythm of their lives, when the faithful give themselves over to the timings of prayer they acknowledge through their devotional outpourings that God's time is greater.

THE FORM OF PRAYER

> Yet we cannot ignore the important consideration that the posture of the body is a real factor in determining the attitude of the mind.
> —Muhammad Iqbal, *The Reconstruction of Religious Thought in Islam*[19]

With head bowed and hands unfolded to heaven, the faithful whisper their supplications with the subtlest movement of lips and the softest words of the heart. This is *duʿāʾ*, the open supplication, one of the barest forms of prayer. What is important is that even this simple kind of prayer has a *form*. When we beseech God, we have been taught to assume a posture and make a gesture that shifts both our bodies and our minds into an appropriate disposition. Even when you cannot change your environment or circumstances—even when you cannot silence the din around you—you can, at the very least, transform your mindset by undertaking the simplest and slightest of gestures: bow your head and upturn your hands. These small acts can deliver the seeking soul into a different space altogether. The world recedes, leaving the supplicant alone before the Creator. By assuming a form, we open ourselves up to hear and be heard.

Consider now how dramatic the transformation is when the worshiper performs the daily ritual prayer that entails one's standing, bowing, kneeling, and prostrating in a pattern and cycle connected to the time of day. As the faithful move their bodies in accordance with the recitation of prescribed words, time and space gradually melt away. The present moment swells to the fore. Worshipers are transported in prayer to the very threshold of the divine audience. In this place of intricate folds of body and soul, revelation and supplication meet. Here in the throes of prayer the faithful learn what it means to be *with* God. Here we see that all things are made possible if we dare to believe.

Imagine, then, what it means to stand before God. Imagine what it means that for each and every prayer we begin by rising to our feet rather than falling to our knees. The standing reminds us that one day we will all be raised up from our graves to gather and stand in trembling throngs before our Lord. It is a reminder that we will each have to stand on our own before God so that we may be judged for all that we have done and all that we have failed to do. The standing is also an expression of our devotion, our desire to rise to the occasion, namely to stand at the ready as servants of the Almighty. Whether we stand with a congregation or alone, we are standing on our own—of our own volition—filled with faith or fervently seeking it. Indeed, we stand to remember that we stand for God foremost of all.

The standing is also a humbling reminder. We are commanded to stand so that we never forget that there lies within us an inclination to arrogance. As faithful as we may become, our lot is never far removed from that of Satan, who so easily succumbed to pride. *And they prostrated except Iblīs; he refused and waxed proud* (Q. 2:34). *He said [to God], "I am better than him [Adam]. You created me from fire, while You created him from clay"* (Q. 7:12).[20] In dangerously similar fashion, we imagine ourselves towering over the rest of creation. Is a confidence in human superiority not implicated by our self-designation as *homo sapiens*, "wise" human beings? The name sets us standing above *homo erectus*, ignoring that God created us to be worshipful servants endowed with pliant bodies so that we might fold over in devotion. The mantle of stewardship of the earth—granted by God to humankind—should not be seen as a right that is deserved, but rather as a responsibility for which God will hold humankind accountable.[21] To stand in prayer is to remember our inclination to haughtiness.

The standing of prayer, however, only signals the beginning. Whatever pride we might fear to lurk within is displaced when the words of the Qur'an are recited. Whether what is recited is the briefest of verses or the longest of chapters, the fullness of God's word drowns out whatever pride might be entertained within. Then, with the weight of revelation bearing down upon reciting tongues, we are brought downward to bow in deference to God. In this position with backs bent, the world no longer stretches out endlessly before our sight. The illusion of human mastery over the earth is dispelled. Instead we are forced to gaze with humility upon that meager patch of earth that we occupy. This is our place in the world, small and fleeting, which God has granted to us for only a short time.

After reaching this point of recognition, we rise to stand again, but with our state of being transformed. We rise not as supposed masters of the world, but as servants of God. Our purpose in the world is not to stand for ourselves but to stand for others as God has called us to do. This second standing, however, lasts for the briefest of moments, unlike the first. It serves to dramatize the next performance, the prostration—

the primordial posture where our humanity finds fulfillment. We rise to our fullest height so that we may fall to our lowest depths.

Here in this basest of positions, prostration, we find our effacement. Our face is erased figuratively as it is pressed to the earth. Our sense of self is given over to God entirely and willingly. We submit in the fullest sense of the word. To prostrate once, however, is not enough. In the cycle of ritual prayer we prostrate twice so that we might behold that both our creation and our death lie with God Almighty. We fall in prostration in the first instance so that we may come face-to-face with the substance of our being. As Chittick describes, "The prostration, then, marks the point where the servant returns to that which belongs to himself, which is clay. . . . It is the servant's recognition and experience of his own nothingness. It is his annihilation (*fanāʾ*) in the light of God."[22] There at the bottom of prostration is the base substance of our beginning. Were it not for the breath of God— . . . *and I breathed into him from My spirit* (Q. 38:72)—we would be nothing more than muddied dust, a languid lump of flesh.[23] Lying prostrate and facing the nature of our creation do we discover the ground—that low, earthly ground—from which we can respond to God. We are only able to respond to Him because He has placed a measure of His spirit, a mere breath's worth, within us. The divine breath that speaks *Be!* and brings us into being, giving life to clay, is the same divine breath that speaks eternally in the dialectic of revelation and makes our response to God possible. *Then He fashioned him and breathed into him His spirit, and He placed in you hearing, sight, and hearts* (Q. 32:9). We find our words when we come to realize that we are nothing without God. This is what prostration reveals. It is not the power of our intellect that allows us to speak but our fundamental servanthood. *He sends His spirit from His command upon whom He wills of His servants to warn of the Day of Meeting* (Q. 40:15). God has given us the first words with which we might respond to Him. These words, however, are not uttered with the tongue but with the whole of the praying body.

From the cradle of the first prostration, we bring ourselves up to rest upon our knees. We sit kneeling in a moment of quiet respite. Then we lower ourselves down just as profoundly as before into the second prostration, but this time the earth we face is not of our beginning but of our end. In the second prostration is a prefiguration of our death to come. Our faces confront the hard earth into which we will one day be laid.

And they fall upon on their faces weeping and it increases them in humility (Q. 17:109). In this future tomb we shall lie, waiting in tremulous expectation of God, the Abaser and the Exalter, who will resurrect the dead in both body and soul. With each prostration we are brought before God, the Bestower of Life and the Bringer of Death. With our bent backs and bowed heads, we proceed symbolically from one door of existence to the next.

The life of faith lies between these two prostrations that mark respectively the valley of our birth and the valley of our death. That short span afforded between the two is a time of reflection. As Iqbal writes, "Prayer as a means of spiritual illumination is a normal vital act by which the little island of our personality suddenly discovers its situation in a larger whole of life."[24] Resting upon our knees between prostrations is our time to assess the life that we are living. What will we do back in the world when our prayer concludes?

The prayer, however, does not end with our symbolic passage from cradle to grave. As powerful and poignant as the second prostration may be, our journey is not yet complete. A final station waits. What follows the second prostration—that last descent into death—is a final rising, our resurrection. *Truly shall the Hour come, there is no doubt in it, and truly shall God resurrect those who are in their graves* (Q. 22:7). When at last we rise to sit and kneel for the final time, we rise with a vision of the life that is still to come. Here in the aftermath of all that prayer has rendered, the faithful behold the Day of Reckoning that awaits. It is a future time that has yet to come. Until that moment arrives, the end of every prayer asks, what will you do with the time that remains? The final sitting, then, is not really about the end, but about redemptive possibilities. The last kneeling marks our imminent return to the world of the living, where the life of faith is still ongoing and within reach. Then, with a single cycle of prayer completed, either rise to perform it all over again or depart with the expectation that its repetition is not far off in the future. We do not return to our everyday lives with the naiveté or pride of before. Rather, we return hopefully made anew by all that we have experienced in prayer and mindful of the future that is in store. Such is the nature of our lives, to do and do again lest we forget. Such is the nature of our place in the back-and-forth of God's revelation and our human response, to respond and respond again so that the word of God is made to live within us.

THE PROSTRATION OF RESPONSE

> *Whosoever is in the heavens and earth prostrates to God, willingly or unwillingly, as do their shadows in the morning and evening.*
> —Qur'an 13:15

The Qur'an refers to human beings as servants of God with incredible frequency, but servanthood is not a trait unique to humankind. As the Qur'an also emphasizes, all of creation serves God. This service is described as the glorification or praise of God: *Whatever is in the heavens and whatever is on earth is glorifying God, He is the Almighty, the All-Wise* (Q. 59:1); *Whatever is in the heavens and whatever is on earth glorifies God, the Sovereign, the Divine, the Almighty, the All-Wise* (Q. 62:1); *The seven heavens and the earth and whatever is therein glorifies Him and there is no thing save that it glorifies His praise, but you do not understand how they glorify Him. Truly He is the All-Forbearing, the All-Forgiving* (Q. 17:44). Each creature and every created thing, human beings included, glorifies God in their own respective way. Nonetheless, as the last-cited verse indicates, it is not always clear how this is so. There is another verse, however, that entices the imagination with a striking metaphor: *Whosoever is in the heavens and earth prostrates to God, willingly or unwillingly* (Q. 13:15). It is as if all of creation is engaged in the act of worship, whether they are conscious of it or not. God is glorified through the rhythm of the natural world. It is as if our whole lives—and not just the moments in which we pray—are an act of prostration to God. Or rather, it is how our lives *ought* to be.

While nearly all of creation worships God by dint of their God-given natures, human beings stand apart. In possession of free will, humanity has the capacity to pursue ends other than the one for which God created it, to worship and serve Him. Human beings, then, are servants of God through supreme effort. Easily distracted, humankind is constantly leading itself astray. Forgetfulness lies at the root of human failings. Prayer, this gift from God, serves as a corrective reminder. By performing the rites of prayer, the faithful have the means to overcome themselves and recover their rightful orientation toward God once more. Whether one prays for the first time or for the thousandth, the descent into prostration returns a soul to its primordial form, curled over like infants in the womb. Down there in that fetal position, revelation reverberates more loudly. Prostration allows the faithful to hear the word of God with all of their being. It attunes both body and soul not only to hear revelation, but also to respond.

To think of prostration, then, as purely an act of submission is too passive an understanding. Prayer fundamentally entails choice. It is an act of witness that a person chooses to undertake, and prostration embodies an active commitment to that witnessing. With every preformed prayer, the human being joins the chorus of creation in glorifying God. With each prostration the faithful are simultaneously answering their Creator and addressing the world in which they live, because to turn to God necessarily precipitates a change in how one lives. Each act of prayer may come to an end, but a *life* of prayer is continuous. God is still addressing the faithful even after they rise, and they must still respond even after the ardor of praying fades. Indeed, one's commitment to God can only be truly carried out in prostration's aftermath. Faith may find its form in the cradle of prostration, but its fulfillment can only be wrought in the throes of life itself and the many relationships that it entails. God calls all of humankind to bring prayer and righteousness together.

THE PROSTRATION OF PROTEST

> The spirit of all true prayer is social.
> —Muhammad Iqbal, *The Reconstruction of Religious Thought in Islam*[25]

> *Have you seen the one who forbids*
> *A servant when he prays?*
> *Have you seen if he relies on guidance,*
> *Or enjoins reverence?*
> *Have you seen if he denies and turns away?*
> *Does he not know that God sees?*
> *No! But if he ceases not We shall seize him by the forelock—*
> *A denying, sinning forelock!*
> *So let him call upon his cohorts;*
> *We shall call upon the guardians of Hell.*
> *No! Obey him not, but prostrate and draw near.*
> —Qur'an 96:9–19

The righteous stand in protest. They lie down in protest. They cast their bodies before others who would do ill. They speak and shout so that all might hear. They spend of what they have and they suffer what they must so that others—the world itself—might be made right, even if only by a little. All such acts of protestation, whether great or small, have their share of righteousness. *Truly God loves the just* (Q. 49:9; 60:8). All these many acts feed the fire of righteousness that burns within the human soul. Imagine, then, what it might mean to prostrate in protest. Imagine how brightly that fire would blaze were it fueled by every performed prayer and prostration. Such were the ways of the prophets and messengers of God. Through their ardent prostrations and their fervent protestations, they set the world afire.

The ritual prayer is not an act intended to isolate and insulate a person of faith from the world. The timing and form of prayer anchors prayer to the circumstances of a person's existence. When the faithful pray, they do so in the midst of the world where they strive, struggle, and suffer. It compels them to face their situation and confront the difficulties and challenges therein. *The true faithful are those who have faith in God and His Messenger, then doubt not, but struggle with their wealth and their persons in the way of God. It is they who are truthful* (Q. 49:15). In order to speak heavenward we must understand our place upon this earth. The gift of ritual prayer, then, is more than our response to God. It is also our response to the world. As intimate and personal an offering as prostration is to our Creator and Sustainer, it is also an outcry against the condition of the world, which brings us to the brink of prayer in the first place. When we face devastation, ruin, and that which seems insurmountable, unfathomable, and unbearable, prayer is an ever-present recourse. When we face oppression and injustice, prayer is a light against the darkness. It can be a firebrand to be wielded against the iniquities that cover this world and afflict this life. To pray in the face of despair, then, does not signal surrender, but instead declares one's commitment to rendering righteousness in the world. Just as prostration marks how we respond to the incredible burden of God's revelation, it also punctuates how we address the brokenness of the world that surrounds us. Prayer gives voice to our righteous discontent as much as it embodies our devotion and faith.

Indeed, faith and righteousness are inseparable. God calls humanity to both. Time after time God admonishes humankind to be among *those who have faith and do righteous deeds* (Q. 2:25, passim). The faithful servants of God are asked to bear both in all that they do. As God discloses, faith and righteous works define and fulfill each other. The link between the two is intimate. A faith fostered in the heart alone yearns for more. It seeks expression in action and desires to be manifest in the world. Likewise, deeds done in righteousness are difficult to sustain without the energy of faith to fuel them from within. Works wrought without substance or center diminish with time. Faith and righteous deeds, when kindled carefully, propel one another to greater heights.

God also repeatedly commands humankind to *enjoin the right and forbid the wrong* wherever and whenever they may be. Each and every soul is asked to do so individually. *Perform prayer, enjoin the right and forbid the wrong, and patiently persevere over whatever befalls you* (Q. 31:17). The divine imperative also addresses humanity collectively. *Let there be from among you a community calling to goodness, enjoining the right and forbidding the wrong. It is they who are the successful* (Q. 3:104). It is not that some must stand forth, while others abstain. It is not for any person to delay or dither. All who are united in faith are called to be that enjoining and forbidding community of God. The obligation must be both pursued personally and fulfilled communally.

Throughout the past, God has sent prophets and messengers to show humankind that faith and righteousness are necessary and inseparable. *Indeed We have sent Our messengers with clear proofs and We have sent down the Scripture and the Balance with them so that humankind could uphold justice* (Q. 57:25). The prophets walked and lived among us so that we would come to know with directness and intimacy what God asks of His dutiful servant. They taught and embodied that faith and righteousness go hand in hand. The prophet Moses stood against the tyranny of the people of Pharaoh—*who afflicted you with terrible torment slaughtering your sons and sparing your women* (Q. 2:49). The prophet Ṣāliḥ stood against the reckless excessiveness of the people of Thamūd. *And obey not the command of the intemperate, who sow corruption upon the earth, doing not what is right!* (Q. 26:151–52). The prophet Hūd stood against the monumentalism and self-aggrandizement of the people of ʿĀd. *Do you build on every height a sign to amuse yourselves? And do you occupy strongholds thinking that you may live forever? And when you strike out, do you strike out as tyrants?* (Q.

26:128–30). The prophet Shuʿayb stood against the exploitation and avarice of the people of Madyan. *Give full measure and be not of those who give less, and weigh with a true balance* (Q. 26:181–82). The prophets David and Jesus stood against the most rebellious transgressors from among their respective peoples. *That was because they disobeyed and transgressed persistently* (Q. 5:78).

The Prophet Muhammad stood too against the very blood of his blood, the Quraysh of Mecca, so that the poor, downtrodden, and marginalized might find favor and dignity in this life and the next. In fact, during his days as a young man prior to prophethood, he responded to the call of justice by partaking in the Alliance of the Virtuous, a pact made to ensure the collective dispensation of justice for all those treated unfairly in Mecca.[26] The Prophet Muhammad was among those who pledged to be like "a single hand with the oppressed and against the oppressor."[27] Years later, after the mantle of prophethood had arrived, the Prophet Muhammad affirmed his continued commitment to the pact. He testified, "I was present in the house of ʿAbd Allah ibn Judʿan at so excellent a pact [the Alliance of the Virtuous] that I would not exchange it for a herd of red camels; [the clans of] Hashim, Zuhrah and Taym swore to side with the oppressed till the sea drenched wool and if now, in Islam, I were summoned unto it, I would gladly respond."[28] In so saying, the Prophet Muhammad was declaring that he would stand by all who were victims of injustice regardless of creed, association, or inclination.

The prophets altogether lived to exemplify the will of the Creator: *Truly God enjoins justice, virtue, and generosity to kinsfolk and He forbids indecency, wrong, and wickedness* (Q. 16:90) Through these many God-sent exemplars, we have come to learn how to join the fire of our faith in God and the fire of our righteous indignation against the darknesses and iniquities of the world. We partake in the ongoing prophetic experience when we choose to emulate them. We stand with them when we make their tradition the form of our life.

God granted us prayer so that we might find yet another way to experience the joining of faith and righteousness as the prophets did. No prophet strode in righteousness without also bowing in devotion. We join their exalted ranks, then, with every prostration we perform. Our heads come to touch the same earth that theirs did. Our bodies bend as theirs did in ages past. More than that, our hearts are made to burn with the same fire that fueled their mission and gave life to their righteous and salvific words. May we live and pray like the prophets of God.

Imagine, then, that when we prostrate we demonstrate our devotion to our Lord while simultaneously voicing our protest against the injustices of life around us. We respond to God and the world at once. However much we commit to God, we are setting ourselves in equal proportion and measure against those who dare to be ungodly. As we give ourselves over to our Creator, we are marshaling simultaneously our strength to resist those who seek to undo the goodness of creation with their wanton destruction, exploitation, and corruption. As we utter our ardent and searching response to the eternal Almighty, we are voicing at the same time our fervent outcry against those who wield their temporal might wickedly and oppressively. As we prostrate our bodies before the truth that is God the Real, we are turning our backs in effect upon all those who have given themselves over to deception and falsehood. With every prostration we challenge those who would dare to enjoin the wrong and forbid the right. With every prayer we partake of the prophetic experience.

With every prayer we do not bow down alone. We join the multitude of the faithful and faith-seeking who follow in the wake of God's messengers and prophets. To prostrate, then, is to pray like the prophets. More than that, it is to pray *with* the prophets. Through prayer, we join a vast and rich tradition of righteous resistance that has emerged over the centuries from out of the ongoing prophetic experience. We are bowing and bending with the hosts of the pious who would not let worldly power eclipse heavenly promise. When we prostrate, we join Aḥmad b. Ḥanbal in his resistance to political power that would see faith bend before it. When we prostrate, we join Abū Ḥāmid al-Ghazālī in his resistance to the trappings of prestige and exalted position. When we prostrate, we join el-Hajj Malik el-Shabazz, Malcolm X, in his resistance to the systemic inhumanity that racialized power would impose over us all. When we prostrate, we join the throngs who struggle still to establish righteousness in the world wherever it is needed.

Prostrate, then, so that all may know that we commit ourselves to that which is greater than ourselves and greater than all else. In prayer we prostrate to God alone. We will bow to no other power. In prayer we place ourselves before the Almighty as His faithful servants. We will cower before no oppressor. In prayer we bend with the arc of revelation, accompanying its mighty descent—that terrible and eternal hammer fall—into the world. We fall *with* the word of God like a crashing wave against the iniquities that swell up from below. Then, when prayer ends, our lot is to rise up and struggle onward. To pray and prostrate is only a beginning; it is not an end in and of itself.

Theology only finds true fulfillment when lived boldly in the temperamental moments of the everyday. In the aftermath of prayer, we must give voice and form to the words we found in the depths of our prostrations. We must learn to embody those fervent words so that the foulness and falsity that afflicts us knows that faith and righteousness are greater. The mighty and thunderous course of revelation shows us the way. Let us pray that the theologies we live by have the boldness and humility to follow.

PRAY AS THOUGH IT IS YOUR LAST PRAYER

> When you stand for your prayer, then pray as though it is your farewell prayer. Do not say anything for which you must apologize and abandon the desire for what is in the hands of other people.
> —Hadith of the Prophet Muhammad[29]

> Anyway, now, each day I live as if I am already dead.
> —Malcolm X[30]

The words of the Prophet Muhammad and Malcolm X, though spoken centuries apart in drastically different contexts, lead to the same end, namely that one's orientation toward prayer and life ought to be one and the same. The words of the Prophet cited above are often paraphrased as a common refrain during many congregational prayers: "Pray as though it is your last prayer." With these words, worshipers are invited to approach prayer with the graveness of their mortality before their eyes. They are asked to pray *as though* it were their last. This particular invocation of the religious imagination by the Prophet Muhammad is particularly poignant because it pivots upon an unavoidable truth: every prayer one offers might very well be one's last. As the Qur'an repeatedly discloses, all of creation has its term of life that God has appointed—a *specified term* (Q. 39:42; 40:67). Nonetheless, no one knows when their short span will end or how it will end. It is with this reality in mind that the Prophet offers his admonition, "Pray as though it is your last prayer." He is urging the faithful to approach each prayer with the magnitude that it deserves. He is reminding his community that the form and depth of their prayers ought to echo the imminence of one's last breath. Should not every moment in this world be treated as precious? Should every prayer not be offered as though it might be the last since the time of our return to our Lord could transpire at any moment?

The counsel of the Prophet Muhammad, however, does not end here. He adds, "Do not say anything for which you must apologize and abandon the desire for what is in the hands of other people." To approach prayer as if it is your last is not simply a matter of how one will face the Creator should this prayer indeed be the last. To approach your last prayer also entails bidding farewell to the world in a good and righteous manner. How the worshiper enters prayer is just as important as the prayer itself. In what standing are the bonds, ties, and relationships that one would leave behind? Did one live with faith and righteousness, or were the schemes of ambition, covetousness, and complicity stronger? If the present prayer is to be the last, then know, the Prophet warns, that the final accounting will hinge upon what one did with the short span of life that one was given.

Similarly, Malcolm X, a voice of justice and renewal, knew well the urgency of the present. His words speak just as poignantly to the imminence of the end. As he felt his last days rapidly approaching, he confessed to writer Alex Haley, "Anyway, now, each day I live *as if* I am already dead."[31] The expectation of his death, however, was not a new revelation to him. He felt the certainty of it from early on. "It has always been my belief that I, too, will die by violence."[32] What Malcolm reveals with his words "each day I live as if I am already dead" is that he had come to accept his fate. The manner of his acceptance, however, was not some reckless embrace of Thanatos, the death drive, like the path of self-destruction that he followed in his earlier life of crime and depravity. Rather, Malcolm was *living* with the recognition that each moment he experienced was a moment of great value and potential. There was work to be done while God granted him life. There were truths about our racialized realities that still needed to be said while his voice could still be heard. Although death loomed immensely large, the specter of it did not cow him. During the last days of Malcolm's appointed term, that short span left to him, he was living—not dying—with deliberative purpose.

Indeed, as the impending arrival of Malcolm's end gained greater clarity and focus, so too did his voice of righteousness. He had to speak the truth so long as he still drew breath. With every borrowed day, Malcolm continued to resist the very powers that threatened his existence. He continued to struggle and speak out until the moment of his death so that the world he left behind might be made right. Righteousness, however, was not his only concern at this time. His sense of justice was tempered by his pursuit of faith. Even though Malcolm knew his time was quickly expiring, he journeyed to Mecca, the "Holy World," so that he could stand before the house of God. He took the time to learn painstakingly the form of ritual prayer. He struggled to understand as best he could what it meant to truly prostrate to God. His tireless pursuit of righteousness did not preclude the life of faith but embraced it. For Malcolm, prayer and speaking truth to power went hand in hand. Folded in Malcolm's bent and bowed form, inscribed in his prostrate body, was an ethos of protest—of righteousness joined to faith.

The Prophet Muhammad urged us to approach every prayer with the fullness and finality of life keenly in mind. Malcolm X demonstrated to us that even when the end of life looms large, our measure of righteousness is magnified when joined with searching faith and sincere prayer. Although their words speak of death, they were uttered to spur us to embrace the life that we have left. Every prayer ought to be offered with urgency. Every action ought to accord with righteousness. The time for faith and righteousness cannot wait. We have but the present moment with no assurance of another. Recall too the words of the Prophet Muhammad from before: "Worship God as though you see Him, for though you do not see Him, He sees you." Sincere worship has no end. It is not confined to the short time that we set aside for prayer. Nor is it restricted to the small space that our limbs carve out in prayer's performance. Sincere worship—a life of worship—precedes the call to prayer that signals the start. It continues long after the greetings of peace that marks a prayer's conclusion. What the Prophet Muhammad and Malcolm X disclose is that for the faithful servant of God life and prayer ought to be lived as one.

Let it be clear that this is not an enjoinment to spend every waking moment in devotion and supplication. While we may find our primordial form in the cradle of prostration, we were not created to abide perpetually down in those prayerful depths. We are also God's servants created to live for a time upon the horizon of God's creation. To live life and prayer as one is to pursue life *as though* we are always praying. It is to proceed into the world *as though* we are always in prostration. It is to approach every situation with the immensity of God's word always bearing down upon us. It is to bring to every encounter we experience the same humility and servanthood that we bring to every prostration we perform. The spirit of prayer should infuse the words we choose to speak. It should guide the actions we choose to undertake. Until our departure from this life, we must strive to make every moment both a testament to our faith in God and a witness to the good we try to render in the world around us. So let us not simply pray as though each prayer is our last. Let us live as though each moment may be our last—that final moment before we find ourselves standing before our Creator at the end of all things.

NOTES

1. Chittick, *In Search of the Lost Heart*, 24.

2. Numerous Muslim scholars, including seminal commentators like al-Ṭabarī (d. 310/923) and al-Thaʿlabī (d. 427/1035), understood Q. 17:1 to refer to the Prophet's Night Journey (*isrāʾ*) and Heavenly Ascension (*miʿrāj*) that transpired during his prophetic mission in Mecca. Both Vuckovic and Colby have provided broad-ranging analyses of exegetical traditions concerning Q. 17:1. Al-Ṭabarī, *Jāmiʿ al-bayān*, 15:5–22; al-Thaʿlabī, *Al-Kashf wa-l-bayān*, 6:54–69; Brooke Vuckovic, *Heavenly Journeys, Earthly Concerns: The Legacy of the Miʿrāj in the Formation of Islam* (New York: Routledge, 2005); Frederick S. Colby, *Narrating Muḥammad's Night Journey: Tracing the Development of the Ibn ʿAbbās Ascension Discourse* (Albany: State University of New York Press, 2008).

3. The Qur'an commentaries differ as to the meaning of the events mentioned in the first eighteen verses of *sūrat al-najm* (Q. 53:1–18). Some understand the passage to reference at least two different divine encounters by the Prophet Muhammad. Some commentators, like the Sufi mystic and Ashʿarī theologian al-Qushayrī (d. 465/1072), speculated that at least the second en-

counter is a reference to the Heavenly Ascension. Al-Ṭabarī, *Jāmiʿ al-bayān*, 27:50–69; al-Thaʿlabī, *Al-Kashf wa-l-bayān*, 9:134–44; Nguyen, *Sufi Master and Qur'an Scholar*, 173–83; Martin Nguyen, "Qushayrī's Exegetical Encounter with the Miʿrāj," in *The Spirit and the Letter: Approaches to the Esoteric Interpretation of the Qur'an*, ed. Annabel Keeler and Sajjad Rizvi (Oxford: Oxford University Press, 2016), 241–66.

4. The prescription for the ritual prayer is related in the literature related to the Heavenly Ascension as well as prophetic biographies.

5. Malcolm X and Haley, *Autobiography*, 170.

6. Malcolm X and Haley, *Autobiography*, 170.

7. Malcolm X and Haley, *Autobiography*, 170.

8. Malcolm X and Haley, *Autobiography*, 171.

9. Malcolm X and Haley, *Autobiography*, 171.

10. Malcolm X and Haley, *Autobiography*, 171.

11. Malcolm X and Haley, *Autobiography*, 171.

12. Malcolm X and Haley, *Autobiography*, 171.

13. Malcolm X and Haley, *Autobiography*, 331–32.

14. Malcolm X and Haley, *Autobiography*, 334.

15. According to Islamic ritual law, one should perform prostration when a Qur'anic verse containing its mention is recited. The schools of law differ as to the number of verses for which prostration is called, ranging from eleven to fifteen. The schools of law also differ as to when prostration is deemed obligatory (*wājib*) for a verse or merely recommended (*mustahab*).

16. Malcolm X and Haley, *Autobiography*, 391.

17. Aileen Vincent Barwood, "A Gift from the Kingdom," *Aramco World Magazine* 36, no. 5 (September/October 1985): 23.

18. Hāmān is a servant of Pharaoh mentioned twice in the Qur'an. *Pharaoh said: O notables! I know of no god for you other than myself. O Hāmān! Light for me a fire to bake clay, then set up for me a tower so that I may behold the God of Moses, though truly do I think he is among the liars* (Q. 28:38).

19. Iqbal, *Reconstruction*, 74.

20. During the course of his study of the Qur'anic Iblīs-Satan narrative, Bodman draws upon the Qur'an commentaries of major exegetes like al-Ṭabarī and al-Qurṭubī (d. 671/1272). For the two verses cited here, see Bodman, *Poetics of Iblīs*, 203–36.

21. Al-Ṭabarī, *Jāmiʿ al-bayān*, 1:174–79; al-Thaʿlabī, *Al-Kashf wa-l-bayān*, 1:228–30. In the Qur'an, God creates Adam to be God's vicegerent or *khalīfa* upon the earth (Q. 2:30–33). This has been understood by commentators to represent a mantle of stewardship (*khilāfa*). Elsewhere in the Qur'an, humankind is described as undertaking a trust from God that the rest of creation refuses. Moreover, humankind undertakes that trust irresponsibly. *Indeed, We*

offered the trust to the heavens, the earth, and the mountains and they declined to undertake it and feared it, yet humanity undertook it. Indeed, it is unjust and ignorant (Q. 33:72). Tlili has analyzed classical and modern interpretations concerning the idea of *khilāfa* in Q. 2:30 as well as Q. 33:72 in an important study of human and nonhuman animals in the Qur'an. I agree with Tlili's analysis "that many of the themes occurring in the *istikhlāf* verses disproves the claim that this concept imparts any significant status to human beings." Sarra Tlili, *Animals in the Qur'an* (Cambridge: Cambridge University Press, 2012), 115–22, 237–41, quotation on 122.

22. Chittick, *In Search of the Lost Heart*, 26.

23. Al-Ṭabarī, *Jāmiʿ al-bayān*, 23:216–17; Murata and Chittick, *Visions of Islam*, 100–101.

24. Iqbal, *Reconstruction*, 72.

25. Iqbal, *Reconstruction*, 73.

26. Ch. Pellat, "*Ḥilf al-fuḍūl*," in *Encyclopaedia of Islam*, 3:389; Ibn Saʿd, *Kitāb al-Ṭabaqāt al-kabīr*, 1:106–7.

27. Pellat, "*Ḥilf al-fuḍūl*," 3:389.

28. Quoted in Esack, *Qurʾān, Liberation and Pluralism*, 194; Ibn Saʿd, *Kitāb al-Ṭabaqāt al-kabīr*, 1:107.

29. Ibn Majah, *Sunan Ibn Majah bi-sharḥ al-imām Abī al-Ḥasan al-Ḥanafī al-maʿrūf al-Sindī al-mutawaffā 1137 Ḥ wa-bi-ḥāshiya taʿlīqāt Miṣbāḥ al-zujāja fī Zawāʾid Ibn Majāh li'l-Būṣīrī*, ed. Khalīl Maʾmūn Shīḥā, 5 vols. (Beirut: Dār al-Maʿrifa, 1417/1996), 4:455, *kitāb al-zuhd, bāb al-ḥikma*, no. 4171.

30. Malcolm X and Haley, *Autobiography*, 387.

31. Malcolm X and Haley, *Autobiography*, 387, emphasis added.

32. Malcolm X and Haley, *Autobiography*, 2.

CONCLUSION

WHERE WE HAVE BEEN

> Hence, although we have a final religion, we cannot have a final understanding of religion. And although, we have a perfect religion . . . we do not have perfect religious knowledge. There is a great distance and difference between attesting to the fact that Islam (intrinsically and in itself) is complete and suggesting that the disciplines of *fiqh*, exegesis, ethics, etc. are all complete; just as there is a world of difference between the flawlessness of nature and the flawlessness of the sciences of nature.
>
> —Abdulkarim Soroush, *The Expansion of Prophetic Experience*[1]

As my present theological venture comes to a close, a recapitulation of the preceding chapters is in order. The rhythm of the natural world resonates with the worship of the Divine. Humankind, however, stands apart. Although God has created us as servants of God, the fulfillment of our worshipful purpose requires our deliberative effort. To worship God with our prayers and throughout our lives is a struggle and test while we abide upon this earth. We do not, however, enter this test alone. We are members of communities and inheritors of histories from which we can draw lessons, inspiration, and succor. We are, in sum, part of a tradition—an expansive and dynamically adapting tradition. Nonetheless, greater still are the workings of our Lord. *And thus We have made you a justly balanced community so that you may be witnesses over humankind* (Q. 2:143). God, Almighty and Wise, cleaves closely to both tradition and our individual selves. *And We have already created the human being and know what his soul whispers to him, and We are closer to him than his jugular vein* (Q. 50:16). Neither the life of tradition nor the life of the individual soul unfolds beyond the course of God's divine decree.

Furthermore, out of love and mercy, God has spoken to us in order to ease our way. Throughout all of history, even in the seemingly direst of times, God has sent revelation and prophets to guide us back to the Divine. Even unto the present, God has never left our side. The Qur'an, though revealed to the Prophet Muhammad in his historical moment, is an ongoing revelation that continues to speak to each and every one of us still. It continues to speak to us even though we may not hear it through the noise of our modern times or the cacophony of our personal lives. The life of faith that we experience depends upon how we form our response to God's revelation. To this end, I have contended throughout this book, we ought to take recourse to the imagination, divinely endowed within us all. Through its exercise we might hear clearly the word of God once more. With its aid, as the tradition demonstrates, we can form new and vibrant theologies of response.

Indeed, all that we do in life forms our response to God. Prayer merely marks an important point of entry for us. There is incredibly more in life that we ought to imagine and engage for the sake of developing our responses to God, our respective personal theologies. However we choose to pursue this end, a theology of true engagement cannot be aimed at God and the Hereafter alone. Although faith is formed in relation to the Creator first and foremost, the engagement that God asks of us is also formed in relation to God's creation. To engage the world, the Qur'an repeatedly informs us, entails that we *uphold justice* (Q. 57:25), *enjoin the right and forbid the wrong* (Q. 31:17), and *do righteous deeds* (Q. 2:25) to the utmost of our ability. While we ought to prostrate with these divine imperatives inscribed upon our hearts, we must also rise to enact them in the world.

There is urgency to the task. Malcolm X understood this well when he wrote these words: "They say insha Allah [if God wills it] and then wait; and while they are waiting the world passes them by."[2] We cannot let this world pass us by. With our time in this world so short, we cannot afford to tarry for long uncommitted and uncritical of what we do. Nor can we live in expectation of God because God is already with us. God has spoken and speaks still. His revelation—His eternal speech—the Qur'an, has broken into this world and we, who live in its thunderous wake, have been called to stand and respond.

The task of our reply, however, is not as impossible as it seems. Our response can issue from many quarters. My reimagining of prayer and prostration as a form of practical theology was meant to serve as a evocative and hopefully memorable demonstration of what can be achieved if we take theology and the imagination seriously. The fact of the matter is that my preceding treatment entails only some of the ways that we might conceive of a theology of prostration. My aim was never to articulate a theology for all times or for all communities, but rather to present a theology that might speak to those of us struggling in common cause in the here and now. While God's speech is eternal, the words of our response are not. The nature of our reply will change as much as we do. Accordingly, there are innumerable other ways that we might have constructed and construed what a theology of prostration, or any theology for that matter, might entail. Our words of response might have been otherwise for they *have been* otherwise, to be sure, as our enduring and ever-changing tradition reveals. Ultimately, we must each find our own way of answering God. We must each come to discover and live a transformative and faith-affirming theology of our own, one suited to our respective time, place, condition, and crises so that we might draw closer to God from wherever we are. Most assuredly, wherever we turn, God will be there. *To God belong the East and the West. Wherever you turn there is the face of God. God is the All-Encompassing, the All-Knowing* (Q. 2:115).

WHERE WE SHALL GO

> Theology is—or should be—a species of poetry, which read quickly or encountered in a hubbub of noise makes no sense. You have to open yourself to a poem with a quiet, receptive mind, in the same way as you might listen to a difficult piece of music. . . . You have to give it your full attention, wait patiently upon it, and make an empty space for it in your mind. And finally the work declares itself to you, steals deeply into the interstices of your being, line by line, note by note, phrase by phrase, until it becomes part of you forever. —Karen Armstrong, *The Spiral Staircase*[3]

From our humble human vantage, the horizon ahead appears overwhelming in its expansiveness. The possibilities for a life of faith are incredibly varied and manifold. This book was only intended as a beginning, or rather as a new link in the chain of the tradition. Truth be told, we cannot know where God will take us. We cannot foresee how our tradition will continue to unfold. As Christian theologian and ethicist Stanley Hauerwas writes, "Our future is in God's hands. We had best not try to anticipate what God is doing and is going to do to us. Indeed, it is not even clear what a century might mean in God's time. We had best keep on keeping on hoping in the hope God can make use of us in ways that we cannot imagine."[4] What we do know is that our future rests with God. God alone knows where the community of faith will go until the ending of all things. He alone knows the path that each of us faces until the hour of our death. To God do we turn in faith and to God do we offer our prayers and our labor.

With the unfathomable future unfolding before us, I end this venture with a proposition concerning how we might proceed theologically from here. I propose that the character of our theological expression ought to embrace the beautiful. Ours is a time in need of poetry. To pursue beauty in theology is not to give in to vanity or earthly distraction. Instead, we are seeking to find accord with the beauty of the Creator. As the Prophet Muhammad attests, "God is beautiful and loves beauty."[5]

Our theologies, then, ought to be attentive to aesthetics, that field of inquiry attentive to the nature of beauty. To this end, we have no better example than revelation itself. As thunderous and terrible as revelation may be—a sign of God's glory—it is, at the same time, breathtaking and magnificent to behold—a sign of God's beauty. When God speaks, His words issue with sonorous eloquence. The call to faith and righteousness is delivered with poetic splendor. Moreover, God's revelation admonishes us to do likewise. *And speak to them with penetrating words about their selves* (Q. 4:63). Our responses ought to emulate as fully as humanly possible the excellence of revelation.

The speech of God penetrates hearts deeply because of the perfection of its expression and the dynamism of its imagery. Many have turned to give ear because of the vim and vigor of the Qur'an's locution and delivery. Imagine the potency and enduring power that such a theology would bear if it were expressed poetically. Would it not steal into the interstices of our being as Armstrong suggests? Would it not transport us further? To be attentive to the aesthetics of theology is to allow the beauty of faith and righteousness to wend its way to the core of who we are and from therein transform us.

In the end, this book is an invitation to partake more deliberately and thoughtfully in the ongoing work of theology. It is a proposal for the community of faith to undertake the practice of theology with greater care, courage, and imagination. In our times, it is often not enough simply to strive to live piously and righteously. We must take the time to discern the meaning behind the life we choose to live. We must reflect deeply on what it means to serve our Lord here and now. Let us dare to imagine theology, then, as an invigorating and meaningful mode of life. Let us seek out as earnestly as we can the life of faith.

To live as though always praying, to hear God as though always bowed, to go forth into the world as though ever prostrating, to worship God as though we can see Him—these are but some of the humble responses that a theology of imagination, faithful reflection, and genuine engagement makes possible. It is time to see where else the revelation of God shall take us. May the peace and mercy of God be upon you.

> *Say, "Believe in it or do not believe." Indeed those who were given knowledge before it fall upon their faces in prostration when it is recited to them.*
> —Qur'an 17:107

NOTES

1. Soroush, *Expansion of Prophetic Experience*, 52.
2. Marable, *Malcolm X*, 310.
3. Karen Armstrong, *The Spiral Staircase: My Climb Out of Darkness* (New York: Anchor Books, 2004), 284.
4. Stanley Hauerwas, *Approaching the End: Eschatological Reflections on Church, Politics, and Life* (Grand Rapids, MI: Wm. B. Eerdmans, 2013), 87.
5. Muslim, *Ṣaḥīḥ*, 1:93, *kitāb al-īmān, bāb taḥrīm al-kibr*, no. 147; Muslim and al-Nawawī, *Ṣaḥīḥ Muslim bi-sharḥ al-Nawawī*, 2:88–89.

BIBLIOGRAPHY

ARABIC TEXTS

ʿAbd al-Raḥmān, Ṭāhā. *Fī uṣūl al-ḥiwar wa-tajdīd ʿilm al-kalām*. Casablanca: al-Muʾassasa al-Ḥadītha, 1987.

———. *Al-Ḥaqq al-Islāmī fī-l-ikhtilāf al-fikrī*. Casablanca: al-Markaz al-Thaqāfī al-ʿArabī, 2005.

Abū Dāwūd al-Sijistānī, Sulaymān b. al-Ashʿath al-Azdī. *Sunan Abī Dāwūd*. Edited by Shuʿayb al-Arnaʾūṭ and Muḥammad Kāmil Qarabalalī. 7 vols. Beirut: Dār al-Risāla al-ʿĀlamiyya, 2009.

Abū Ḥanīfa. *Kitāb al-ʿĀlim wa-l-mutaʿallim: riwāyat Abī Muqātil ʿan Abī Ḥanīfa rādiya Allāh ʿanhumā wa-yalīhi Risālat Abī Ḥanīfa ilā ʿUthmān al-Battī thumma al-Fiqh al-absaṭ riwāyat Abī Muṭīʿ ʿan Abī Ḥanīfa raḥimahum Allāh*. Edited by Muḥammad Zāhid al-Kawtharī. Cairo: Maṭbaʿat al-Anwār, 1368/[1949].

al-Bāqillānī, Abū Bakr b. al-Ṭayyib. *Al-Inṣāf fī mā yujab iʿtiqāduhu wa-lā yajūzu al-jahl bi-hi*. Edited by Muḥammad Zāhid b. al-Ḥasan al-Kawtharī. Cairo: Maktabat al-Khānjī, 2001.

al-Bazdawī, Abū al-Yusr Muḥammad. *Uṣūl al-dīn*. Edited by Hans Peter Linss. Cairo: al-Maktabat al-Azhariyya li-l-Turāth, 2003.

al-Bukhārī, Abū ʿAbd Allāh Muḥammad b. Ismāʿīl. *Ṣaḥīh al-imām al-Bukhārī al-musammā al-jāmiʿ al-musnad al-ṣaḥīḥ al-mukhtaṣar min umūr rasūl Allāh wa-sunanihi wa-ayyāmihi*. Edited by Muḥammad Zuhayr b. Nāṣir al-Nāṣir. 9 vols. Beirut: Dār Ṭawq al-Najāh, 2002.

al-Dhahabī, Shams al-Dīn Muḥammad b. Aḥmad b. ʿUthmān. *Tārīkh al-islām*. Edited by ʿUmar ʿAbd al-Salām Tadmūrī. 53 vols. Beirut: Dār al-Kitāb al-ʿArabī, 1990–2000.

al-Ghazālī, Abū Ḥāmid Muḥammad b. Muḥammad. *Iḥyāʾ ʿulūm al-dīn*. Edited by Muḥammad Wahbī Sulaymān and Usāma ʿAmūra. 5 vols. Damascus: Dār al-Fikr, 2006.

———. "*Al-Munqidh min al-ḍalāl*." In *Majmūʿat rasāʾil al-imām al-Ghazālī*, 537–64. Beirut: Dār al-Fikr, 2003.

Ibn Abī Yaʿlā al-Baghdādī al-Ḥanbalī, Abū al-Ḥusayn Muḥammad. *Ṭabaqāt al-ḥanābila*. Edited by ʿAbd al-Raḥmān b. Sulaymān al-ʿUthaymīn. 3 vols. Riyadh: al-Mamlaka al-ʿArabiyya al-Saʿūdiyya al-Amāna al-ʿĀmma li-l-Iḥtifāl bi-Murūr Miʾat ʿĀmʿalā Taʾsīs al-Mamlaka, 1999.

Ibn ʿAjība. *Al-Baḥr al-madīd fī tafsīr al-Qurʾān al-majīd*. Edited by ʿUmar Aḥmad al-Rāwī. 8 vols. Beirut: Dār al-Kutub al-ʿIlmiyya, 1999.

Ibn Ḥanbal, Aḥmad. *Al-Musnad*. Edited by Aḥmad Muḥammad Shākir. 8 vols. Cairo: Dār al-Ḥadīth, 1995.

Ibn Hishām, Abū Muḥammad ʿAbd al-Malik al-Muʿāfirī. *Al-Sīra al-nabawiyya li-Ibn Hishām*. Edited by Walīd b. Muḥammad b. Salāma and Khālid b. Muḥammad b. ʿUthmān. 4 vols. Cairo: Maktabat al-Ṣafā, 2001.

Ibn Majah. *Sunan Ibn Majah bi-sharḥ al-imām Abī al-Ḥasan al-Ḥanafī al-maʿrūf al-Sindī al-mutawaffā 1137 Ḥ wa-bi-ḥāshiya taʿlīqāt Miṣbāḥ al-zujāja fī Zawāʾid Ibn Majāh liʾl-Būṣīrī*. Edited by Khalīl Maʾmūn Shīḥā. 5 vols. Beirut: Dār al-Maʿrifa, 1417/1996.

Ibn Qutayba, ʿAbd Allāh b. Muslim. *Taʾwīl mushkil al-Qurʾān*. Edited by al-Sayyid Aḥmad Ṣaqr. 2nd ed. Cairo: Dār al-Turāth, 1393/1973.

Ibn Saʿd al-Zuhrī, Abū ʿAbd Allāh Muḥammad. *Kitāb al-Ṭabaqāt al-kabīr*. Edited by ʿAlī Muḥammad ʿUmar. 11 vols. Cairo: Maktabat al-Khānjī, 2001.

al-Juwaynī. *Kitāb al-Irshād ilā qawāṭiʿ al-adilla fī uṣūl al-iʿtiqād*. Edited by Muḥammad Yusūf Mūsā and ʿAlī ʿAbd al-Muʿnim ʿAbd al-Ḥamīd. Cairo: Maktabat al-Khanjī, 2002.

Mālik b. Anas. *Al-Muwaṭṭāʾ*. Edited by Muḥammad ʿAbd al-Raḥmān al-Marʿashlī. Beirut: Dār Iḥyāʾ al-Turāth al-ʿArabī and Muʾassasat al-Tārīkh al-Gharbī, 2003.

al-Muḥāsibī, al-Ḥārith. *Kitāb al-Tawahhum*. Edited by A. J. Arberry. Cairo: Maṭbaʿat al-Taʾlīf waʾl-Tarjama waʾl-Nashr, 1937.

Muslim b. al-Ḥajjāj, Abū al-Ḥusayn al-Qushayrī al-Naysabūrī. *Ṣaḥīḥ Muslim*. Edited by Muḥammad Fuʾād ʿAbd al-Bāqī. 5 vols. Cairo: Dār Iḥyāʾ al-Kutub al-ʿArabiyya, 1955–1956.

Muslim b. al-Ḥajjāj and Yaḥyā b. Sharaf al-Nawawī. *Ṣaḥīḥ Muslim bi-sharḥ al-Nawawī*. 18 vols. Cairo: al-Maṭbaʿat al-Miṣriyya bi-l-Azhar, 1347–1349/1929–1930.

al-Nasafī, Abū al-Muʿīn Maymūn b. Muḥammad. *Baḥr al-kalām*. Edited by Walī al-Dīn Muḥammad Ṣāliḥ al-Farfūr. Damascus: Maktabat Dār al-Farfūr, 2000.

al-Nawawī, Yaḥyā b. Sharaf. *Al-Tibyān fī adāb ḥamalat al-Qurʾān*. Edited by ʿAbd al-ʿAzīz ʿIzz al-Dīn al-Sayrawān. Beirut: Dār al-Nafāʾis, 1984.

al-Qushayrī, Abū al-Qāsim ʿAbd al-Karīm b. Hawāzin. *Laṭāʾif al-ishārāt: Tafsīr ṣūfī kāmil li-l-Qurʾān al-karīm*. Edited by Ibrāhīm Basyūnī. 6 vols. Cairo: Dār al-Kitāb al-ʿArabī, 1968.

———. *Al-Risāla al-Qushayriyya*. Edited by ʿAbd al-Ḥalīm Maḥmūd and Maḥmūd b. al-Sharīf. 2 vols. Cairo: Dār al-Kutub al-Ḥadītha, 1966.

al-Shawkānī. *Fatḥ al-qadīr: al-Jāmiʿ bayna fannī al-riwāya wa-l-dirāya min ʿilm al-tafsīr*. Edited by ʿAbd al-Raḥmān ʿUmayra. 6 vols. Cairo: Dār al-Wafāʾ, 1994.

al-Ṭabarī, Abū Jaʿfar Muḥammad b. Jarīr. *Jāmiʿ al-bayān ʿan taʾwīl al-Qurʾān al-maʿrūf tafsīr al-Ṭabarī*. Edited by Maḥmūd Shākir. 30 vols. Beirut: Dār Iḥyāʾ al-Turāth al-ʿArabī, 2001.

———. *Tārīkh al-umam wa-l-mulūk: Tārīkh al-Ṭabarī*. Edited by Abū Ṣuhayb al-Karamī. Amman: Bayt al-Afkār wa-l-Dawliyya, n.d.

al-Taftazānī, Saʿd al-Dīn. *Sharḥ ʿaqāʾid al-Nasafiyya*. Edited by Aḥmad Ḥijāzī al-Saqqā. Cairo: Maktabat al-Kulliyāt al-Azhāriyya, 1987.

al-Thaʿlabī, Abū Isḥāq Aḥmad b. Muḥammad. *Al-Kashf wa-l-bayān ʿan tafsīr al-Qurʾān*. Edited by Abū Muḥammad b. ʿĀshūr and Naẓīr al-Sāʿīdī. 10 vols. Beirut: Dār Iḥyāʾ al-Turāth alʿArabī, 2002.

———. *Qiṣaṣ al-anbiyāʾ al-musammā ʿarāʾis al-majālis*. Edited by ʿAbd al-Laṭīf Ḥasan ʿAbd al-Raḥmān. Beirut: Dār al-Kutub al-ʿIlmiyya, 2009.

al-Tirmidhī, Abū ʿĪsā Muḥammad b. ʿĪsā. *Al-Jāmiʿ al-kabīr*. Edited by Bashshār ʿAwwād Maʿrūf. 6 vols. Beirut: Dār al-Gharb al-Islāmī, 1996.

al-Wāḥidī. *Al-Tafsīr al-basīṭ*. Edited by Muḥammad ibn Ṣāliḥ ibn ʿAbd Allāh al-Fawzān. 25 vols. Saudi Arabia: Jāmiʿat al-Imām Muḥammad b. Saʿūd al-Islāmiyya, 1430/[2009].

Yāqūt ibn ʿAbd Allāh al-Ḥamawī. *Muʿjam al-buldān*. 5 vols. Beirut: Dār al-Ṣādir, 1397/1977.

al-Zarnūjī. *Taʿlīm al-mutaʿallim ṭarīq al-taʿallum*. Khartoum: Dār al-Sūdāniyya li-l-Kutub, 2004.

GENERAL SOURCES

110 Ahadith Qudsi: Sayings of the Prophet Having Allâhs Statements. Edited by Ibrahim M. Kunna. Translated by Syed Masood-ul-Hasan. 3rd ed. Riyadh: Darussalam, 2006.

Abd-Allah Wymann-Landgraf, Umar F. *Mālik and Medina: Islamic Legal Reasoning in the Formative Period*. Leiden: Brill, 2013.

Abdul-Matin, Ibrahim. *Green Deen: What Islam Teaches about Protecting the Planet*. San Francisco: Berrett-Koehler, 2010.

Abrahamov, Binyamin. *Islamic Theology: Traditionalism and Rationalism*. Edinburgh: Edinburgh University Press, 1998.

Abu-Rabi', Ibrahim M. *Intellectual Origins of Islamic Resurgence in the Modern Arab World*. Albany: State University of New York Press, 1996.

Abu Zayd, Nasr Hamid. *Reformation of Islamic Thought: A Critical Historical Analysis*. Amsterdam: Amsterdam University Press, 2006.

Adamson, Peter. "Abū Bakr al-Rāzī on Animals." *Archiv für Geschichte der Philosophie* 94, no. 3 (2012): 249–73.

Adonis. *An Introduction to Arab Poetics*. Translated by Catherine Cobham. London: Saqi Books, 1990.

Ahmed, Rumee. *Narratives of Islamic Legal Theory*. Oxford: Oxford University Press, 2012.

Akhtar, Shabbir. *The Final Imperative: An Islamic Theology of Liberation*. London: Bellew, 1991.

Ali, Kecia. *Sexual Ethics and Islam: Feminist Reflections on Qur'an, Hadith, and Jurisprudence*. Oxford: Oneworld, 2006.

Aristotle. *Nicomachean Ethics*. In *The Complete Works of Aristotle: The Revised Oxford Translation*, edited by Jonathan Barnes, 2:1729–1867. 2 vols. Princeton, NJ: Princeton University Press, 1995.

Arkoun, Mohammed. *Islam: To Reform or to Subvert?* 2nd ed. London: Saqi Books, 2006.

———. *The Unthought in Contemporary Islamic Thought*. London: Saqi Books, 2002.

Armstrong, Karen. *The Spiral Staircase: My Climb Out of Darkness*. New York: Anchor Books, 2004.

Asad, Talal. *The Idea of an Anthropology of Islam*. Washington, DC: Center for Contemporary Arab Studies, Georgetown University, 1986.

al-Ash'arī, Abū al-Ḥasan. *The Theology of al-Ash'arī: The Arabic Texts of al-Ash'arī's Kitāb al-Luma' and Risālat Istiḥsān al-Khawḍ fī 'Ilm al-Kalām*. Edited and translated by Richard McCarthy. Beirut: Imprimerie Catholique, 1953.

'Aṭṭār, Farīd al-Dīn. *The Conference of the Birds*. Translated by Afkham Darbandi and Dick Davis. New York: Penguin, 1984.

al-Attas, Syed Muhammad Naquib. *The Concept of Education in Islam: A Framework for an Islamic Philosophy of Education*. Kuala Lumpur: International Institute of Islamic Thought and Civilization, 1999.

———. *Islam and Secularism*. Kuala Lumpur: International Institute of Islamic Thought and Civilization, 1978.

———. *On Quiddity and Essence: An Outline of the Basic Structure of Reality in Islamic Metaphysics*. Kuala Lumpur: International Institute of Islamic Thought and Civilization, 1990.

——— *Prolegomena to the Metaphysics of Islām: An Exposition of the Fundamental Elements of the Worldview of Islām*. Kuala Lumpur: International Institute of Islamic Thought and Civilization, 1995.

Awn, Peter. *Satan's Tragedy and Redemption: Iblīs in Sufi Pyschology*. Leiden: Brill, 1983.

Ayoub, Mahmoud M. *The Crisis of Muslim History: Religion and Politics of Early Islam*. Oxford: Oneworld, 2003.

———. *A Muslim View of Christianity: Essays on Dialogue*. Edited by Irfan A. Omar. Maryknoll, NY: Orbis, 2007.

Azadpur, Mohammad. *Reason Unbound: On Spiritual Practice in Islamic Peripatetic Philosophy*. Albany: State University of New York Press, 2011.

Barlas, Asma. *"Believing Women" in Islam: Unreading Patriarchal Interpretations of the Qur'an*. Austin: University of Texas Press, 2002.

Barwood, Aileen Vincent. "A Gift from the Kingdom." *Aramco World Magazine* 36, no. 5 (September/October 1985): 18–23.

Berkey, Jonathan P. *Popular Preaching and Religious Authority in the Medieval Islamic Near East.* Seattle: University of Washington Press, 2001.

Bodman, Whitney S. *The Poetics of Iblīs: Narrative Theology in the Qur'an*. Cambridge, MA: Harvard University Press, 2011.

Brockis, Victor. *Muhammad Ali: In Fighter's Heaven*. London: Hutchinson London, 1998.

Brown, Daniel W. *Rethinking Tradition in Modern Islamic Thought.* Cambridge: Cambridge University Press, 1996.

Brown, Jonathan. *The Canonization of al-Bukhārī and Muslim: The Formation and Function of the Sunnī Ḥadīth Canon.* Leiden: Brill, 2007.

———. *Hadith: Muhammad's Legacy in the Medieval and Modern World.* Oxford: Oneworld, 2009.

Brown, Norman O. *The Challenge of Islam: The Prophetic Tradition, Lectures, 1981*. Santa Cruz, CA: New Pacific Press, 2009.

Browne, Edward G. *A Literary History of Persia*. Vol. 2, *From Firdawsí to Sa'dí*. Cambridge: Cambridge University Press, 1956.

Bulliet, Richard W. *Hunters, Herders, and Hamburgers*. New York: Columbia University Press, 2005.

Cassirer, Ernst. *An Essay on Man: An Introduction to a Philosophy of Human Culture*. New Haven, CT: Yale University Press, 1944.

Chittick, William C. *The Heart of Islamic Philosophy: The Quest for Self-Knowledge in the Teachings of Afḍal al-Dīn Kāshānī*. New York: Oxford University Press, 2001.

———. *Imaginal Worlds: Ibn al-'Arabī and the Problem of Religious Diversity*. Albany: State University of New York Press, 1994.

———. *In Search of the Lost Heart: Explorations in Islamic Thought*. Edited by Mohammed Rustom, Atif Khalil, and Kazuyo Murata. Albany: State University of New York Press, 2012.

———. *Science of the Cosmos, Science of the Soul: The Pertinence of Islamic Cosmology in the Modern World*. Oxford: Oneworld, 2007.

———. *The Sufi Path of Knowledge: Ibn al-'Arabi's Metaphysics of Imagination*. Albany: State University of New York, 1989.

———. "Worship." In *The Cambridge Companion to Classical Islamic Theology*, edited by Tim Winter, 218–36. Cambridge: Cambridge University Press, 2008.

Chodkiewicz, Michel. *An Ocean without Shore: Ibn Arabi, the Book, and the Law*. Translated by David Streight. Albany: State University of New York Press, 1993.

Colby, Frederick S. *Narrating Muḥammad's Night Journey: Tracing the Development of the Ibn 'Abbās Ascension Discourse*. Albany: State University of New York Press, 2008.

Cone, James H. *Martin and Malcolm and America: A Dream or a Nightmare.* Maryknoll, NY: Orbis, 1991.

Corbin, Henry. *Alone with the Alone: Creative Imagination in the Sūfism of Ibn 'Arabī.* Princeton, NJ: Princeton University Press, 1997.

Cragg, Kenneth. *The Event of the Qur'ān: Islam in Its Scripture*. Oxford: Oneworld, 1994.

Daulatzai, Sohail. *Black Star, Crescent Moon: The Muslim International and Black Freedom Beyond America.* Minneapolis: University of Minnesota Press, 2012.

De Blois, F. C. "Ta'rīkh, I. Dates and Eras in the Islamic World." In *Encyclopaedia of Islam*, 2nd ed., edited by P. J. Bearman, Th. Bianquis, C. E. Bosworth, E. van Donzel, and W. P. Heinrichs, 10:257–64. 12 vols. Leiden: Brill, 1960–2005.

DeCaro, Louis A., Jr. *Malcolm and the Cross: The Nation of Islam, Malcolm X, and Christianity*. New York: New York University Press, 1998.

———. *On the Side of My People: A Religious Life of Malcolm X.* New York: New York University Press, 1996.

De Goeje, M. J. *Mémoire sur les Carmathes du Bahraïn et les Fatimides*. Leiden: E. J. Brill, 1886.

Druart, Thérèse-Anne. "Al-Razi's Conception of the Soul: Psychological Background to his Ethics." *Medieval Philosophy and Theology* 5, no. 2 (1996): 245–63.

Dutton, Yasin. *The Origins of Islamic Law: The Qur'an, the Muwaṭṭa' and Madinan 'Amal*. Surrey, UK: RoutledgeCurzon, 1999.

El-Bizri, Nader. *The Phenomenological Quest between Avicenna and Heidegger*. Binghamton, NY: Global Publications, 2000.

Eliade, Mircea. *The Sacred and the Profane: The Nature of Religion*. Translated by Willard R. Trask. San Diego: Harcourt Brace & Company, 1959.

Elias, Norbert. *The Loneliness of the Dying*. Translated by Edmund Jephcott. New York: Continuum, 1985.

El Shamsy, Ahmed. "Rethinking *Taqlīd* in the Early Shāfi'ī School." *Journal of the American Oriental Society* 128, no. 1 (2008): 1–23.

Ernst, Carl W. *Sufism: An Introduction to the Mystical Tradition of Islam*. Boston: Shambhala, 2011.

Esack, Farid. *On Being a Muslim: Finding a Religious Path in the World Today*. Oxford: Oneworld, 2009.

———. *Qur'ān, Liberation and Pluralism: An Islamic Perspective of Interreligious Solidarity against Oppression*. Oxford: Oneworld, 1997.

Fakhry, Majid. *A History of Islamic Philosophy*. 2nd ed. New York: Columbia University Press, 1983.

Fancy, Nahyan. *Science and Religion in Mamluk Egypt: Ibn al-Nafīs, Pulmonary Transit and Bodily Resurrection*. New York: Routledge, 2013.

al-Faruqi, Isma'il R. *Islāmization of Knowledge: General Principles and Work Plan*. Washington, DC: International Institute of Islāmic Thought, 1982.

Filiu, Jean-Pierre. *Apocalypse in Islam*. Translated by M. B. DeBevoise. Berkeley: University of California Press, 2011.

Frank, Richard M. "Elements in the Development of the Teaching of al-Ash'ari." *Le Museon* 54 (1991): 101–90.

Gadamer, Hans-Georg. *Truth and Method*. 2nd ed. Translated by Joel Weinsheimer and Donald G. Marshall. New York: Continuum, 2002.

Garden, Kenneth. *The First Islamic Reviver: Abū Ḥāmid al-Ghazālī and His Revival of the Religious Sciences*. Oxford: Oxford University Press, 2014.

al-Ghazālī. *The Book of Knowledge—Kitāb al-'ilm: Book 1 of the Iḥyā' 'ulūm al-dīn—The Revival of the Religious Sciences*. Translated by Kenneth Honerkamp. Louisville, KY: Fons Vitae, 2015.

———. *Deliverance from Error: Five Key Texts including His Spiritual Autobiography, al-Munqidh min al-Dalal*. Translated by R. J. McCarthy. Louisville, KY: Fons Vitae, 1980.

———. *The Faith and Practice of al-Ghazālī*. Translated by W. Montgomery Watt. Chicago: Kazi Publications, 1982.

———. *Al-Ghazali's Path to Sufism: His Deliverance from Error—al-Munqidh min al-Dalal*. Translated by R. J. McCarthy. Louisville, KY: Fons Vitae, 2000.

———. *The Niche of Lights*. Translated by David Buchman. Provo, UT: Brigham Young University Press, 1998.

———. *The Remembrance of Death and the Afterlife—Kitāb dhikr al-mawt wa-mā ba'dahu: Book XL of the Revival of the Religious Sciences—Iḥyā' 'ulūm al-dīn*. Translated by T. J. Winter. Cambridge: Islamic Texts Society, 1989.

Giddens, Anthony. *The Consequences of Modernity*. Stanford, CA: Stanford University Press, 990.

Goldziher, Ignaz. *Introduction to Islamic Theology and Law*. Translated by Andras and Ruth Hamori. Princeton, NJ: Princeton University Press, 1981.

Graham, William A. *Divine Word and Prophetic Word in Early Islam*. The Hague: Mouton, 1977.

Gray, John. *Straw Dogs: Thoughts on Humans and Other Animals*. London: Granta Books, 2002.

Grewal, Zareena. *Islam Is a Foreign Country: American Muslims and the Global Crisis of Authority*. New York: New York University Press, 2014.

Griffel, Frank. *Al-Ghazālī's Philosophical Theology*. Oxford: Oxford University Press, 2009.

Gutas, Dimitri. *Greek Thought, Arabic Culture: The Graeco-Arabic Translation Movement in Baghdad and Early 'Abbāsid Society (2nd–4th/8th–10th centuries)*. New York: Routledge, 1998.

al-Haddad, 'Abdallah Ibn 'Alawi. *The Book of Assistance*. Translated by Mostafa al-Badawi. Louisville, KY: Fons Vitae, 2003.

———. *The Lives of Man: A Sufi Master Explains the Human States; Before Life, in the World, and after Death*. Translated by Mostafa al-Badawi. Louisville, KY: Fons Vitae, 1991.

Ḥaddād, Gibrīl Fouād. *The Four Imams and Their Schools: Abū Ḥanīfa—Mālik—al-Shāfi'ī—Aḥmad*. London: Muslim Academic Trust, 2007.

Hauerwas, Stanley. *Approaching the End: Eschatological Reflections on Church, Politics, and Life*. Grand Rapids, MI: Wm. B. Eerdmans, 2013.

———. "Should Suffering Be Eliminated? What the Retarded Have to Teach Us (1984)." In *The Hauerwas Reader*, edited by John Berkman and Michael Cartwright, 569–74. Durham, NC: Duke University Press, 2001.

Hidayatullah, Aysha. *Feminist Edges of the Qur'an*. Oxford: Oxford University Press, 2014.

Hodgson, Marshall G. S. *The Venture of Islam: Conscience and History in a World Civilization*. Vol. 1, *The Classical Age of Islam*. Chicago: University of Chicago Press, 1974.

Hobsbawm, Eric. "Introduction: Inventing Traditions." In *The Invention of Traditions*, edited by Eric Hobsbawm and Terence Ranger, 1–14. Cambridge: Cambridge University Press, 1983.

Horkheimer, Max. *Eclipse of Reason*. New York: Seabury Press, 1947.

Hoyland, Robert G. *Arabia and the Arabs: From the Bronze Age to the Coming of Islam*. London: Routledge, 2001.

Ibn al-'Arabī. *The Meccan Revelations*. Vol. 1, *Selected Texts of al-Futūhāt al-Makkiya*. Edited by Michel Chodkiewicz. Translated by William C. Chittick and James W. Morris. New York: Pir Press, 2002.

Ibn Isḥāq. *The Life of Muhammad: A Translation of Isḥāq's Sīrat Rasūl Allāh*. Translated by A. Guillaume. Oxford: Oxford University Press, 1955.

Ibn al-Jawzī, 'Abd al-Raḥmān. *The Attributes of God (Daf' Shuhab al-Tashbīh bi-Akaff al-Tanzīh)*. Translated by 'Abdullāh b. Ḥamīd 'Alī. Bristol: Amal Press, 2006.

Ibn Khaldūn. *The Muqaddimah: An Introduction to History*. Edited by N. J. Dawood. Translated by Franz Rosenthal. Princeton, NJ: Princeton University Press, 1967.

Ibn Ṭufayl. *Ibn Ṭufayl's Ḥayy ibn Yaqẓān: A Philosophical Tale*. Translated by Lenn Evan Goodman. Los Angeles: Gee Tee Bee, 1983.

Iqbal, Muhammad. *Complaint and Answer of Iqbal*. Translated by A. J. Arberry. Lahore: Sh. Muhammad Ashraf, 1997.

———. *The Reconstruction of Religious Thought in Islam*. Edited by M. Saeed Sheikh. Stanford, CA: Stanford University Press, 2012.

Izetbegovic, 'Alija 'Ali. *Islam between East and West*. Indianapolis: American Trust Publications, 1993.

Izutsu, Toshihiko. *The Concept of Belief in Islamic Theology: A Semantic Analysis of Īmān and Islām*. Kuala Lumpur: Islamic Book Trust, 2006.

———. *God and Man in the Qur'an: Semantics of the Qur'anic Weltanschauung*. Kuala Lumpur: Islamic Book Trust, 2002.

Jackson, Sherman. *Islam and the Problem of Black Suffering*. Oxford: Oxford University Press, 2009.

———. *On the Boundaries of Theological Tolerance in Islam: Abū Ḥāmid al-Ghazālī's Fayṣal al-Tafriqa Bayna al-Islām wa al-Zandaqa*. Karachi: Oxford University Press, 2002.

———. *Sufism for Non-Sufis? Ibn 'Aṭā' Allāh al-Sakandarī's Tāj al-'Arūs*. Oxford: Oxford University Press, 2012.

———. "*Taqlīd*, Legal Scaffolding and the Scope of Legal Injunctions in Post-Formative Theory: *Muṭlaq* and *'Āmm* in the Jurisprudence of Shihāb al-Dīn al-Qarāfī." *Islamic Law and Society* 3, no. 2 (1996): 165–92.

Jambet, Christian. *The Act of Being: The Philosophy of Revelation in Mullā Sadrā*. Translated by Jeff Fort. New York: Zone Books, 2006.

John of Damascus. *Writings: The Fountain of Knowledge*. Translated by Frederic H. Chase Jr. Washington, DC: Catholic University of America Press, 1970.

Jones, Linda G. *The Power of Oratory in the Medieval Muslim World*. Cambridge: Cambridge University Press, 2012.

al-Juwayni. *A Guide to Conclusive Proofs for the Principles of Belief: Kitāb al-irshād ilā qawāṭiʿ al-adilla fī uṣūl al-iʿtiqād*. Translated by Paul E. Walker. Reading, UK: Garnet, 2000.

Kamali, Mohammad Hashim. *Principles of Islamic Jurisprudence*. 3rd ed. Cambridge: Islamic Text Society, 2003.

Kaufman, Gordon D. *The Theological Imagination: Constructing the Concept of God*. Philadelphia: Westminster Press, 1981.

Kennedy, Hugh. *The Prophet and the Age of the Caliphates: The Islamic Near East from the Sixth to the Eleventh Century*. London: Longman, 1986.

Kermani, Navid. *God Is Beautiful: The Aesthetic Experience of the Quran*. Translated by Tony Crawford. Cambridge: Polity, 2015.

———. "Revelation in Its Aesthetic Dimension: Some Notes about Apostles and Artists in Islamic and Christian Culture." In *The Qurʾan as Text*, edited by Stefan Wild, 213–24. Leiden: E. J. Brill, 1996.

Khalil, Mohammad Hassan. *Islam and the Fate of Others: The Salvation Question*. Oxford: Oxford University Press, 2012.

Knysh, Alexander D. *Ibn ʿArabi in the Late Islamic Tradition: The Making of a Polemical Image in Medieval Islam*. Albany: State University of New York Press, 1999.

Koselleck, Reinhart. *Futures Past: On the Semantics of Historical Time*. Translated by Keith Tribe. New York: Columbia University Press, 2004.

Lamptey, Jerusha Tanner. *Never Wholly Other: A Muslima Theology of Religious Pluralism*. Oxford: Oxford University Press, 2014.

Lange, Christian. *Justice, Punishment, and the Medieval Muslim Imagination*. Cambridge: Cambridge University Press, 2008.

Leaman, Oliver, and Sajjad Rizvi. "The Developed *Kalām* Tradition." In *The Cambridge Companion to Classical Islamic Theology*, edited by Tim Winter, 77–96. Cambridge: Cambridge University Press, 2008.

Lowry, Joseph E. *Early Islamic Legal Theory: The Risāla of Muḥammad ibn Idrīs al-Shāfiʿī*. Leiden: Brill, 2007.

Luhmann, Niklas. *Risk: A Sociological Theory*. Translated by Rhodes Barrett. New York: A. de Gruyter, 1993.

Lukacs, John. *Historical Consciousness or the Remembered Past*. New York: Harper & Row, 1968.

MacDonald, D. B. "*Wahm* in Arabic and Its Cognates." *Journal of the Royal Asiatic Society* 4 (October 1922): 505–21.

MacIntyre, Alasdair. *After Virtue*. 3rd ed. Notre Dame, IN: University of Notre Dame Press, 2007.

———. *Whose Justice? Which Rationality?* Notre Dame, IN: University of Notre Dame Press, 1988.

Madelung, W. "Māturīdiyya." In *Encyclopaedia of Islam*, 2nd ed., edited by P. J. Bearman, Th. Bianquis, C. E. Bosworth, E. van Donzel, and W. P. Heinrichs, 6:847–48. 12 vols. Leiden: Brill, 1960–2005.

———. "The Spread of Māturīdism and the Turks." In *Actas do IV Congresso de Estudos Árabes e Islâmicos Coimbra-Lisboa*, 109–68. Leiden: Brill, 1971.

———. *Religious Trends in Early Islamic Iran*. Albany, NY: Bibliotheca Persica, 1988.

Madigan, Daniel. *The Qurʾân's Self-Image: Writing and Authority in Islam's Scripture*. Princeton, NJ: Princeton University Press, 2001.

Makdisi, George. "Ashʿārī and the Ashʿarites in Islamic Religious History II." *Studia Islamica* 18 (1963): 19–39.

Malamud, Margaret. "Gender and Spiritual Self-Fashioning: The Master-Disciple Relationship in Classical Sufism." *Journal of the American Academy of Religion* 64 (1996): 89–117.

Mālik b. Anas. *Al-Muwatta of Imam Malik ibn Anas: The First Formulation of Islamic Law*. Translated by Aisha Abdurrahman Bewley. Inverness, UK: Madinah Press, 2004.

Marable, Manning. *Malcolm X: A Life of Reinvention*. New York: Viking, 2011.

Marable, Manning, and Garrett Felber, eds. *The Portable Malcolm X Reader*. New York: Penguin, 2013.

Martin, Richard C., Mark R. Woodward, and Dwi S. Atmaja. *Defenders of Reason in Islam: Mu'tazilism from Medieval School to Modern Symbol*. Oxford: Oneworld, 1997.

al-Māturīdī, Abū Manṣūr. *Kitāb al-Tawḥīd*. Edited by Bekir Topaloğlu and Muhammad Aruçi. Ankara: İSAM, Türkiye Diyanet Vakfı, İslâm Araştırmaları Merkezi, 2005.

Mir, Mustansir. *Iqbal*. London: I. B. Tauris, 2006.

Moosa, Ebrahim. *Ghazālī and the Poetics of the Imagination*. Chapel Hill: University of North Carolina Press, 2005.

Murad, Abdal Hakim. *Commentary on the Eleventh Contentions*. Cambridge: Quilliam Press, 2012.

Murata, Sachiko, and William C. Chittick. *The Vision of Islam*. St. Paul, MN: Paragon House, 1994.

Musa, Aisha Y. *Ḥadīth as Scripture: Discussions on the Authority of Prophetic Traditions in Islam*. New York: Palgrave Macmillan, 2008.

Nasr, Seyyed Hossein. *Ideals and Realities of Islam*. Rev. ed. Chicago: Kazi, 2000.

———. *Man and Nature: The Spiritual Crisis of Modern Man*. Chicago: ABC International Group, 1997.

———. *Sufi Essays*. 3rd ed. Chicago: ABC International Group, 1999.

al-Nawawī. *Etiquette with the Quran: Al-Tibyān fī Ādāb Ḥamalat al-Qur'ān*. Translated by Musa Furber. Chicago: Starlatch Press, 2003.

———. *An-Nawawī's Forty Hadith: An Anthology of the Sayings of the Prophet Muhammad*. Translated by Ezzeddin Ibrahim and Denys Johnson-Davies. Cambridge: Islamic Texts Society, 1997.

Nayed, Aref. *Growing Ecologies of Peace, Compassion and Blessing: A Muslim Response to "A Muscat Manifesto."* Dubai: Kalam Research & Media, 2009.

Nguyen, Martin. "Could the Kaaba Represent Tradition?" *Renovatio: The Journal of Zaytuna College*, February 6, 2018. https://renovatio.zaytuna.edu/article/could-the-kaaba-represent-tradition.

———. "Exegesis of the *ḥurūf al-muqaṭṭa'a*: Polyvalency in Sunnī Traditions of Qur'anic Interpretation." *Journal of Qur'anic Studies* 14, no. 2 (2012): 1–28.

———. "Modern Scripturalism and Emergent Theological Trajectories: Moving beyond the Qur'an as Text." *Journal of Islamic and Muslim Studies* 1, no. 2 (November 2016): 61–79.

———. "Qushayrī's Exegetical Encounter with the Mi'rāj." In *The Spirit and the Letter: Approaches to the Esoteric Interpretation of the Qur'an*, edited by Annabel Keeler and Sajjad Rizvi, 241–70. Oxford: Oxford University Press, 2016.

———. *Sufi Master and Qur'an Scholar: Abū'l-Qāsim al-Qushayrī and the Laṭā'if al-ishārāt*. Oxford: Oxford University Press, 2012.

Nykl, A.R. *Hispano-Arabic Poetry and Its Relations with the Old Provencal Troubadours*. Baltimore, MD: J. H. Furst, 1946.

Ogle, Vanessa. *The Global Transformation of Time: 1870–1950*. Cambridge, MA: Harvard University Press, 2015.

———. "Whose Time Is It? The Pluralization of Time and the Global Condition, 1870s–1940s." *American Historical Review* 118, no. 5 (Dec. 2013): 1376–1402.

Pellat, Ch. "*Ḥilf al-fuḍūl*." In *Encyclopaedia of Islam*, 2nd ed., edited by P. J. Bearman, Th. Bianquis, C. E. Bosworth, E. van Donzel, and W. P. Heinrichs, 3:389. 12 vols. Leiden: Brill, 1960–2005.

Picken, Gavin. "Ibn Ḥanbal and al-Muḥāsibī: A Study of Early Conflicting Scholarly Methodologies." *Arabica* 55 (2008): 337–61.

Pieper, Josef. *Tradition: Concept and Claim*. South Bend, IN: St. Augustine's Press, 2008.

Qadhi, Yasir. "Mecca Under Siege: The Juhayman Crisis of 1979." Paper presented at the Fifth International Conference on Islamic Legal Studies, Lawful and Unlawful Violence in Islamic Law and History, Harvard Law School, Cambridge, MA, September 10, 2006.

The Qur'an. Translated by M. A. S. Abdel Haleem. Oxford: Oxford University Press, 2005.

The Qur'an: A New Translation. Translated by Tarif Khalidi. London: Penguin, 2008.

al-Qushayrī. *Al-Qushayri's Epistle on Sufism*. Translated by Alexander D. Knysh. Reading, UK: Garnet, 2007.

Renard, John, ed. and trans. *Knowledge of God in Classical Sufism: Foundations of Islamic Mystical Theology*. Mahwah, NJ: Paulist Press, 2004.

Ricoeur, Paul. *Figuring the Sacred: Religion, Narrative, and Imagination*. Edited by Mark I. Wallace. Translated by David Pellauer. Minneapolis: Fortress Press, 1995.

Rustomji, Nerina. *The Garden and the Fire: Heaven and Hell in Islamic Culture*. New York: Columbia University Press, 2008.

Saeed, Abdullah. *Interpreting the Qur'ān: Towards a Contemporary Approach*. London: Routledge, 2006.

Saleh, Walid A. *The Formation of the Classical Tafsīr Tradition: The Qur'ān Commentary of al-Tha'labī (d. 427/1035)*. Leiden: Brill, 2004.

Saliba, John A. *"Homo Religiosus" in Mircea Eliade: An Anthropological Evaluation*. Leiden: E. J. Brill, 1976.

Saul, John Ralston. *On Equilibrium: Six Qualities of the New Humanism*. New York: Four Walls Eight Windows, 2004.

Schacht, Joseph. "An Early Murci'ite Treatise: The *Kitāb al-'Ālim wal-Muta'allim*." *Oriens* 17 (1964): 96–117.

Schimmel, Annemarie. *Gabriel's Wing: A Study into the Religious Ideas of Sir Muhammad Iqbal*. Lahore: Iqbal Academy Pakistan, 2000.

al-Shāfi'ī, Muḥammad b. Idrīs. *The Epistle on Legal Theory*. Edited and translated by Joseph E. Lowry. New York: New York University Press, 2013.

Shah, Zulfiqar Ali. *The Astronomical Calculations and Ramadan: A Fiqhi Discourse*. Washington, DC: International Institute of Islamic Thought, 2009.

Shah-Kazemi, Reza. *The Other in Light of the One: The Universality of the Qur'ān and Interfaith Dialogue*. Cambridge: Islamic Text Society, 2006.

Shakir, Zaid. "EVENT INVITE: May 18, 2013 Zaid Shakir, Think Outside the Cube." YouTube video, May 10, 2013. https://www.youtube.com/watch?v=Sy8_0uXMOJQ.

Shariati, Ali. *Religion vs. Religion*. Translated by Laleh Bakhtiar. Chicago: ABC International Group, 2000.

———. *School of Thought and Action*. Translated by Cyrus Bakhtiar. Chicago: ABC International Group, 2000.

Siddiqui, Mona. *Christians, Muslims, and Jesus*. New Haven, CT: Yale University Press, 2014.

———. *Hospitality in Islam: Welcoming in God's Name*. New Haven, CT: Yale University Press, 2015.

Silvers, Laury. "The Teaching Relationship in Early Sufism: A Reassessment of Fritz Meier's Definition of the *shaykh al-tarbiya* and the *shaykh al-ta'līm*." *Muslim World* 93 (2003): 69–97.

Smith, James K. A. *Imagining the Kingdom: How Worship Works*. Grand Rapids, MI: Baker Academic, 2013.

Smith, Jane Idleman, and Yvonne Yazbeck Haddad, *The Islamic Understanding of Death and Resurrection*. Oxford: Oxford University Press, 2002.

Smith, Wilfred Cantwell. *Faith and Belief*. Princeton, NJ: Princeton University Press, 1979.

———. *The Expansion of Prophetic Experience: Essays on Historicity, Contingency and Plurality in Religion*. Edited by Forough Jahanbakhsh. Translated by Nilou Mobasser. Leiden: Brill, 2009.

Soroush, Abdolkarim. *Reason, Freedom, and Democracy in Islam: Essential Writings of 'Abdolkarim Soroush*. Edited and translated by Mahmoud Sadri and Ahmad Sadri. Oxford: Oxford University Press, 2000.

Sourdel, Dominique. "Une Profession de Foi de l'Historien al-Ṭabarī." *Revue des Études Islamiques* 36, no. 2 (1968): 177–97.
Stark, Rodney. "A Theory of Revelation." *Journal for the Scientific Study of Religion* 38, no. 2 (1999): 286–307.
The Study Quran: A New Translation and Commentary. Translated by Seyyed Hossein Nasr, Caner K. Dagli, Maria Massi Dakake, Joseph E. B. Lumbard, and Mohammed Rustom. New York: HarperCollins, 2013.
al-Ṭabarī. *The History of al-Ṭabarī*. Vol. 1, *General Introduction and From the Creation to the Flood*. Translated by Franz Rosenthal. Albany: State University of New York Press, 1989.
———. *The History of al-Ṭabarī*. Vol. 6, *Muḥammad at Mecca*. Translated by W. Montgomery and M. V. McDonald. Albany: State University of New York Press, 1988.
———. *The History of al-Ṭabarī*. Vol. 17, *The First Civil War*. Translated by G. R. Hawting. Albany: State University of New York Press, 1996.
———. *The History of al-Ṭabarī*. Vol. 19, *The Caliphate of Yazīd b. Muʿāwiyah*. Translated by I. K. A. Howard. Albany: State University of New York Press, 1990.
———. *The History of al-Ṭabarī*. Vol. 21, *The Victory of the Marwānids*. Translated by Michael Fishbein. Albany: State University of New York Press, 1990.
Taftazani. *A Commentary on the Creed of Islam: Saʿd al-Dīn al-Taftazānī's Commentary on the Creed of Najm al-Dīn al-Nasafī*. Translated by Earl Edgar Elder. New York: Columbia University Press, 1950.
al-Thaʿlabī, Abū Isḥāq Aḥmad b. Muḥammad. *ʿArāʾis al-majālis fī qiṣaṣ al-anbiyāʾ or "Lives of the Prophets."* Translated by William M. Brinner. Leiden: Brill, 2002.
Taylor, Charles. *The Language Animal: The Full Shape of the Human Linguistic Capacity*. Cambridge, MA: Harvard University Press, 2016.
Tlili, Sarra. *Animals in the Qur'an*. Cambridge: Cambridge University Press, 2012.
Touati, Houari. *Islam and Travel in the Middle Ages*. Translated by Lydia G. Cochrane. Chicago: University of Chicago Press, 2010.
Tritton, A. S. *Muslim Theology*. Bristol, UK: Luzac & Company, 1947.
Trofimov, Yaroslav. *The Siege of Mecca: The 1979 Uprising at Islam's Holiest Shrine*. New York: Doubleday, 2007.
Vasalou, Sophia. *Ibn Taymiyya's Theological Ethics*. Oxford: Oxford University Press, 2016.
———. *Moral Agents and Their Deserts: The Character of Muʿtazilite Ethics*. Princeton, NJ: Princeton University Press, 2008.
Vuckovic, Brooke. *Heavenly Journeys, Earthly Concerns: The Legacy of the Miʿrāj in the Formation of Islam*. New York: Routledge, 2005.
Wadud, Amina. *Inside the Gender Jihad Women's Reform of Islam*. Oxford: Oneworld, 2006.
———. *Qur'an and Woman: Rereading the Sacred Text from a Woman's Perspective*. Oxford: Oxford University Press, 1999.
Walbridge, John. *God and Logic in Islam: The Caliphate of Reason*. New York: Cambridge University Press, 2011.
Waldman, Marilyn Robinson. "Tradition as a Modality of Change: Islamic Examples." *History of Religions* 25, no. 4 (May 1986): 318–40.
Watt, W. Montgomery. *Early Islam: Collected Articles*. Edinburgh: Edinburgh University Press, 1990.
———, trans. *Islamic Creeds: A Selection*. Edinburgh: Edinburgh University Press, 1994.
Weiss, Bernard G. *The Spirit of Islamic Law*. Athens: University of Georgia Press, 1998.
Wensinck, A. J. *The Muslim Creed: Its Genesis and Historical Development*. New Delhi: Oriental Books Reprint Corporation, 1979.
Wensinck, A. J., and A. Rippin. "Waḥy," In *Encyclopaedia of Islam*, 2nd ed., edited by P. J. Bearman, Th. Bianquis, C. E. Bosworth, E. van Donzel, and W. P. Heinrichs, 11:53–56. 12 vols. Leiden: Brill, 1960–2005.
Wheeler, Brannon. *Mecca and Eden: Ritual, Relics, and Territory in Islam*. Chicago: University of Chicago Press, 2006.
Winter, Tim. "Introduction." In *The Cambridge Companion to Classical Islamic Theology*, edited by Tim Winter, 1–16. Cambridge: Cambridge University Press, 2008.

Wolfson, Harry Austryn. "The Internal Senses in Latin, Arabic, and Hebrew Philosophic Texts." *Harvard Theological Review* 28, no. 2 (April 1935): 69–133.

X, Malcolm. *February 1965: The Final Speeches*. New York: Pathfinder, 1992.

———. *Malcolm X Speaks: Selected Speeches and Statements*. Edited by George Breitman. New York: Grove Press, 1965.

X, Malcolm, and Alex Haley. *The Autobiography of Malcolm X*. New York: Grove Press, 1965.

Yusuf, Hamza. *Agenda to Change Our Condition*. Hayward, CA: Zaytuna Institute, 2001.

———. *Caesarian Moon Births: Calculations, Moon Sighting, and the Prophetic Way*. Louisville, KY: Fons Vitae, 2008.

———. *Imam Muḥammad b. Nāṣir al-Darʿī's The Prayer of the Oppressed: The Sword of Victory's Lot over Every Tyranny and Plot*. Translated by Hamza Yusuf. Danville, CA: Sandala, 2010.

Yusuf, Hamza, and Zaid Shakir. *Agenda to Change Our Condition*. N.p.: Sandala, 2013.

Zargar, Cyrus Ali. *The Polished Mirror: Storytelling and the Pursuit of Virtue in Islamic Philosophy and Sufism*. London: Oneworld, 2017.

al-Zarnūjī. *Instruction of the Student: The Method of Learning*. Rev. ed. Translated by G. E. von Grunebaum and Theodora M. Abel. Chicago: Starlatch Press, 2003.

Ziai, Hossein. "Islamic Philosophy (*falsafa*)." In *The Cambridge Companion to Classical Islamic Theology*, edited by Tim Winter, 55–76. Cambridge: Cambridge University Press, 2008.

INDEX OF QUR'ANIC VERSES

INDEX

ABOUT THE AUTHOR

Martin Nguyen is associate professor of religious studies, faculty chair for diversity, and director of the Islamic World Studies Minor Program at Fairfield University. He earned his master's of theological studies from Harvard Divinity School and then obtained his Ph.D. from Harvard University's Center for Middle Eastern Studies. He has researched and published on Muslim theology, the Qur'an and its interpretation, and Islamic spirituality. Among his publications is the book *Sufi Master and Qur'an Scholar: Abū'l-Qāsim al-Qushayrī and the Laṭā'if al-ishārāt*. He serves on the boards of the Society for the Study of Muslim Ethics and the journal *Teaching Theology and Religion* from the Wabash Center.

Religion in the Modern World

Series Advisors
Kwok Pui-lan, Episcopal Divinity School
Joerg Rieger, Southern Methodist University

This series explores how various religious traditions wrestle with the dynamic and changing role of religion in the modern world and examines how past changes reflect on today's critical issues. Accessibly and engagingly written, books in this series will look at secularization, global society, gender, race, class, sexuality and their relation to religious life and religious movements.

Titles in Series

Not God's People: Insiders and Outsiders in the Biblical World by Lawrence M. Wills
The Food and Feasts of Jesus: The Original Mediterranean Diet, with Menus and Recipes by Douglas E. Neel and Joel A. Pugh
Occupy Religion: Theology of the Multitude by Joerg Rieger and Kwok Pui-lan
The Politics of Jesús: A Hispanic Political Theology by Miguel A. De La Torre